高职高专商务英语、应用英语专业规划教材

国际贸易操作实训

主　编　董佩佩　王　珍

副主编　李　琳　袁　清　蒋伟娟

Foreign Trade Practice

ZHEJIANG UNIVERSITY PRESS

浙江大学出版社

编 者 说 明

随着我国经济发展和高等教育体系的逐步完善，高等职业技术教育越来越显示出它的重要地位。根据高职教育对人才培养的要求，高职院校担负着培养在技术和经济领域中直接参与生产实践的应用型人才的重任。如何在以基础理论够用为度的原则指导下，注重培养学生的实际操作能力，适应具体的工作岗位要求，是目前高职教学中需要迫切解决的一个问题。

为满足社会对应用型和技能型人才的需要，服务于高职教学，我们编写了这本能满足高职高专应用英语、商务英语专业教学所需的操作性很强的国际贸易操作实训教材。

本教材以进出口外贸业务程序为主线，包括出口贸易与进口贸易两大板块。其中出口贸易具体涉及：出口准备、交易磋商、外销合同签订、支付方式选择、备货与货物出运、货物报验、货物投保、出口报关、出口制单结汇与出口核销退税等十个方面的内容。进口贸易流程包括：进口准备、进口交易磋商、申请进口许可证、信用证业务、进口运输、进口报验、进口投保、进口报关与进口付汇核销等九部分内容。具有内容充实、体系完整的特点。在每一个实训环节，分别设置了实训目标、操作实例及解析、操作指南等方面的内容，有利于指导学生每一流程的上机实习。

教材突出强调了内容的全面性、完整性，不仅涵盖了出口与进口两大模块，同时在编写上融合了"外贸实务"、"外贸函电"、"商务文秘英语"、"国际结算"、"电子商务"等课程的综合知识；案例选取力求贴近真实的外贸实际业务，具有较强的针对性与实用性，案例新颖、精炼，富有代表性，并将相关理论融入大量的例题中，以例释理；拓展训练部分可以充分调动学生在实训实践环节中的自主操作性，提升对知识的理解与消化。

本教材是为高职高专应用英语、商务英语专业编写的专用教材，也可以作为"国际贸易实务"课程的配套用书。

本教材由董佩佩和王珍任主编，李琳、袁清、蒋伟娟任副主编。各实训章节的编写人员分工如下：董佩佩编写了出口部分的实训一；王珍编写了出口部分的实训四、实训五、实训六和实训七；李琳编写了出口部分的实训二、实训三和实训八，以及进口部分的实训五、实训七和实训八；袁清编写了进口部分的实训一、实训二和实训四；蒋伟娟编写了出口部分的实训九和实训十，进口部分的实训三、实训六和实训九。全书由董佩佩和李琳负责审核和统稿。

由于编者水平有限，书中不足之处难以避免，恳切希望读者批评指正。

编　者

2008 年 12 月

CONTENTS 目　录

高职高专商务英语、应用英语专业规划教材◇◇◇

Export Procedure

出口贸易流程

PRACTICE 1

Preparation for Export
出口准备

Learning Objective 学习目标

◇ To be familiar with the preparation before export business 熟悉出口贸易前的准备工作

Example & Analysis 操作实例及解析

◆ Case Lead-in

Ningbo Sakai Pet Co., Ltd. was established in 2000. It is a professional exporter specializing in pet products and pet articles. The company is located in Ningbo, Zhejiang Province. Nowadays, the company has been the most important export enterprise in the field of pet products. In the spring of this year, Wang Li, the salesman of the company, joined in the Guangzhou Foreign Trade Fair with his manager. At the trade fair, the company showed off their own products such as pet house, pet clothes and so on. With humanized design and updated fashion style, the products from Sakai Pet Corporation drew attention of foreign clients. Some of them were expressed their desire to place order if price was reasonable.

One of them was from the USA. From the Internet, Wang Li got some detailed information about the buyer.

ABF International Co., Ltd. is one of the first companies that dealing with pet products in North America. And it has clients and sales channel all over the world.

Add: 35 Forest Avenue, Miami, USA

Tel: 001-523-6277820

Fax: 001-523-6277825

Email: Barbur@ABF.com

◆ **案例导入**

宁波井通宠物用品有限公司成立于 2000 年，是一家专业经营宠物用品的公司。公司位于浙江省宁波市。经过几年的努力，目前公司已经成为了在宠物用品领域最重要的出口企业。今年春天，业务员王立随同经理参加了广交会。在广交会上，公司向国外客户展示了公司的特色产品，包括宠物穿的衣服、宠物住的小房屋等，产品人性化的设计以及时尚的款式，吸引了不少国外客户。现场就有客户表示如果价格合理的话愿意下订单。

其中一位客户是来自于美国 ABF 国际贸易有限公司。王立通过网络获悉了该公司的一些基本资料。ABF 国际贸易有限公司是北美地区最早经营宠物产品的公司之一，公司拥有遍及全球的客户和销售网络。

Directions 操作指南

在出口交易磋商前，外贸企业必须认真做好交易前的各项准备工作，准备工作做得越充分、越细致，在商订合同过程中也会越主动和顺利。

◆ **市场调研**

在出口交易磋商前，要加强对国外市场的调查研究，应通过各种途径广泛了解供求情况、价格动态、各国有关的贸易政策法规、措施和习惯做法，从中选择适当的目标市场。对国外市场调研主要有三个方面：国别调研、市场调研和客户调研。其中，市场调研，是以具体出口商品为对象，了解市场对该商品花色、品种、规格、质量、包装等的需求和习惯爱好等。在对市场调研的基础上，根据国家的外贸政策和扩大出口市场的需要和可能，适当选择和安排市场。市场不宜过分集中，也不宜过分分散，同时必须注意开拓新市场。

◆ **制定出口商品经营方案**

在进行市场调研的基础上，有针对性地、系统地对调研的相关信息进行整理分析，据此制定出口经营方案。出口经营方案内容因商品不同而不一，大致包括以下几个方面：

货源情况：包括实际生产能力、可供出口的数量，以及出口商品的品质、规格和包装等；

国外市场情况：包括国外市场需求和价格变动趋势；

出口经营情况：包括出口成本、创汇率等情况，并提出经营的具体意见和安排；

推销计划和措施：按照品种、数量或金额列明推销的计划进度，以及按推销计划采取的措施，诸如，对客户的了解、贸易方式、收汇方式的运用，对佣金和折扣的把握等。

◆ **寻找商机——寻找潜在客户**

寻找潜在客户的途径包括：

(1) 展览会、博览会等。比如每年春季召开的华交会，一年两届的广交会为出口企业寻找客户提供了平台。

(2) 各种媒体，包括报纸、电视、电台、杂志期刊、互联网络等，其中比较多的会利用互联网络，通过一些商务网站来达成交易，比如阿里巴巴网站等。

(3) 行业协会、商会、银行、领事馆参赞处等。

Practice 操作练习

假设你自己创办一家进出口公司，生产经营某类出口商品，请尝试对自己经营的产品作一番市场调研，确定商品的目标市场，并制订相应的出口经营方案。

PRACTICE 2
Business Negotiation for Export
出口交易磋商

Learning Objectives 学习目标

◇ To be familiar with each step of international trade for negotiation, including enquiry, offer, counter-offer and acceptance, and learn how to write business correspondence between exporter and importer independently and skillfully 熟悉国际贸易合同磋商的基本步骤，独立并熟练撰写交易磋商过程中的往来函电

◇ To master the method of quotation calculation and how to apply the commonly used international trade price terms to the real situations 熟悉价格术语的应用，掌握报价核算方法

Business negotiation is an important part of concluding a transaction. It is the dealings between the buyer and the seller in order to reach an agreement on price, payment, quantity, quality, and other terms or conditions of a sale. In most cases, it needs going through four stages: inquiry, offer, counter-offer and acceptance. Of course, it is not necessary to have all the four steps taken for every transaction. Sometimes, only offer and acceptance will do.

交易磋商是达成一项交易的重要组成部分。它是买卖双方就价格、付款、数量、质量以及其他条款或条件方面达成协议。在大多数情况下，需要经过四个步骤：询盘、发盘、还盘和接受。当然，不是每笔交易都有这四个步骤的。有时，只有发盘和接受这两个步骤。

Example & Analysis 操作实例及解析

◆ Case Lead-in

Ningbo Sakai Pet Co., Ltd. negotiated with ABF International Co., Ltd. USA about pet care products by email. Ningbo Sakai Pet Co., Ltd. calculated price after receiving the inquiry, and then made a favorable offer to their client. Finally, they succeeded in making a deal.

◆ **案例导入**

宁波井通宠物用品有限公司(ADD: 118 Zhongshan Road, Ningbo, China, TEL: 0574-88762018, FAX: 0574-88762020, Email: Jessica@Sakai.com)在本年度广交会上获悉美国 ABF International Co., Ltd. (ADD: 35 Forest Avenue, Miami, USA, TEL: 001-523-6277820, FAX: 001 523 6277825, Email: Barbur@ABF.com)对公司的宠物护理用品很感兴趣，随即与美国 ABF International Co., Ltd. 就宠物护理用品的各项交易条件用电子邮件进行磋商，井通公司在收到客商询盘后进行了价格核算，并向客商发盘，经过一番讨价还价，双方终于达成交易。

Task 1 Establishing Business Relationship 建立业务关系

A foreign-trade firm needs extensive business connection to maintain or expand its business activities, so the establishment of business relations is one of the most important undertakings in foreign trade. The following is the example of establishing business relations from the seller.

Sender: Jessica@Sakai.com

Receiver: Barbur@ABF.com

Subject: Establish business relationship

Dear Sir,

Thank you for visiting our booth in the 103rd China Import & Export Fair in this April. It was a pleasure to meet you, and we hope to build a strong partnership with you. Thank you for your interest in our Fashion-Sweater.

We, Ningbo Sakai Pet Co., Ltd., are a well experienced pet care products company in China. With strong expertise in design and development of pet products, we are expert in developing and manufacturing super quality pet products to worldwide markets.

Our philosophy of creating value by developing innovative and high quality products and services enhances customers' competitiveness. We commit to establishing long-term business partnership with our esteemed customers.

By owning design team, product development team and research team, we develop custom-made quality products to different markets and clients. We could also provide standard products fitting to the mass markets.

Our Winter Fashion Series catalogue is coming. We will send you soon. Should you have any questions, please feel free to contact me. Your opinion is sincerely welcome. We look forward to your reply and doing business with you in the coming future.

Thanks & regards.

Yours faithfully,

×××

Directions 操作指南

> **Generally speaking, letters on establishing business relationship must be friendly and helpful. The letter should include all of the following information:** 一封规范的建立业务关系函电应包括以下内容:

- The letter begins by telling your client or the addressee the source of your information, that is how his name is known. 信息来源,即从何处获得对方信息。

- The second step is to write down your objectives, expressing your desire or interest in having a connection to open up business. 致函目的。

- Then some general information should be given as to the lines of business being handled. The writer should state simply, clearly and concisely what he can sell or what he expects to buy. 公司自述与产品介绍。

- State your expectation to receive the reply as soon as possible. 期盼答复。

> **Useful sentences 典型例句**

- We write to introduce ourselves as exporter of health tea having over 30 years' experience in this line of business.

- We have learned from China Council for the Promotion of International Trade that you are in the market of Chinese Cotton Piece Goods.

- Your company has been introduced to us by the Bank of China as prospective buyers of electronic products. As we deal in the items, we shall be pleased to establish direct business relations with you.

- It will be to our mutual benefit to develop business between us.

Task 2　Calculation of Quotation 出口报价核算

Information

Art No.	DC-212-10018	DC-210-10019	DC-210-10020
Commodity	Flocking Sweater with Chick Pattern	Flocking Sweater with Lion Pattern	Flocking Sweater with Dog Head Pattern
Packing	25 PC/CTN	25 PC/CTN	25 PC/CTN
M	0.14308CBM 30×42CM/PC	0.14308CBM 30×42CM/PC	0.14308CBM 30×42CM/PC
G.W.	13KG	13KG	13KG

Information:	VAT Rate 17%, Export Duty Reimbursement 13%
Local Charge:	Inland Transport Charge　　　　　¥60 per cubic meter
	Customs Declaration Charges　　　¥200 per sale

	Customs Censoring Charges		￥200 per sale	
	Verification Charges		￥10 per sale	
Ocean Freight:	From Ningbo, China to Copenhagen, Denmark			
	LCL (MTQ)	LCL (TNE)	FCL (20')	FCL (40')
Basic Freight:	$151	$216	$2290	$3410
Banking Charges:	Export L/C Advising Fee		￥200 per sale	
	L/C Amendment Fee		￥100 per sale	
	Negotiation Charge		0.13% of contract price	
	D/A Charge		0.1% of contract price	
	D/P Charge		0.1% of contract price	
Marine Cargo Insurance:	For 110% of CIF Value against All Risks as per PICC Dated 1/1/1981			
	FPA		0.5%	
	WPA		0.6%	
	ALL RISKS		0.8%	
Exchange Rate:	1USD=7RMB			

出口预算表(budget)

Item 项目	Estimated Amount 预算金额
Purchase Cost 采购成本	￥39,780/sale
Tax Reimbursement for Export 出口退税收入	￥4,420/sale
Inland Freight 内陆运费	￥20,160/sale
Customs Censoring Charges 报检费	￥200/sale
Customs Declaration Charges 报关费	￥200/sale
Ocean Freight 海洋运费	￥518/carton
Verification Charge 核销费	￥10/sale
Insurance Premium 保险费	￥438.72/sale
Banking Charges 银行费用	￥365/sale
Fixed Charges 业务定额费	￥747.81/sale
Lump Sum 包干费	￥10,800/sale

Directions 操作指南

- 出口商品价格构成

    出口商品价格=成本+费用+利润

- 成本核算公式

    实际成本=采购成本－出口退税额

    　　　　=采购成本/(1+增值税率)×(1+增值税率－出口退税率)

公式推导：

采购成本=货价+增值税额

=货价+货价×增值税率

=货价×(1+增值税率)

货价=采购成本/(1+增值税率)

实际成本=采购成本－出口退税额

=货价×(1+增值税率)－货价×出口退税率

=货价×(1+增值税率－出口退税率)

=采购成本/(1+增值税率)×(1+增值税率－出口退税率)

出口退税额=货价×出口退税率

=采购成本/(1+增值税率)×出口退税率

- 海洋运费的计算

计算步骤：

首先要根据报价数量计算产品体积与重量，比照集装箱规格，如果报价数量正好够装整箱(20 英尺集装箱或 40 英尺集装箱)，则直接取单位包箱费率为基本运费；如果不够装整箱，则用产品总体积(或总重量，或取两者较高者)×拼箱运费率来算出海运费。

(1) 班轮运费的计算

计算公式：$F=F_b×(1+\sum S)×Q$

F 为班轮运费总额，F_b 为基本运费率，$\sum S$ 为附加费率之和，Q 为总货运量。

(2) 集装箱运费的计算

以集装箱为运费的单位，20'集装箱的有效容积为 25CBM，限重 17.5TNE，40'集装箱的有效容积为 55CBM，限重 24.5TNE。

常见的包箱费率有三种：

FAK 包箱费率(Freight for All Kinds)，对每个集装箱部分货物种类统一收取运费。

FCS 包箱费率(Freight for Class)，按不同货物的等级制定的包箱费率。

FCB 包箱费率(Freight for Class & Basis)，按不同货物的等级或货物类别以及计算标准制定的费率。

- 保险费的计算

保险金额=CIF(或 CIP)×(1+投保加成率)

保险费=保险金额×保险费率

- 银行手续费

银行手续费是银行向客户提供汇兑、结算等相关服务时所收取的费用。

计算方式一般为：按每笔交易收取，按报价或成交价格的一定百分比收取。

- 业务定额费

业务定额费是出口商对业务操作中诸如：邮电通讯、交通差旅、招待客户等业务费用。计算方式一般为：定额费=采购成本×定额费率

- 出口关税的计算

出口货物应纳关税=出口货物完税价格×出口货物关税税率

其中：按照 FOB 价格成交，出口货物的完税价格=FOB/(1+出口关税税率)

按照 CFR 价格成交，出口货物的完税价格=(CFR－运费)/(1+出口关税税率)

按照 CIF 价格成交，出口货物的完税价格

=(CIF－运费－保险费)/(1+出口关税税率)

● 利润的计算

销售利润=销售价格×利润率

成本利润=采购成本×利润率

Analysis:

以货号 DC-212-10018 为例：

CIF 报价=成本+费用+利润

实际成本=采购成本/(1+增值税率)×(1+增值税率－出口退税率)

=16.8/(1+17%)×(1+17%－13%)=14.9RMB

国内费用=报关费+报检费+核销费+内陆运费

=200+200+10+60×0.14308×2400=20,570RMB

银行费用=信用证通知费+信用证修改费+议付费

=200+100+CIF 价格×0.13%=365RMB

海洋运费=0.14308×24×151=518RMB

货运保险=CIF 价格×(1+10%)×0.8%=438.72RMB

业务定额费=1.5%×7122×7=747.81RMB

包干费=4.5×2400=10800RMB

计算结果：货号为 DC-212-10018 的 CIF 报价为每件 3.09 美元。

Task 3　Offer 出口发盘

An offer is a proposal of terms and conditions presented in a potential contract by one party to another party. The following letter is an offer for reference.

Sender: Jessica@Sakai.com

Receiver: Barbur@ABF.com

Subject: Quotation

Dear Sir,

Thank you for your inquiry.

As you have mentioned that you would like to get the quotation of Sweater, we are now sending this email herewith the quotation of Sweater.

Unit price:

Art No. DC-212-10018	Flocking Sweater with Chick Pattern	600pcs	@USD3.09/pc
Art No. DC-210-10019	Flocking Sweater with Lion Pattern	600pcs	@USD3.64/pc
Art No. DC-210-10020	Flocking Sweater with Dog head Pattern	1,200pcs	@USD2.57/pc

The above all quotations are based on the stated order quantity.

Packing: to be packed in cartons of 24pcs each

Shipment: not later than July, 2008

Insurance: to be covered by the buyer for 110PCT of the invoice value against all risks

Payment: by irrevocable L/C payable by draft at sight

We are looking forward to your favorable reply.

Thanks & regards.

Yours faithfully,

×××

Directions 操作指南

➢ **In response to an enquiry, quotations may be sent. A satisfactory quotation will include the following: 让客户满意的发盘应包括如下内容:**

● An express of thanks for the enquiry. 对客户询盘表示感谢。

● Details of prices, terms of payment, quantity, packing, shipment, insurance, etc. 准确阐明各项主要交易条件，如价格、数量、包装、装运、付款、保险等。

● A statement or clear indication of what the prices cover. 对报价组成部分的明确表述。

● The period for which the quotation is valid. 规定发盘的有效期及其他约束条件。

● Advise your client to place an order as soon as possible owing to the increase of demand or other reason. 鼓励对方订货并尽早下订单。

➢ **Use ful sentences 典型例句**

● We have learnt that there is a good demand for walnuts in your market, and take this opportunity of enclosing our quotation sheet for your consideration.

● As prices are steadily rising, we would advise you to place your order without delay.

● We have received your inquiry of… and wish to make the following offer.

● We have learnt from your letter dated… that you are going to place an order with us for 2,000 metric tons of chemical fertilizers. We are pleased to quote as follows:

Task 4   Acceptance 接受

One illustration of letter of acceptance is given below.

Sender: Jessica@Sakai.com

Receiver: Barbur@ABF.com

Subject: Acceptance

Dear Sir,

　　We have received your letter of April 28th, 2008.

　　After due consideration, we have pleasure in confirming offer and accepting it. We will draw up sales contract and send it to you as soon as possible.

Thanks & regards.

Yours faithfully,

×××

Practice 操作练习

Case No. 1

1. 操作信息

　　宁波新鑫进出口公司(ADD: 56 Jianfang Road, Ningbo, China, TEL: 0574-88773210)是宁波市一家颇具规模的进出口贸易公司，经营的主要产品包括纺织品和服装等，在欧美、日本等国际市场上享有一定的声誉。公司业务员 Eric 在互联网上获悉美国 Principal Co., Ltd. (ADD: 12th Ave, New York, USA, TEL: 212-350-6787)对女式衬衫很感兴趣，于是及时与对方取得联系并进行贸易磋商。

(1) 4 月 10 日 Principal 公司来函称：

　　"对你方衬衫很感兴趣，请报价格。"

(2) 4 月 15 日新鑫收到对方公司的询盘，核算出口商品的价格，核算资料如下：

　　供货价格 25 元/件，单价均包含 17%的增值税，出口退税率为 6%。

国内费用：

　　海洋运费：从宁波出口纺织服装品至美国纽约，一个 20 英尺集装箱的包箱费率为 1900 美元，一个 40 英尺集装箱的包箱费率为 2500 美元，散货基本运费为每运费吨 116 美元，计算标准为 W/M。

　　商检费 200 元，报关费 200 元，核销费 10 元。

　　货运保险：CIF 基础上加成 10%投保中国人民保险公司海运货物保险条款中的一切险，费率为 0.8%。

　　报价利润：报价的 10%。

　　汇率：7 元人民币兑换 1 美元。

(3) 4 月 25 日新鑫公司向 Principal 发报价函："女式衬衫 4000 件，CIF 纽约，不可撤销即期信用证，每件装一个塑料袋，每 20 件装一个纸箱，交货时间不迟于 2008 年 7 月。"

(4) 5 月 3 日宁波新鑫公司发接受函，双方达成交易，进入签订合同阶段。

2. 操作要求

(1) 请你以业务员的身份，根据上述资料计算每件衬衫的 CIF 价格。

(2) 请你以业务员的身份，根据上述资料用英语拟写一份询盘函与发盘函。

Case No. 2

1. 操作信息

杭州威然贸易有限公司(HANGZHOU WEIRAN TRADING CO., LTD., ADD: NO. 819 SHANGTANG ROAD, HANGZHOU, CHINA, TEL: 0571-83840566)，公司主要经营家用电器、通讯设备等进出口业务。2008 年威然公司参加了上海华交会，获悉加拿大家用电器进口集团(ELECTRIC HOUSEHOLD APPLIANCES IMPORTER CORP., ADD: 40 ST. GEORGE STREET, TORONTO, CANADA, TEL: 416-9226560)急需一批 29 英寸纯平彩电。

2. 操作要求

请你以业务员的身份，根据以下资料作出口报价核算：

(1) 29 英寸纯平彩电出厂价：3500 元/台。

(2) 40'集装箱包箱费率(上海—多伦多)：每箱 3200 美元。

(3) 40'集装箱国内成本：运杂费=1800 元，商检费=200 元，报关费=200 元，港杂费=1600 元，业务定额费=2000 元，银行费用=FOB 价格的 2%，其他杂费=700 元。

(4) 货物按发票金额的 110%投保一切险，保险费率为 0.5%。

(5) 增值税率 17%，出口退税率 6%，出口报价利润是 FOB 价格的 20%。

(6) 汇率：7.2 人民币兑换 1 美元。

*P*RACTICE *3*

Signing the Contract
签订外销合同

Learning Objectives 学习目标

◇ To be familiar with the structure, content and main clause of Sales Contract 熟悉外销合同的结构、内容及各项条款

◇ To be able to sign a Sales Contract with importer 掌握进出口贸易合同的填制方法及技巧

Example & Analysis 操作实例及解析

◆ Case Lead-in

After several rounds of negotiations by email, on May, 2008, Ningbo Sakai Pet Co., Ltd. finally succeeded in signing a Sales Contract with ABF International Co., Ltd. USA about Flocking Sweater.

◆ 案例导入

经过几个回合的往来函电磋商，宁波井通宠物用品有限公司在 2008 年 5 月与美国 ABF International Co., Ltd. 就宠物用植绒毛衣签订了一份贸易合同。

1. 售货确认书
SALES CONFIRMATION

2. 编号
Contract No.: <u>ST08020</u>
日期
Date: <u>MAY 26th, 2008</u>
地点
Place: <u>NINGBO, CHINA</u>

The Sellers:

NINGBO SAKAI PET CO., LTD.

118 ZHONGSHAN ROAD

NINGBO, CHINA

The Buyers:

ABF INTERNATIONAL CO., LTD.

35 FOREST AVENUE

MIAMI, USA

3. 下列签字双方同意按以下条款达成交易

The undersigned Sellers and Buyers have agreed to close the transaction according to the following terms and conditions.

4. 品名及规格 COMMODITY AND SPECIFICATIONS	5. 数 量 QUANTITY	6. 单 价 UNIT PRICE	7. 金 额 AMOUNT
		CIF MIAMI	
FLOCKING SWEATER WITH CHICKEN PATTERN	600 PCS	USD3.09/PC	USD1,854.00
FLOCKING SWEATER WITH LION PATTERN	600 PCS	USD3.64/PC	USD2,184.00
FLOCKING SWEATER WITH DOG HEAD PATTERN	1,200 PSCS	USD2.57/PC	USD3,084.00

8. SHIPPING MARK:
    ABF
    ST08020
    MIAMI
    C/NO.: 1-UP			

			USD7,122.00

9. 总值

TOTAL VALUE: SAY U.S. DOLLARS SEVEN THOUSAND ONE HUNDRED AND TWENTY-TWO ONLY.

10. 包装

PACKING: ALL THE PRODUCTS ARE PACKED IN THE STANDARD EXPORT CARTON BOXES. EACH TO BE PACKED IN A TRANSPARANT POLYBAG, 24 PIECES TO ONE CARTON.

11. 目的地

DESTINATION: FROM NINGBO TO MIAMI BY SEA.

12. 装运期限

SHIPMENT: IN JULY, 2008, WITH PARTIAL SHIPMENT AND TRANSSHIPMENT ALLOWED.

13. 保险

INSURANCE: TO BE COVERED BY THE SELLER FOR 110PCT OF THE INVOICE VALUE AGAINST ALL RISKS AS PER CIC.

14. 付款方式

PAYMENT: BY IRREVOCABLE L/C PAYABLE BY DRAFT AT SIGHT OPENED BY THE BUYER THROUGH A BANK ACCEPTABLE TO THE SELLER TO REACH THE SELLER 30 DAYS BEFORE TIME OF SHIPMENT AND REMAIN VALID FOR NEGOTIATION UNTIL THE 15TH DAY AFTER THE DATE OF SHIPMENT.

买方(The Buyers)   卖方(The Sellers)

Directions 操作指南

书面合同的基本内容通常包括约首、本文和约尾三个部分。

1. 约首部分(Preamble)

合同的约首通常包括合同名称、合同编号、缔约双方公司名称和地址、签约日期、签约地点等内容。合同编号最好能用代码反映出签约部门和客户、签约年份和编号，以便日后的管理和参考。

2. 本文部分(Body)

本文是合同的主体，包括买卖货物的品名、品质规格、成交数量、价格、包装、运输、支付和保险等条款。

(1) 品名条款。通常合同中品名条款比较简单，通常是在(name of commodity)"商品名称"或"品名"的标题下，列明交易双方成交货物的名称。有时为了省略起见，也可不加标题，只在合同的开头部分，列明交易双方同意买卖的某种货物。

但有的货物具有不同的规格、等级和型号，为了明确起见，有必要把有关的具体规格、等级和型号等概括性的表述包含在品名中，做进一步的限定，这种情况下，常常使用"货物描述"(description of goods)来标明商品的具体细节。

(2) 品质条款。品质条款是构成商品说明的重要组成部分，也是交易双方在交接货物时对货物品质界定的主要依据。在国际贸易中，决定商品品质的方法一般有两种：一种是用实物来表示商品的品质，另一种是用文字说明表示商品的品质。

(3) 数量条款。数量是指用一定的度量衡制度表示出的商品的重量、个数、长度、面积、容积等的量。数量条款中最基本的内容，主要是交易的数量和计量单位。

(4) 价格条款。国际贸易合同中的价格条款通常包括单价(unit price)和总值(amount)两个项目。商品的单价通常由计量单位、单位价格金额、计价货币和贸易术语四个部分组成。在合同中，单价的各个组成部分必须表述清楚。总值是指单价同成交商品数量的乘积，即一笔交易的货款总金额。若合同允许数量溢短装，则总金额也应该有相应的增减幅度。

(5) 包装条款。包装条款的主要内容包括包装方式、规格、包装材料和运输标志。

(6) 运输条款。一般应根据价格条件订明装运时间及批次、装运港和卸货港、运输方式、分批和转运条款等内容。装运港和目的港是贸易术语和合同中的要件，决定着买卖双方的责任、费用与风险的划分。如果没有相关规定，一般应在合同中订明"允许分批装运"或"允许转船"。

(7) 支付条款。合同中的支付条款根据不同的支付方式而内容各异，使用汇付方式时，应明确规定具体的汇付方式、汇付的时间和金额；使用托收方式时，应明确规定交单条件、方式和买方付款或承兑责任以及付款期限；使用信用证方式时，主要内容应包括信用证种类、开证银行、开证时间、信用证有效期及到期地点等。

(8) 保险条款。一般根据贸易术语明确由买方或卖方负责投保，保险条款必须订明办理保险的当事人、保险险别、保险金额的确定、采用的保险条款并注明生效日期等事项。在 CIF 术语下，如没有特殊说明，由卖方根据保险公司条款按发票总值 110% 投保最低险别，卖方在替买方投保后应把保险权益及时转让给买方。

3. 约尾部分(End)

约尾是合同的结尾部分，一般包括合同文字效力的规定、合同份数的说明、适用法律条款的规定以及订约日期、地点和双方当事人签字等内容。

空白合同样式如下：

1. **售货确认书**
SALES CONFIRMATION

2. 编号
Contract No.: _____
日期
Date: _____
地点
Place: _____

The Sellers:

The Buyers:

3. 下列签字双方同意按以下条款达成交易

The undersigned Sellers and Buyers have agreed to close the transaction according to the following terms and conditions.

4. 品名及规格 COMMODITY AND SPECIFICATIONS	5. 数 量 QUANTITY	6. 单 价 UNIT PRICE	7. 金 额 AMOUNT
8. SHIPPING MARK:			

9. 总值

TOTAL VALUE:

10. 包装

PACKING:

11. 目的地

DESTINATION:

12. 装运期限

SHIPMENT:

13. 检验

INSPECTION:

14. 保险

<u>INSURANCE:</u>

15. 付款方式

<u>PAYMENT:</u>

OTHER TERMS:

1. 异议：品质异议须于货到目的口岸之日起 30 天内提出，数量异议须于货到目的口岸之日起 15 天内提出，但均须提供经卖方同意的公证行的检验证明。如责任属于卖方者，卖方于收到异议 20 天内答复买方并提出处理意见。

　　Discrepancy: In case of quality discrepancy, claim should be lodged by the Buyers within 30 days after the arrival of the goods at the port of destination, while for quantity discrepancy, claim should be lodged by the Buyers within 15 days after the arrival of the goods at the port of destination. In all cases, claims must be accompanied by Survey Reports of Recognized Public Surveyors agreed to by the Sellers. Should the responsibility of the subject under claim be found to rest on the part of the Sellers, the Sellers shall, within 20 days after receipt of the claim, send their reply to the Buyers together with suggestion for settlement.

2. 信用证内应明确规定卖方有权可多装或少装所注明的百分数，并按实际装运数量议付(信用证之金额按本售货合约金额增加相应的百分数)。

　　The covering Letter of Credit shall stipulate the Sellers' option of shipping the indicated percentage more or less than the quantity here by contracted and be negotiated for the amount covering the value of quantity actually shipped. (The Buyers are requested to establish the L/C in amount with the indicated percentage over the total value of the order as per this Sales Contract.)

3. 信用证内容须严格符合本售货合约的规定，否则修改信用证的费用由买方负担，卖方并不负因修改信用证而延误装运的责任，并保留因此而发生的一切损失的索赔权。

　　The contents of the covering Letter of Credit shall be in strict conformity with the stipulations of the Sales Contract. In case of any variation there of necessitating amendment of the L/C, the Buyers shall bear the expenses for effecting the amendment. The Sellers shall not be held responsible for possible delay of shipment resulting from awaiting the amendment of the L/C and reserve the right to claim from the Buyers for the losses resulting therefrom.

4. 除经约定保险归买方投保者外，由卖方向中国的保险公司投保。如买方需增加保险额及/或需要加保其他险，可于装船前提出，经卖方同意后代为投保，其费用由买方负担。

　　Except in cases where the insurance is covered by the Buyers as arranged, insurance is to be covered by the Sellers with a Chinese insurance terms is required by the Buyers, prior notice to this effect must reach the Sellers before shipment and is subject to the Sellers' agreement, and the extra insurance premium shall be for the Buyers' account.

5. 因人力不可抗拒事故使卖方不能在本售货合约规定期限内交货或不能交货，卖方不负责任，但是卖方必须立即以电报通知买方。如果买方提出要求，卖方应以挂号函向买方提供由中国国际贸易促进委员会或有关机构出具的证明，证明事故的存在。买方不能领到进口许可证，不能被认为系属人力不可抗拒范围。

The Sellers shall not be held responsible if they fail, owing to Force Majeure cause or causes, to make delivery within the time stipulated in this Sales Contract or cannot deliver the goods. However, the Sellers shall inform immediately the Buyers by cable. The Sellers shall deliver to the Buyers by the China Council for the Promotion of International Trade or by any competent authorities, attesting the existence of the said cause or causes. The Buyers' failure to obtain the relative Import License is not to be treated as Force Majeure.

6. 仲裁：凡因执行本合约或有关本合约所发生的一切争执，双方应以友好方式协商解决；如果协商不能解决，应提交中国国际经济贸易仲裁委员会，根据该会的仲裁规则进行仲裁。仲裁裁决是终局的，对双方都有约束力。

Arbitration: All disputes arising in connection with this Sales Contract or the execution there of shall be settled by way of amicable negotiation. In case no settlement can be reached, the case at issue shall then be submitted for arbitration to the China International Economic and Trade Arbitration Commission in accordance with the provisions of the said Commission. The award by the said Commission shall be deemed as final and binding upon both parties.

7. 附加条款(本合同其他条款如与本附加条款有抵触时，以本附加条款为准)。

Supplementary Condition(s) (Should the articles stipulated in this Contract be in conflict with the following supplementary condition(s), the supplementary condition(s) should be taken as valid and binding.)

_____   _____

买方(The Buyers)   卖方(The Sellers)

Practice 操作练习

Case No. 1

1. 操作信息

杭州华辰纺织服装进出口公司(HANGZHOU HUACHEN TEXTILE GARMENT IMP. & EMP. CO., LTD., ROOM 308-310 JINMAO BUILDING, NO. 819 XUEYUAN ROAD, HANGZHOU, CHINA)从事纺织服装等产品进出口业务，公司产品主要销往欧洲、美洲等地区。美国 ROSBRO SPORTWEAR INTERNATIONAL CORP. 欲求购一批中国产的女士全棉上衣(LADIES COTTON BLAZER)。

(1) 2008 年 3 月 2 日，ROSBRO 公司传真一份制作女士全棉上衣(LADIES COTTON BLAZER)的指示书，并邮寄面料、色样及一件成衣样品给华辰公司，要求 2008 年 6 月 20 日前交货，并回寄面料、色样及成衣样品确认。

(2) 2008 年 3 月 7 日，华辰公司收到该样件后，立即联络杭州临平天羽制衣有限公司，根据 ROSBRO 提供的样件打品质样和色卡，然后用 DHL 邮寄给 ROSBRO 公司确认。

(3) 2008 年 3 月 13 日，ROSBRO 公司收到华辰公司寄去的样件，回复确认合格，要求华辰公司再寄送成衣样品供其确认。收到邮件后，华辰公司立即联络临平天羽制衣赶制成衣样品。3 月 17 日，天羽制衣将成衣样品送到华辰公司，当天华辰公司就将该样品用 DHL 邮寄给 ROSBRO 公司确认。

(4) 2008 年 3 月 22 日，ROSBRO 公司收到华辰公司寄去的成衣样品，确认合格，要求华辰公司报价。当天，华辰公司根据要求，以制衣厂的报价、交易费用、公司利润等为基础向 ROSBRO 公司报价。

(5) 经过多次磋商，3 月 25 日，双方最终确定报价为，2500 件女士全棉上衣，货号：46-301A，50 件装一纸箱，每件 USD12.80 FOB 上海，不可撤销信用证，2008 年 6 月 20 日前从上海装运至美国。ROSBRO 公司要求华辰公司根据该份报价单制作合同传真其会签。

补充资料：

合同编号：LCB05127，投保一切险，不允许分批装运，允许转运，从中国运至美国长滩港口。

2. 操作要求

(1) 请你以业务员杨琳 LINDA YANG 和 MR. PETER 的身份，根据上述信息用英语拟写询盘函与发盘函。

(2) 缮制一份出口销售确认书。

1. 售货确认书
SALES CONFIRMATION

2. 编号
Contract No.: _____
日期
Date: _____
地点
Place: _____

The Sellers:

The Buyers:

3. 下列签字双方同意按以下条款达成交易

The undersigned Sellers and Buyers have agreed to close the transaction according to the following terms and conditions.

4. 品名及规格 COMMODITY AND SPECIFICATIONS	5. 数　量 QUANTITY	6. 单　价 UNIT PRICE	7. 金　额 AMOUNT
8. SHIPPING MARK:			

9. 总值
TOTAL VALUE:
10. 包装
PACKING:
11. 目的地
DESTINATION:
12. 装运期限
SHIPMENT:
13. 检验
INSPECTION:
14. 保险
INSURANCE:
15. 付款方式
PAYMENT:

买方(The Buyers)   卖方(The Sellers)

Case No. 2

1. 操作信息

客户询盘

　　INTERESTED IN MODEL CHD3050 PLEASE OFFER CIF TORONTO.

客户还盘

　　YOUR PRICE IS MUCH ON THE HIGH COUNTER-OFFER USD PLEASE REPLY.

客户接受

　　1,000 SETS OF COLOUR TELEVISION USD420.00 PER SET CIF TORONTO OCT. SHIPMENT PARTIAL SHIPMENT AND TRANSSHIPMENT ALLOWED INSURANCE AMOUNT 110 PCT INVOICE VALUE AGAINST ALL RISKS PAYMENT BY IRREVOCABLE LETTER OF CREDIT AT SIGHT WILL BE OPENED THROUGH THE CANADIAN IMPERIAL BANK OF COMMERCE.

SUPPLEMENT:
PACKING: 1SET/ CARTON
CONTRACT NO.: LH08106

2. 操作要求

　　根据实训二 Case No. 2 报价资料和上述往来函电，缮制一份出口销售确认书。

1. 售货确认书
SALES CONFIRMATION

2. 编号
Contract No.: _____
日期
Date: _____
地点
Place: _____

The Sellers:
The Buyers:

3. 下列签字双方同意按以下条款达成交易

The undersigned Sellers and Buyers have agreed to close the transaction according to the following terms and conditions.

4. 品名及规格 COMMODITY AND SPECIFICATIONS	5. 数　量 QUANTITY	6. 单　价 UNIT PRICE	7. 金　额 AMOUNT
8. SHIPPING MARK:			

9. 总值

TOTAL VALUE:

10. 包装

PACKING:

11. 目的地

DESTINATION:

12. 装运期限

SHIPMENT:

13. 检验

INSPECTION:

14. 保险

INSURANCE:

15. 付款方式

PAYMENT:

_____   _____

买方(The Buyers)   卖方(The Sellers)

PRACTICE 4

Execution of a Contract (I)
—Terms of Payment
履行合同（1）——选择支付方式

Example & Analysis 操作实例及解析

◆ Case Lead-in

After friendly negotiation, Ningbo Sakai Pet Co., Ltd. signed a Sales Contract with ABF International Co., Ltd. USA on May 26th, 2008, the terms of which read like this: Shipment to be effected from Ningbo to Miami by sea in July, 2008 with partial shipment and transshipment allowed. Payment to be made by irrevocable L/C payable by draft at sight to reach the sellers 30 days before time of shipment and remain valid for negotiation until the 15th day after the date of shipment. Ningbo Sakai Pet Co., Ltd. rushed ABF International Co., Ltd. to open the L/C and wrote to them asking for the amendment to the L/C upon examination. Finally, they received the amendment to the L/C and began to get the goods ready for shipment.

◆　**案例导入**

　　宁波井通宠物用品有限公司于 2008 年 5 月 26 日和美国 ABF 国际有限公司签订一外销合同，合同规定：2008 年 7 月装运，支付方式为不可撤销的即期信用证，信用证须在装运前一个月到达卖方，装运后 15 天在中国议付有效。井通公司催促对方开立信用证，在收到 L/C 后即审核并发函要求修改。最终，他们收到了信用证的修改通知书，开始备货。

Task 1　Rushing the Establishment of the L/C 催开信用证

　　In an L/C practice, the buyer should instruct his bank to open an L/C within the time stipulated in the contract. But for one reason or another (the price fluctuation, the importer's trouble in capital flow, etc.), he may fail to have the L/C opened on time. The seller should write to the buyer to urge him for the establishment of the L/C. It is the end of June but Ningbo Sakai Pet Co., Ltd. has not received the L/C yet. So they write the following letter to urge ABF International Co., Ltd. USA to issue the L/C.

Dear Sirs,

Referring to the 2,400 pieces of Flocking Sweaters under our S/C No. ST08020, we wish to call your attention to the fact that the date of shipment is drawing near, but we have not received the covering L/C up to now. Please do your utmost to expedite its establishment, so as to enable us to execute the order within the stipulated time.

For your information, there is a direct vessel sailing for your port around the middle of next month. If we have your L/C before the end of this month, we might catch the steamer.

In order to avoid subsequent amendments, please see to it that the L/C stipulations are in strict conformity with the terms and conditions of the contract.

We look forward to your L/C at an early date.

Yours faithfully,

×××

Directions 操作指南

➢　**Generally speaking, a letter rushing the establishment of L/C should be written in a courteous way. The letter should include the following information: 催证信函的写信要点如下：**

●　State the time stipulated by the S/C to open the L/C. 陈述合同规定的开证时间。

- Ask the buyer to expedite the establishment of the L/C. 要求速开信用证。
- Care to be taken by the buyer in opening the L/C. 开证注意事项。
- Express your expectation to receive the L/C. 盼早日收到信用证。

➢ **Useful sentences** 典型例句

- Referring to the 500 pieces of Sewing Machines under our S/C No. 668, we would draw your attention to the fact that the date of shipment is approaching, but we haven't received your L/C up to date. 关于我方第 668 号合同项下的 500 台缝纫机，我们拟提请你方注意，交货日期日益逼近，而有关的信用证至今未到。

- With reference to our S/C No. 367 dated Jan. 15th, 2009, we regret to find that your L/C has failed to arrive here within the time stipulated. 关于我方于 2009 年 1 月 15 日签订的第 367 号合同，我们很遗憾你方的信用证未能在规定的时间开达我方。

- As stipulated in our Sales Confirmation No. 667, the covering L/C should reach us not later than the end of this month and we hope you will open it in time so as to ensure early shipment. 按照第 667 号销售确认书，有关信用证应该不迟于本月底前到达我方，希望你们及时开证，以确保早日装运。

- As the goods are ready for shipment, please expedite your L/C so that we may effect shipment by S.S. "Peace". 由于货已备好待运，请速开信用证以便这批货能赶上"和平"号轮。

- In order to avoid subsequent amendments, please see to it that the L/C stipulations are in exact accordance with the terms of the contract. 为避免日后修改，务请做到信用证条款与合同条款完全相符。

- If you do not establish the L/C in time, you will be responsible for the loss resulting from the delay. 如果你方不能及时开出信用证，你方将承担由于耽搁所造成的一切损失。

- If your L/C fails to reach us by the end of July, we will be forced to cancel your order. 如果你方未能在七月底前将信用证开到，我方将被迫取消你方订单。

Task 2 Examining the L/C with the S/C 审核信用证

Upon receipt of the L/C, the exporter should pay special attention to checking the credit to see if all the terms and conditions in the credit are in strict conformity with S/C stipulations and if not, amendments should be made well in advance of shipment of the goods. Otherwise the exporter may run the risk of his draft being dishonored by the bank. The following is the L/C opened by STANDARD BANK LTD., USA.

Issue of a Documentary Letter of Credit

51A: Issuing Bank	:	STANDARD BANK LTD., USA
40A: Form of Doc. Credit	:	REVOCABLE
20: No. of Doc. Credit	:	BOC070325

31C: Date of Issue	:	080628
31D: Expiry	:	DATE 080810 PLACE MIAMI USA
50: Applicant	:	ABF INTERNATIONAL CO., LTD. USA
59: Beneficiary	:	NINGBO SAKAI PET CO., LTD.
		118 ZHONGHUA ROAD, NINGBO, CHINA
		TEL: 0574-88762018, FAX: 0574-88762020
32B: Amount	:	USD5,935.00 (SAY U.S. DOLLARS FIVE THOUSAND NINE HUNDRED AND THIRTY-FIVE ONLY.)
27: Pos./Neg. Tol. (%)	:	5/5
41D: Available with/by	:	ANY BANK IN ADVISING COUNTRY BY NEGOTIATION
42C: Draft at	:	DRAFT AT 30 DAYS SIGHT
42A: Drawee	:	ABF INTERNATIONAL CO., LTD. USA
43P: Partial Shipment	:	NOT ALLOWED
43T: Transshipment	:	NOT ALLOWED
44A: Loading in Charge	:	NINGBO
44B: For Transport to	:	MIAMI, USA
44C: Latest Date of Shipment	:	JULY 30TH, 2008
45A: Descrip. of Goods	:	2,400PCS OF FLOCKING SWEATERS AS PER S/C NO. ST08020 DD MAY 26TH, 2008.
46A: Documents Required	:	

46A: Documents Required :

- COMMERCIAL INVOICE IN 4 FOLD.
- PACKING LIST IN DUPLICATE.
- FULL SET OF CLEAN ON BOARD MARINE BILLS OF LADING MADE OUT TO ORDER MARKED "FREIGHT PREPAID" AND NOTIFY APPLICANT.
- CERTIFICATE OF ORIGIN IN ONE ORIGINAL AND ONE COPY.
- INSURANCE POLICY OR CERTIFICATE BLANK ENDORSED FOR 120% OF THE INVOICE VALUE, STATING CLAIMS PAYABLE IN MIAMI FOR THE CURRENCY OF THE DRAFT(S), COVERING OCEAN MARINE CARGO ALL RISKS AND WAR RISKS AS PER CIC CLAUSE.
- COPY OF FAX/EMAIL SENT BY BENEFICIARY TO APPLICANT WITHIN TWO DAYS FROM B/L ON BOARD DATE EVIDENCING: VALUE OF GOODS AND THEIR QUANTITY (FOR EACH STYLE, SIZE AND COLOR), FEEDER AND OCEANIC VESSEL NAME, PORT OF LOADING AND PORT OF DISCHARGE, CONTAINER IDENTIFICATION NUMBER, SAILING DATE AND E.T.A.
- COPY OF SIGNED DECLARATION ISSUED BY THE COMPANY

WHO LOADED THE GOODS ON THE CONTAINER STATING THAT ALL THE GOODS INDICATED ON THE SHIPPING DOCUMENTS (COMMERCIAL INVOICE AND PACKING LIST) HAVE BEEN REALLY LOADED ON THE CONTAINER.

- COPY OF FAX/EMAIL SENT BY APPLICANT TO BENEFICIARY STATING THAT ALL SHIPPING DETAILS HAVE BEEN SUPPLIED BY BENEFICIARY.

47A: Additional conditions :
- ALL DOCUMENTS MUST BEAR THIS L/C NUMBER.
- SHIPPING MARKS: ABF/ST08020/MIAMI/C/NO.1-UP
- NOTWITHSTANDING THE PROVISIONS OF UCP 600, IF WE GIVE NOTICE OF REFUSAL OF DOCUMENTS PRESENTED UNDER THIS CREDIT, WE SHALL HOWEVER RETAIN THE RIGHT TO ACCEPT A WAIVER OF DISCREPANCIES FROM THE APPLICANT AND, SUBJECT TO SUCH WAIVER WITHOUT REFERENCE TO THE PRESENTER PROVIDED THAT NON-WRITTEN INSTRUCTIONS TO THE CONTRARY HAVE BEEN RECEIVED BY US FROM THE PRESENTER BEFORE THE RELEASE OF THE DOCUMENTS. ANY SUCH RELEASE PRIOR TO RECEIPT OF CONTRARY INSTRUCTIONS SHALL NOT CONSTITUTE A FAILURE ON OUR PART TO HOLD THE DOCUMENTS AT THE PRESENTER'S RISK AND DISPOSAL, AND WE WILL HAVE NO LIABILITY TO THE PRESENTER IN RESPECT OF ANY SUCH RELEASE.

71B: Charges :
- ALL COMM. AND CHARGES OUTSIDE USA, INCLUDING UNUTILIZED COMM./CHARGES, AND ALL AMENDMENT COMM./ CHRGS (OURS AND YOURS), PLUS USD60 DISCRE-PANCY FEES, IF ANY, ARE FOR BENEFICIARY'S ACCOUNT.

48: Presentation Period : 15 DAYS AFTER ISSUANCE DATE OF SHIPPING DOCUMENTS.

49: Confirmation : WITHOUT

78: Inst. to Payg/Accptg/ Negotg Bank :
- UPON RECEIPT OF COMPLIED DOCUMENTS AT OUR COUNTERS WE SHALL CREDIT NEGOTIATING BANK ACCORDING TO THEIR INSTRUCTIONS.
- DOCS TO BE SENT TO US IN TWO CONSECUTIVE SETS: FIRST BY DHL COURIER, SECOND BY REGISTERED AIRMAIL.

Sender to Receiver Information : SUBJECT TO UCP 2006 REV. I.C.C. PUB. NO. 600

Directions 操作指南

Letter of Credit is based on documents. Whether the exporter can get paid depends entirely on the documents he presents to the bank. It will put the exporter in great trouble if the terms and conditions in the L/C are not in compliance with the S/C terms. His draft will be dishonored by the bank if his documents do not comply with the L/C terms. And this means he has broken the contract, the importer will lodge a claim against him. If he doesn't conform to the S/C stipulations, his draft will be dishonored by the opening bank. So examining the L/C with the S/C is a vitally important step under an L/C practice.

➢ **Items to be examined in the L/C**

1. 信用证的种类必须与合同规定一致

　　按 UCP600 规定，凡是可撤销的信用证必须注明"revocable"字样，如未注明，则视为不可撤销。

2. 信用证中的两个主要当事人，即开证人和受益人的名称必须准确无误。

3. 信用证中的合同号码是否正确。

　　信用证中一般有两个号码，一个是信用证号码，一个是合同号码。信用证中所述的合同号码必须与所签的合同号码完全一致。

4. 信用证是否生效。

　　有些信用证规定以进口许可证的签发或以收到卖方样品等为生效条件。这类有保留条件或限制性条件的信用证实际上并未生效。因此，在信用证生效之前，受益人不可贸然准备装船。

5. 信用证的金额是否与合同一致。

　　信用证的金额绝对不能低于合同金额，所用货币种类要与合同规定的一致，金额的大小写要一致。

6. 信用证的有效期和有效地

　　信用证应规定一个有效期，到期地点尽量要求在我国。根据 UCP600 规定，若信用证没有规定有效期，视为无效信用证。

7. 信用证的装运期和有效期

　　信用证的装运期一般应规定为最迟(LATEST)某年某月。

　　若来证没有规定装运期，根据 UCP600 的规定，可理解为"双到期"，即有效期和装运期在同一天。

8. 汇票条款

　　若信用证为即期付款，其汇票条款为"CREDIT AVAILABLE BY YOUR DRAFT(S) AT SIGHT FOR 100% OF INVOICE VALUE DRAWN ON…"。若信用证为远期付款，要分清是真远期还是假远期，真远期的汇票条款一般为"AVAILABLE BY YOUR DRAFT(S) AT 30 DAYS SIGHT DRAWN ON US FOR 100% OF THE INVOICE VALUE"；而假远期的汇票条款一般为

"USANCE DRAFT ON SIGHT BASIS, DISCOUNT CHARGES, ACCEPTANCE COMMISSION ARE FOR APPLICANT'S ACCOUNT"。

9. 装运港和目的港

　　装运港和目的港必须符合合同要求。

10. 分批装运及转运

　　UCP600 规定，除非信用证另有规定，允许分批装运及转运；

　　UCP600 规定，运输单据表面注明货物系使用同一运输工具并经同一路线运输的，即使每套运输单据注明的装运日期不同及/或装货港、接受监管地、发运地不同，只要运输单据注明的目的地相同，也不视为分批装运；

　　UCP600 规定，除非信用证特别授权，如信用证规定在指定时期内分期装运，其中任何一期未按期装运，则信用证对该期和以后各期均告失效；

　　来证不准分批，又没有数量增减条款，则实际装运数量不得少装。但对于散装货，UCP600 规定即使信用证不准分批，数量也可有 5%的增减幅度。

11. 货物描述

　　来证所列货物的品名、货号、规格、数量、单价、总值、包装等必须符合合同规定。佣金和折扣的规定也要符合合同要求。

12. 单据要求

(1) 商业发票

　　来证要求出具两份不同买主名称的商业发票时，应要求改证。

(2) 海运提单

　　以 FOB 成交时，提单应显示"FREIGHT COLLECT"，如来证要求显示"FREIGHT PREPAID"，则应要求修改。

(3) 保险单

　　信用证中保险单的保险条款、险别、保险加成、保险人和理赔人等内容应与合同相符。如信用证要求合同条款外的险别且不明确说明额外保费由开证人负担，则应要求修改。

(4) 产地证

　　可由出入境检验检疫局或贸促会出具，但要求上述两家机构互相加具证明的不能接受。

(5) 普惠制产地证格式 A

　　出入境检验检疫局是我国签发普惠制产地证格式 A 的唯一机构，如来证要求由其他机构签发，则应要求改证。

(6) 受益人证明书

　　受益人证明书主要有寄单证明、电抄本和履约证明等。来证要求出具的受益人证明书应是受益人能够做到的。

13. 信用证中是否存在其他不合理的要求

　　例如：应由开证人负担的费用却要求受益人来负担；应在装运后寄给开证人的提单副本却要求出口人在装运前寄出，等等。

Task 3 Amending the L/C 修改信用证

Upon examination, the seller should contact the buyer by asking for the amendment to the L/C without delay. The following is written by Ningbo Sakai Pet Co., Ltd. to that effect.

Dear Mr. Gray,

We have received your Letter of Credit No. BOC070325 issued by STANDARD BANK LTD., USA with thanks. Upon examination, we found some discrepancies between your L/C and S/C No. ST08020. Please amend the L/C as follows:

- The form of the credit should be irrevocable instead of revocable;
- Amend the expiry date and place to read: 080815 in the place of China;
- Change the beneficiary's address from ZHONGHUA ROAD to ZHONGSHAN ROAD;
- Increase the amount from USD5,935.00 to USD7,122.00;
- The drawee should be STANDARD BANK LTD. USA, not ABF INTERNATIONAL CO., LTD. USA;
- Amend the credit allowing partial shipment and transshipment.
- Turn the insurance amount from 120% of the invoice value to 110% of the invoice value.

The time of shipment is approaching. Please amend the L/C accordingly ASAP to enable us to execute the S/C smoothly.

Yours faithfully,

XXX

Directions 操作指南

➢ 修改信用证的注意事项

信用证经审核后，如发现有不符点应及时通知国外买方指示开证行进行修改，应注意以下几点：

- 一份信用证如有几处需要修改，应集中一次通知开证人办理修改，以免浪费时间和费用；
- 对收到的信用证修改通知书要认真审核，如发现内容有误或不能接受的，应及时作出拒绝修改的通知并交通知行；
- UCP600 规定，一份信用证的修改通知书的内容要么全部接受，要么全部拒绝，不能只接受其中的一部分而拒绝另一部分；
- UCP600 规定，信用证的修改通知书必须由原通知行转递或通知。

➢ 改证信函的写信要点

- Confirm your receipt of the L/C but find some discrepancies. 确认收到信用证，经审核存在不符点。
- The items to be amended. 具体要修改的内容。

● Express your wish to receive the amendment at an early date. 尽快修改的意愿。

➢ **Useful sentences in amending the L/C 典型例句**

(1) Thank you very much for your L/C No. 667 which we have duly received. After checking it, however, we would request you to make the following amendments: 我们已收到你方 667 号信用证，谢谢。但经审核，我们要求你方作如下修改：

(2) We are glad to inform you that we have received your L/C No. 345 against S/C No. 987, but find a number of discrepancies. Please amend the L/C as follows: 我们很高兴收到第 987 号合同项下的第 345 号信用证，但发现其中有一些不符点，请对信用证作如下修改：

(3) Please amend the L/C to read/reading... 请修改信用证，改为⋯⋯

(4) Please amend the L/C allowing transshipment and partial shipment. 请改证允许转运和分批装运。

(5) Please delete/cross off/leave out... 请删去⋯⋯

(6) Please insert... 请加上(插入)⋯⋯

(7) To change A into B / To amend A to read B / ... should be B instead of A 将 A 改为 B

(8) To insert B before A / To add B before A 在 A 之前加上 B

(9) To increase the amount from...to... 请将金额由⋯⋯增加到⋯⋯

(10) We shall appreciate it if you will give this matter your immediate attention. / Your amendment to the L/C will be highly appreciated. 请尽快修改信用证为感。

(11) Please amend the L/C at once so as to enable us to effect shipment in time. 请尽快修改信用证以便我方按时装运。

Practice 操作练习

Case No. 1

1. 操作信息

浙江华强经贸有限公司业务员王辉在 2008 年 5 月 1 日和美国大洋贸易有限公司签订一外销合同，合同规定最晚装运期为 2008 年 7 月 30 日，支付方式为不可撤销的即期信用证，信用证须在装运前一个月到达卖方。现已经是 2008 年 6 月 20 日，但王辉还未收到任何关于信用证的消息。

2. 操作要求

请你替王辉写一封催证函，包含以下内容：

● 有关第 123 号合同项下的 5000 辆自行车，交货期逼近，但还未收到相关信用证；

● 为使我方能顺利履行合同，请速开信用证；

● 货已备妥，如果能在 6 月 30 日前收到信用证，则有希望在 7 月底前装运；

● 为避免日后的修改，信用证条款必须和合同条款完全一致；

● 静候佳音。

Case No. 2

1. 操作信息

杭州丽都纺织品进出口公司业务员李强和加拿大温哥华贸易公司于 2008 年 3 月 20 日签订以下合同，加拿大温哥华贸易公司开立了相关信用证，号码为 No. BOC080925。

2. 操作要求

请你替李强审核信用证，找出不符点，并拟一封要求修改信用证的信件。

附1：售货确认书

1. 售货确认书
SALES CONFIRMATION

2. 编号
Contract No.: 07YS88
日期
Date: MARCH 20TH, 2008
地点
Place: HANGZHOU

The Sellers:

LI DU TEXTILES

 IMP./EXP CORP.,

HANGZHOU, CHINA

The Buyers:

VANCOUVER TRADING

 CO., LTD.

VANCOUVER, CANADA

3. 下列签字双方同意按以下条款达成交易

The undersigned Sellers and Buyers have agreed to close the transaction according to the following terms and conditions.

4. 品名及规格 COMMODITY AND SPECIFICATIONS	5. 数 量 QUANTITY	6. 单 价 UNIT PRICE	7. 金 额 AMOUNT
		CFR VANCOUVER	
HALOGEN FITTING W500	9,600PCS	USD3.80/PC	USD36,480.00
Shipping Mark: AT SELLER'S OPTION			
Packing: PACKED IN CARTON OF 5 DOZEN EACH			
			USD36,480.00

8. 总值

TOTAL VALUE: SAY U.S. DOLLARS THIRTY-SIX THOUSAND FOUR HUNDRED AND EIGHTY ONLY.

9. 目的地

DESTINATION: FROM CHINESE MAIN PORT TO VANCOUVER, WITH TRANSSHIPMENT AT HONG KONG

10. 装运期限

SHIPMENT: IN MAY, 2008.

11. 保险

INSURANCE: TO BE COVERED BY THE BUYERS.

12. 付款方式

PAYMENT: BY SIGHT IRREVOCABLE L/C TO BE OPENED 30 DAYS BEFORE SHIPMENT AND TO REMAIN VALID FOR NEGOTIATION IN CHINA UNTIL THE 15TH DAY AFTER SHIPMENT.

THE SELLER   THE BUYER

李　强 (盖章)   JOHN SMITH (盖章)

附 2：信用证

Issue of a Documentary Credit

Issuing Bank	:	STANDARD BANK LTD., CANADA
Form of Doc. Credit	:	REVOCABLE
No. of Doc. Credit	:	BOC080925
Date of Issue	:	080428
Expiry	:	DATE 080510 PLACE CANADA
Applicant	:	VANCOUVER TRADING CO., LTD., VANCOUVER, CANADA
Beneficiary	:	LI DU TEXTILES IMP./EXP. CORP., HANGZHOU, CHINA
Amount	:	USD36,480.00 (SAY U.S. DOLLARS THIRTY-SIX THOUSAND FOUR HUNDRED AND EIGHTY ONLY.)
Pos./Neg. Tol. (%)	:	5/5
Available with/by	:	ANY BANK IN ADVISING COUNTRY BY NEGOTIATION
Draft at	:	DRAFT AT 30 DAYS SIGHT
Drawee	:	ANCOUVER TRADING CO., LTD., VANCOUVE, CANADA
Partial Shipment	:	NOT ALLOWED
Transshipment	:	NOT ALLOWED
Loading in Charge	:	NINGBO
For Transport to	:	VANCOUVER
Latest Date of Shipment	:	MAY 30TH, 2008
Descrip. of Goods	:	960PCS OF HALOGEN FITTING W500, USD6.80 /PC AS PER S/C NO.07YS88 DD MAY 20TH, 2008
Documents Required	:	• COMMERCIAL INVOICE IN 4 FOLD. • PACKING LIST IN DUPLICATE. • FULL SET OF CLEAN ON BOARD MARINE BILLS OF LADING MADE OUT TO ORDER MARKED "FREIGHT PREPAID" AND NOTIFY APPLICANT IN DUPLICATE. • SHIPPMENT ADVICE MUST BE SENT TO APPLICANT WITHIN 2 DAYS AFTER SHIPMENT.
Presentation Period	:	6 DAYS AFTER ISSUANCE DATE OF SHIPPING DOCUMENTS.
Confirmation	:	WITHOUT

Case No. 3

1. 操作信息

附1：售货确认书

SALES CONFIRMATION

NO. SPT-211   **DATE: JAN. 8TH, 2008**

THIS SALES CONFIRMATION IS MADE AND ENTERED INTO BY AND BETWEEN HANGZHOU TIANHUA IMP. & EXP. CORP. 215 HUQIU ROAD, HANGZHOU, CHINA (HEREINAFTER REFERRED TO AS THE SELLERS) AND PETRRCO INTERNATIONAL TRADING CO., LTD., 1,100 SHEPPARD AVENUE EAST SUITE 406, WILLOWDALE ONTARIO, CANADA M2K 2W2 (HEREINAFTER REFERRED TO AS THE BUYERS) WHEREBY THE SELLERS AGREE TO SELL AND THE BUYERS TO BUY THE COMMODITIES MENTIONED IN THIS CONTRACT SUBJECT TO THE TERMS AND CONDITIONS STIPULATED BELOW:

COMMODITY & SPECIFICATION	QUANTITY	UNIT PRICE	AMOUNT
		CIF VANCOUVER	
SBW32　　BASKETBALL	2,000PCS	USD16.95/PC	USD33,900.00
GBW322　FOOTBALL	2,000PCS	USD21.33/PC	USD42,660.00
ERV5　　VOLLEYBALL	1,000PCS	USD12.15/PC	USD12,150.00
		TOTAL	USD88,710.00
TOTAL AMOUNT: SAY U.S. DOLLARS EIGHTY EIGHT THOUSAND SEVEN HUNDRED AND TEN ONLY.			

PACKING: TO BE PACKED IN CARTONS OF 50PCS EACH, TOTAL 100 CARTONS.

SHIPPING MARK: AT THE SELLER'S OPTION.

SHIPMENT: FROM SHANGHAI TO VANCOUVER IN MARCH, 2008 WITH TRANSSHIP MENT AND PARTIAL SHIPMENT ALLOWED.

TERMS OF PAYMENT: BY SIGHT IRREVOCABLE L/C TO BE OPENED 30 DAYS BEFORE SHIPMENT AND TO REMAIN VALID FOR NEGOTIATION IN CHINA UNTIL THE 15TH DAY AFTER SHIPMENT.

INSURANCE: TO BE COVERED BY THE SELLERS FOR 110% OF THE INVOICE VALUE AGAINST ALL RISKS AND WAR RISKS AS PER OCEAN MARINE CARGO AND WAR CLAUSES (CIC) OF THE PEOPLE'S INSURANCE COMPANY OF CHINA DATED 01/01/1981.

THE SELLER   **THE BUYER**

(signature)   (signature)

附 2: 信用证

ISSUE OF A DOCUMENTARY CREDIT

33062 BOCSH CN

ROYAL BANK BCR

OUR L/C NO. PIT310

JANUARY 30, 2008

FROM: THE ROYAL BANK OF CANADA, BRITISH COLUMBIA INTERNATIONAL CENTER, 1055 WEST GEORGIA STREET, VANCOUVER, B.C. V6E 3P3

TO: BANK OF CHINA, HANGZHOU BRANCH

BENEFICIARY: HANGZHOU TIANHUA IMP. & EXP. CORP. 215 HUQIU ROAD, HANGZHOU, CHINA

APPLICANT: PETRRCO INTERNATIONAL TRADING CO., LTD., 1,100 SHEPPARD AVENUE EAST SUITE 406, WILLOWDALE ONTARIO, CANADA M2K 2W2

FOR USD88,710.00 (SAY U.S. DOLLARS EIGHTY EIGHT THOUSAND SEVEN HUNDRED AND TEN ONLY.) TO EXPIRE APRIL 15TH, 2008 AT OUR COUNTRY AVAILABLE BY NEGOTIATION OF YOUR DRAFTS AT 30 DAYS AFTER SIGHT FOR 100% OF THE INVOICE VALUE DRAWN ON ROYAL BANK OF CANADA.

ACCOMPANIED BY THE FOLLOWING DOCUMENTS:

1. COMMERCIAL INVOICE IN QUADRUPLICATE INDICATING THE SALES CONFIRMATION NUMBER
2. PACKING LIST/WEIGHT MEMO IN TRIPLICATE.
3. FULL SET OF CLEAN ON BOARD OCEAN MARINE BILL OF LADING MADE OUT TO ORDER MARKED FREIGHT PREPAID AND NOTIFY APPLICANT.
4. INSURANCE POLICY OR CERTIFICATE IN DUPLICATE ENDORSED IN BLANKED COVERING ALL RISKS AND WAR RISKS FOR 120% OF THE INVOICE VALUE AS PER CIC DATED 01/01/1981.
5. CERTIFICATE OF ORIGIN

COVERING:

5,000PCS OF BASKETBALL, FOOTBAL AND VOLLEYBALL, CIF VANCOUVER AS PER S/C NO. SPT-211 DATED JAN. 8TH, 2008.

SHIPMENT FROM SHANGHAI TO VANCOUVER DURING MARCH 2008.

TRANSSHIPMENT AND PARTIAL SHIPMENT ARE NOT ALLOWED.

GOODS TO BE PACKED IN WOODEN CASES OF 50PCS EACH.

DOCUMENTS TO BE PRESENTED WITHIN 3 DAYS AFTER THE DATE OF ISSUANCE OF THE SHIPPING DOCUMENTS BUT WITHIN THE VALIDITY OF THE L/C.

SPECIAL INSTRUCTIONS:

- T/T REIMBURSEMENT IS NOT ALLOWED.
- DOCUMENTS PRIOR TO THE ISSUANCE OF THE L/C ARE NOT ACCEPTABLE.

WE HEREBY ENGAGE WITH DRAWER AND BONA FIDE HOLDERS THAT DRAFTS DRAWN AND NEGOTIATED IN CONFORMITY WITH THE TERMS OF THIS CREDIT WILL BE DULY HONORDED ON PRESENTATION AND THAT DRAFTS ACCEPTED WITHIN THE TERMS OF THIS CREDIT WILL BE DULY HONORED ON MATURITY.

THIS CREDIT IS ISSUED SUBJECT TO UCP600.

2. 操作要求

根据上述合同审核信用证并写一份改证函。

PRACTICE 5

Execution of a Contract (II)
—Preparing the Goods for Shipment

履行合同（2）——备货与出运

learning Objectives 学习目标

◇ To be able to sign a purchase contract with the manufacturer 与供货商签订内销合同

◇ To be familiar with the procedure of space booking 熟悉租船定舱的流程

◇ To be able to make shipping note 缮制托运单据

Example & Analysis 操作实例及解析

◆ Case Lead-in

Through business correspondence, Ningbo Sakai Pet Co., Ltd. received the following amendment to the L/C. They are now able to sign a purchase contract with the manufacturer and book shipping space.

◆ 案例导入

通过函电往来，宁波井通宠物用品有限公司收到了信用证的修改通知书如下，他们现在可以与生产商签订购货合同，缮制托运单据。

```
------------------------Instance Type and Transmission------------------------
Copy received from SWIFT
Priority: Normal
Message Output Reference: 0028 060316HZCBCN2HAXXX165206355256
Correspondent Input Reference: 1728 060315VRBPIT2VAXXX4594880290
```

------------------------Message Header------------------------

Swift OUTPUT: FIN 700 Amendment to a Documentary Credit

Sender: VRBPIT2VXXX

　　　STANDARD BANK LTD. USA

Receiver: HZCVCN2HXXX

　　　BANK OF CHINA, NINGBO BRANCH, NINGBO, CN

MUR: PG

------------------------Message Text------------------------

20:　　Sender's Reference

　　　1349/86283/VR/05

21:　　Receiver's Reference

　　　SEQUENCE 1/2

26E:　Number of Amendment

　　　　1

59:　　Beneficiary (before amendment)—Nm & Add

　　　NINGBO SAKAI PET CO., LTD.

　　　118 ZHONGHUA ROAD, NINGBO, CHINA

　　　TEL: 0574-88762018　　　FAX: 0574-88762020

40A:　Form of Doc. Credit: IRREVOCABLE

31E:　New Date and Place of Expiry:

　　　080815

59:　　Beneficiary's address: NINGBO SAKAI PET CO., LTD.

　　　　　　　　　118 ZHONGSHAN ROAD, NINGBO, CHINA

32B:　Amount: USD7,122.00 (SAY U.S.DOLLARS SEVEN THOUSAND ONE HUNDRED AND TWENTY-TWO ONLY.)

42C:　Draft at: SIGHT

43P:　Partial Shipment: ALLOWED

43T:　Transshipment: ALLOWED

46A:　Documents Required: INSURANCE AMOUNT NOW TO READ:
　　　　　　　　　"FOR 110% OF THE INVOICE VALUE".

------------------------Message Trailer------------------------

(MAC: 9938A72E)

(CHK: OABB30B3BAFB)

Task 1 Signing a Purchase Contract with the Manufacturer

与供货商签订购货合同

Most of the exporters do not have their own factories. They have to find suitable manufacturers to supply the goods. They should first make investigation into the commercial integrity and production capacity before signing a Purchase Contract with the supplier. Here is the contract signed by and between Ningbo Sakai Pet Co., Ltd. and Ningbo Xinxin Pet's Ware factory.

购销合同

需方：宁波井通宠物用品有限公司

供方：宁波新新宠物用品厂

合同编号：08678

签约日期：2008 年 6 月 15 日

签约地点：宁波

外销合同：ST08020

根据《中华人民共和国合同法》和有关法规，经双方协商签订本合同并信守下列条款：

一、商品

品名及规格	数量	单位	单价(含税)	金额(RMB￥)	交货期
宠物植绒毛衣 No. DC-212-10018(小鸡图案) No. DC-210-10019(狮子图案) No. DC-210-10020(小狗图案)	600 600 1,200	件 件 件	RMB￥16.80 RMB￥20.50 RMB￥14.50	10,080.00 12,300.00 17,400.00 39,780.00	2008 年 7 月 15 日前
总金额(大写)：人民币叁万玖仟柒佰捌拾元整					

二、质量要求：见附页

三、包装要求：每件装一透明塑料袋，每 24 件装一标准出口用纸板箱，详见附页。

四、交货地点：宁波北仑港

五、付款方式：供方凭增值税专用发票，专用税收缴款书、进仓单(送货回单或集装箱单)、购货合同向需方办理收款。

六、责任条款：

    (1) 因供方的责任造成国外客户索赔的，其索赔款及因索赔发生的费用由供方承担。

    (2) 需方已安排供方出产的商品，因外销变化需要作出某些调整或变更的，其修改部分则为合同的组成部分。

七、本合同有效期从 2008 年 6 月 15 日至 2008 年 10 月 30 日。

八、纠纷处理办法及地点：执行本合同过程中如有争议，双方同意通过协商解决；如协商未能取得一致，则由宁波市所辖人民法院管辖。

九、本协议双方签字盖章生效。合同一式两份，供需双方各执一份。

十、备注：

需方授权代表　　　　　　　　　　　　　　供方授权代表

盖　　章　　　　　　　　　　　　　　　　盖　　章

Directions 操作指南

(一) 备货是指卖方根据合同规定的品质、数量、包装和装运时间，进行货物的准备工作。备货工作的主要内容如下：

(1) 与供货商签订购货合同；

(2) 安排生产并核实检查应收货物的品质、数量和包装；

(3) 货物进仓后，在外包装上加刷唛头和其他必要的标志；

(4) 根据出口合同的规定，对货物进行检验。

(二) 在备货过程中应注意的问题：

1. 货物的品质必须与出口合同一致

货物的品质是合同的要约，必须十分重视。

对于凭文字说明成交的合同，卖方所交货物必须与文字说明相符。

对于凭样品成交的合同，卖方所交货物的内在质量与外观形态都必须与样品完全相符。

如果在交易中既凭样品又凭文字说明表示品质，则卖方所交货物的品质既要符合样品，又要与文字说明相符，其中任何一种不符，都构成违约。

2. 货物的数量必须与合同相符

备货时，数量应适当留有余地，以适应合同及信用证规定允许溢短装部分的需要，或装船时可能发生的调换和适应舱容之用。凡按重量计量的货物，且在合同或信用证中未规定按何种方法计量的，按惯例，应以净重计量。

3. 货物的包装和唛头必须符合出口合同和法律规定

货物的包装和唛头，应符合合同和信用证的规定以及运输的要求。如合同中未具体规定，应按同类货物通用的方式装箱或包装，如果没有此种通用的方式，则应按照足以保全或保护货物的方式装箱或包装。唛头的刷制，也应按合同办理。

4. 货物备妥的时间应与合同和信用证规定的装运时间相适应

交货时间是买卖合同的主要条件。延迟装运或提前装运均会导致对方拒收或索赔。合同中如未规定允许分批装运或转运，则应理解为不允许。合同中如规定了每批的数量和装运时间，卖方必须严格照办。如果其中某一期未按合同规定办理，买方可按违约情况要求损害赔偿甚至解除合同。

Task 2　Filling out Booking Note 填制托运单

Procedure for Booking Shipping Space for Ocean Freight
海运租船定舱流程

Under CFR or CIF terms, the seller is responsible for booking shipping space and bear freight charges to port of destination. Sea transport is the most widely used form of transportation in international trade for its low cost. Shipping is estimated to carry about 90% of international trade in terms of volume. The following is the flow for container transportation.

集装箱运输出口程序:

1. 订舱

发货人根据贸易合同或信用证条款的规定,在货物托运前一定时间内填好集装箱货物托运单(Container Booking Note)或出口货物明细单,委托其代理或直接向船公司申请订舱。

2. 接受托运申请

船公司或其代理公司根据自己的运力,航线等具体情况考虑发货人的要求,决定接受与否,若接受申请就着手编制订舱清单,然后分送集装箱堆场(CY),集装箱货运站(CFS),以安排空箱及办理货运交接。

3. 发放空箱

通常整箱货货运的空箱由发货人到集装箱码头堆场领取,有的货主有自备箱;拼箱货货运的空箱由集装箱货运站负责领取。

4. 拼箱货装箱

发货人将不足一整箱的货物交至货运站,由货运站根据订舱清单和场站收据负责装箱,然后由装箱人编制集装箱装箱单(Container Load Plan)。

5. 整箱货交接

由发货人自行负责装箱,并将已加海关封志的整箱货运到集装箱堆场(CY)。CY 根据订舱清单,核对场站收据(D/R)及装箱单验收货物。

6. 集装箱的交接签证

CY 或 CFS 在验收货物和/或箱子,即在场站收据上签字,并将签署后的 D/R 交还给发货人。

7. 装船

集装箱装卸区根据装货情况,制订装船计划,并将出运的箱子调整到集装箱码头前方堆场,待船靠岸,海关放行后即可装船出运。

8. 换取提单

发货人凭 D/R 向集装箱运输经营人或其代理换取提单(Combined Transport Bill of Lading),然后去银行办理结汇。

Directions 操作指南

(一) 出口货物明细单

出口货物明细单是发货人根据买卖合同、信用证和生产出货等实际情况制作的一种货运业务单据，供发货人分析和检查出口货物发运工作的进展以及完成情况的表格，出口货物明细单如下所示，其填写方法可参照集装箱货物托运单。

出口货物明细单

2008 年 7 月 15 日

信用证号码	BOC070325	填制单位编号	2008YN1880
银行编号		外运公司编号	NQ1880

合同(合约)号　ST08020

开证银行	STANDARD BANK LTD., USA	开证日期	JUNE 28TH, 2008	收到日期	JUNE 30TH, 2008
		金额	USD7,122.00	收汇方式	L/C
经营单位（装船人）	NINGBO SAKAI PET CO., LTD. 118 ZHONGSHAN ROAD, NINGBO, CHINA	货物性质		贸易国别	USA
收货人	TO ORDER	中间商名称及地址			

提单或承运收据	抬头人	TO ORDER	出口口岸	NINGBO	目的港	MIAMI
	通知人	ABF INTERNATIONAL CO., LTD. 35 FOREST AVENUE MIAMI, USA	可否转运	Y	可否分批	Y
	运费预付/到付	FREIGHT PREPAID	装运期限	JULY 30TH, 2008	有效期限	AUG. 15TH, 2008

货名规格及货号	HS·CD	件数及包装样式	数量/尺码	毛重(千克)	净重(千克)	价格(成交条件)总价
FLOCKING SWEATERS		100CTNS	24CBM	1,100KGS	1,000KGS	USD7,122.00

标记唛头	ABF ST08020 MIAMI C/NO.: 1-UP				
注意事项	B/L INDICATE THE L/C NO.: BOC070325			总体积	24CBM
				业务员	
				单证员	
				运输员	

(二) 集装箱货物托运单及其缮制

➤ 集装箱货物托运单(Container Booking Note)是出口企业办理海运集装箱货物托运时专用的订舱委托书。一套 12 联，各联的作用如下：

第一联　货主(一般为出口人)留底；

第二联　船代理留底；

第三联　运费通知(1)；

第四联　运费通知(2)；

第五联　装货单(Shipping Order)——场站收据副本；

　　　　附页——缴纳出口货物港务费申请书；

第六联　大副联——场站收据副本；

第七联　场站收据(Dock Receipt, D/R)，货物运至集装箱码头堆场或货运站，由场站业务员在此联上签字并加盖公章后退还发货人，证明货物已收到。发货人凭场站收据换取"收妥待运提单"，或在装船后换取"已装船提单"。

第八联　货代留底；

第九、十联　配舱回单(1)、(2)联；

第十一、十二联　备用联，空白格式。

出口企业根据"出口货物明细单"上规定的内容，参阅"海运出口船期表"中船舶的营运情况，并结合实际的备货情况，填制"海运出口托运单"，并在规定的"截单日"前将托运单送交货运代理公司办理配船定舱。如果需要货运代理派车到仓库提货的，还需将"外销出仓单"(提货联)附在托运单后一并交货运代理公司。

➤ 集装箱货物托运单的内容和缮制方法如下：

1. 托运人(SHIPPER)

出口公司的名称和地址。如果是代理货主办理租船定舱的，要列明代理人名称。

2. 收货人(CONSIGNEE)

在信用证的条件下，对收货人的规定常有两种方法：

(1) 记名收货人。收货人是合同的买方，这类单据不易转让；

(2) 指示收货人。指示收货人有空白指示和记名指示两种，单据可通过背书转让。

3. 受通知人(NOTIFY PARTY)

接受船方发出的到货通知的人的名称和地址。受通知人的职责是接受船方发出的到货通知并将该通知转告真实的收货人，受通知人无权提货。

4. 前程运输(PRECARRIAGE BY)

第一程船名，如果货物不需转运，此栏留空。

5. 收货地点(PLACE OF RECEIPT)

收货的港口名称或地点，如果货物不需转运，此栏留空。

6. 海运船名、航次(OCEAN VESSEL VOY NO.)

实际船名、航次，如果货物需要转运，需填第二程船名。

7. 装运港(PORT OF LOADING)

货物实际装船的港口名称，如果货物需要转运，需填货物中转港口的名称。

8. 卸货港(PORT OF DISCHARGE)

货物卸下最后一艘海轮时的港口名称，一般是目的港。填写时要明确具体，并与信用证描述一致，如有同名港，须注明国家、地区或州、城市。如信用证规定的目的港为选择港，则应是同一航线上的、同一航次挂靠的基本港。

9. 交货地点(PLACE OF DELIVERY)

即最终目的地。如果目的地是一内陆城市，则在此填写此内陆城市的名称；如果目的地就是卸货港，此栏留空。

10. 集装箱号(CONTAINER NO.)

此栏留空。

11. 封志号(SEAL NO.)

此栏留空。

12. 箱数和件数(NO. OF CONTAINERS OR PKGS.)

集装箱的箱数或包装的件数。

13. 包装种类及货名(KIND OF PACKAGES, DESCRIPTION OF GOODS)

包装种类是指货物外包装的种类，如捆、纸箱等。货名的内容允许只写大类名称或统称。但如果同时出口不同的商品，应分别填写，而不允许只填写其中一种数量较多或金额较大的商品。

14. 毛重(GROSS WEIGHT)

货物的实际毛重。如果一次装运的货物中有几种不同的包装材料或完全不同的货物，应分别计算并填写每一种包装材料或每一种货物的毛重，然后合计全部的毛重。一般用千克(公斤)作为计量单位。

15. 尺码(MEASUREMENT)

填写一批货的尺码总数，单位为立方米。总尺码不仅包括各件货物尺码之和，还应包括件与件之间堆放时的合理空隙。

16. 运费与附加费(FREIGHT AND CHARGES)

由船公司填写。

17. 其他各项：按货物性质和信用证规定填写。

Shipper(发货人) **NINGBO SAKAI PET CO., LTD.** **118 ZHONGSHAN ROAD, NINGBO, CHINA**				D/R No. (编号) 第 一 **集装箱货物托运单** 联 货主留底	
Consignee(收货人) **TO ORDER**					
Notify Party(受通知人) **ABF INTERNATIONAL CO., LTD.** **35 FOREST AVENUE, MIAMI, USA**					
Pre-carriage by(前程运输) Place of Receipt(收货地点)					
Ocean Vessel(船名) Voy. No. (航次) Port of Loading(装运港) **NINGBO**					
Port of Discharge(卸货港) Place of Delivery(交货地点) **MIAMI**				Final Destination for Merchant's Reference(目的地)	

Container No. (集装箱号)	Seal No.(封志号), Marks & Nos.(标记与号码)	No. of Containers or Pkgs(箱数或件数) **100CTNS**	Kind of Packages(包装种类), Description of Goods (货名) **100 CARTONS OF FLOCKING SWEATERS**	Gross Weight 毛重(千克) **1,100KGS**	Measurement 尺码(立方米) **24CBM**

TOTAL NUMBER OF CONTAINERS OR PACKAGES (IN WORDS) 集装箱数或件数合计(大写)	**SAY ONE HUNDRED CARTONS ONLY.**		

Freight & Charges (运费与附加费)	Revenue Tons (运费吨)	Rate(运费率) Per(每)	Prepaid (运费预付)	Collect(到付)

Ex Rate(兑换率)	Prepaid at(预付地点) **NINGBO**	Payable at(到付地点)	Place of Issue(签发地点)
	Total prepaid(预付总额)	No. of Original B(s)/L (正本提单份数)	

Service Type on Receiving □-CY, □-CFS, □-DOOR	Service Type on Delivery □-CY, □-CFS, □-DOOR	Reefer Temperature Required.(冷藏温度) ℉ ℃	
Type of Goods (种类)	□Ordinary □Reefer □Dangerous □Auto (普通) (冷藏) (危险品) (裸装车辆) □Liquid □Live Animal □Bulk (液体) (活动物) (散货)	危 险 品	Glass: Property: IMDG Code page: UN NO.
可否转船: **Y**	可否分批: **Y**		
装期: **JULY 30TH, 2008**	效期: **AUG.15TH, 2008**		
金额:			
制单日期: **JULY 20TH, 2008**			

Practice 操作练习

Case No. 1

1. 操作信息

甲方：杭州市大诺服装进出口公司

　　　杭州文秀路 199 号

　　　电话：0571-86936888　　　　传真：0571-86936889

乙方：杭州丽影制衣厂

　　　杭州光华路 188 号

　　　电话：0571-68789999　　　　传真：0571-68789998

加工合同号：DN0888

合同日期：2008 年 6 月 16 日

加工货名：全棉童装

加工数量：3000 套

包装：每套装一塑料袋，每 20 套装一纸箱

加工费：每套 10 元，甲方在签订本合同后 15 天内付 10%定金，其余 90%乙方凭增值税专
　　　用发票，专用税收缴款书、进仓单（送货回单或集装箱单）、购货合同向甲方办理
　　　收款。

产品交付日期：乙方在 2008 年 7 月 15 日之前将货物送到宁波北仑港甲方指定仓库。

2. 操作要求

　　请以杭州市大诺服装进出口公司业务员王立的身份，根据上述资料拟定一份购销合同，
内容正确并签字盖章。

杭州市大诺服装进出口公司

购销合同

需方：杭州市大诺服装进出口公司　　　　　　合同编号：

　　　　　　　　　　　　　　　　　　　　　签约日期：

供方：　　　　　　　　　　　　　　　　　　签约地点：中国杭州

　　　　　　　　　　　　　　　　　　　　　外销合同：

　　根据《中华人民共和国合同法》和有关法规，经双方协商签订本合同并信守下列条款：

一、商品

品名及规格	数量	单位	单价(含税)	金额	交货期
总金额（大写）					

二、质量要求：

三、包装要求：

四、交货地点：

五、付款方式（选择其中一项或两项）

    A. 供方凭增值税专用发票，专用税收缴款书、进仓单(送货回单或集装箱单)、购货合同向需方办理收款。

    B. 待需方收到客户货款后，供方凭增值税专用发票，专用税收缴款书、进仓单(送货回单或集装箱单)、购货合同向需方办理收款。

    C. 其他

六、责任条款：

    A) 因供方的责任造成国外客户索赔的，其索赔款及因索赔发生的费用由供方承担。

    B) 需方已安排供方出产的商品，因外销变化需要作出某些调整或变更的，其修改部分则为合同的组成部分。

七、本合同有效期从   年   月   日至   年   月   日。

八、纠纷处理办法及地点：执行本合同过程中如有争议，双方同意通过协商解决；如协商未能取得一致，则由杭州市所辖人民法院管辖。

九、本协议双方签字盖章生效。合同一式两份，供需双方各执一份。

十、备注：

需方授权代表   供方授权代表

盖   章   盖   章

Case No. 2

1. 操作信息

(1) 信用证条款

CREDIT NUMBER   :   268/2008

DATE OF ISSUE   :   DEC. 27TH, 2008

EXPIRY   :   DATE 080327 PLACE CHINA

APPLICANT   :   NECKMM DE GMBH

67890 FRANKFURT

GERMANY

BENEFICIARY : ZHEJIANG AIDY IMP./EXP. CO., LTD.

23FL., NO. 28 HUAYAN PLAZA,

HANGZHOU, CHINA

AMOUNT : USD79,092.00

PARTIAL SHIPMENT : ALLOWED

TRANSSHIPMENT : ALLOWED

SHIPMENT PERIOD : AT THE LATEST MARCH 27TH, 2008

SHIPMENT FROM : CHINA PORTS

FOR TRANSPORT TO : FRANKFURT, GERMANY

COVERING : 9,825 PCS LADIES' PANTS MADE OF 98% COTTON 2%

ELASTIC.

FOB SHANGHAI

SHIPPING MARKS : N.V./FRANKFURT/G.W.　KGS/C/NO.1-UP

DOCUMENTS REQUIRED :

- FULL SET OF CLEAN ON BOARD OCEAN BILLS OF LADING
  MADE OUT TO ORDER AND NOTIFY APPLICANT, SHOWING
  "FREIGHT COLLECT" MENTIONING THIS L/C NO.

…

ADDITIONAL CONDITIONS: SHIPMENT TO BE EFFECTED BY 1×20' CONTAINER (FCL)

(2) 其他资料

发票号码	75678	托运时间	MAR. 2, 2007
单位毛重	15 KGS/CTN	单位净重	12 KGS/CTN
单位尺码	(60×20×40) CM/CTN	总箱数	471

2. 操作要求

请以受益人业务员的身份，缮制出口货物托运单，向船公司或货运代理定舱。

Shipper(发货人)				D/R No.(编号)		第一联
Consignee(收货人)				集装箱货物托运单 货主留底		
Notify Party(受通知人)						
Pre-carriage by(前程运输)		Place of Receipt(收货地点)				
Ocean Vessel(船名) Voy. No. (航次) Port of Loading(装运港)						
Port of Discharge(卸货港) Place of Delivery(交货地点)				Final Destination for Merchant's Reference(目的地)		

Container No. (集装箱号)	Seal No.(封志号) Marks & Nos.(标记与号码)	No. of Containers or Pkgs(箱数或件数)	Kind of Packages(包装种类) Description of Goods (货名)	Gross Weight 毛重(千克)	Measurement 尺码(立方米)

TOTAL NUMBER OF CONTAINERS OR PACKAGES (IN WORDS) 集装箱数或件数合计(大写)		**SAY ONE HUNDRED CARTONS ONLY.**			
Freight & Charges (运费与附加费)		Revenue Tons (运费吨)	Rate(运费率) Per(每)	Prepaid (运费预付)	Collect(到付)
Ex Rate(兑换率)	Prepaid at(预付地点)		Payable at(到付地点)		Place of Issue(签发地点)
	Total Prepaid(预付总额)		No. of Original B(s)/L (正本提单份数)		

Service Type on Receiving □-CY, □-CFS, □-DOOR	Service Type on Delivery □-CY, □-CFS, □-DOOR	Reefer Temperature Required.(冷藏温度) °F ℃	
Type of Goods (种类)	□Ordinary □Reefer □Dangerous □Auto (普通) (冷藏) (危险品) (裸装车辆) □Liquid □Live Animal □Bulk (液体) (活动物) (散货)	危 险 品	Glass: Property: IMDG Code page: UN NO.
可否转船:	可否分批:		
装期:	效期:		
金额:			
制单日期:			

Case No. 3

1. 操作信息

ALAHLI BANK OF KUWAIT

IRREVOCABLE LETTER OF CREDIT NO. 609/23262

KUWAIT, DATE: MAY 5TH, 2008

BENEFICIARY:	SHANDONG IMPORT & EXPORT CORP.
	7 ZHANSHAN ROAD, QINGDAO, CHINA
ADVISING BANK:	BANK OF CHINA, QINGDAO BRANCH, QINGDAO, CHINA
AMOUNT:	ABOUT USD72,000.00 (ABOUT U.S. DOLLARS SEVENTY-TWO THOUSAND ONLY.)
APPLICANT:	SAMIEH TEXTILE & BLANKET CO., LTD.
	P.O.BOX 299934, SAFAT, KUWAIT
VALID IN:	CHINA
AVAILABLE AT:	SIGHT
VALID UNTIL:	JULY, 15TH 2008
SHIPPING TERMS:	CFR KUWAIT
TRANSSHIPMENT:	PERMITTED

PARTIAL SHIPMENT AT ISRAEL IS PROHIBITED

LOADING IN CHARGE: CHINA

FOR TRANSPORT TO:　KUWAIT

LATEST SHIP DATE:　JUNE 30TH, 2008

NEGOTIATION RESTRICTED TO ADVISING BANK ONLY

SHIPPING MARKS:　ABUZIAO-KUWAIT/CTT/CHH-33/93 MADE IN CHINA

PLEASE ADVISE OUR ABOVE IRREVOCABLE LETTER OF CREDIT AVAILABLE BY BENEFICIARIES' DRAFTS, WITHOUT RECOURSE, DRAWN ON US FOR FULL INVOICE VALUE AND ACCOMPANIED BY THE FOLLOWING DOCUMENTS:

- SIGNED COMMERCIAL INVOICE IN QUINTUPLICATES CERTIFYING THAT EACH PIECE CARTON/ CASE OF THE GOODS CARRIES THE NAME OF COUNTRY OF ORIGIN IN NON-DETACHABLE OR NON-ALTERABLE WAY.

- CERTIFICATE OF ORIGIN SHOWING BENEFICIARIES AS MANUFACTURERS.

- PACKING LIST IN TRIPLICATE SHOWING DESCRIPTION OF GOODS ITEM NO. AS PER HARMONIC SYSTEM NO. OF PACKAGES, KIND OF PACKAGES, CONTENTS OF PACKAGES, GROSS WEIGHT, NET WEIGHT AND TOTAL COST OF EACH ITEM.

- COMPLETE SET OF AT LEAST 3/3 (OF WHICH TWO TO ACCOMPANY THE ORIGINAL SET AND ONE

WITH DUPLICATE SET OF DOCUMENTS) CLEAN "ON BOARD" MARINE BILLS OF LADING ISSUED TO THE ORDER OF ALAHLI BANK OF KUWAIT. K.S.C. NOTIFYING OPENERS AND EVIDENCING "FREIGHT PREPAID".

COVERING

ABOUT 60,000 YARDS ART 032, 65PCT POLYESTER 35 PCT VISCOSE MIXED SUITING FABRIC WEIGHT: ABT. 250 GRAMS PER METER. SIZE: 58"× ABT. 25 YARDS PIECES @ USD. 1.20 PER YARD.

CERTIFIED ON INVOICES THAT ALL OTHER DETAILS OF THE GOODS SHIPPED ARE AS PER INDENT NO. CTT/CH-33/93 S/C: 00JUN30.

SUPPLEMENTS:

1. Commodity: Mixed Suiting Fabric
2. Quantity: 60,000 yards
3. Specifications: Art. 0321 65% polyester 35% viscose

    Weight: ABT. 250 grams per metre

    Size: 58" × abt. 25 yards pieces
4. Price: USD 1.20 per yard CFR Kuwait
5. Packed in cartons of 22 pieces each (No. 1—100) 10 pieces each (101—120), total: 2,400 pieces
6. Gross weight: 1,398 kgs

    Net weight: 1,370 kgs

    Measurement: 24CBM (Container/Seal No.: APLU12346/7658)
7. Shipped per S/S "Maria" No.275
8. Shipping Mark:

    ABUZIAO-KUWAIT

    CTT/CHH-33/93

    MADE IN CHINA

    NO. 1—120
9. Invoice No.: 20MSF43
10. S/C No.: 06YN568 dated Apr. 5th, 2008

2. 操作要求

请以托运人的身份，缮制出口货物明细单。

出口货物明细单

2008 年 7 月 15 日

信用证号码		填制单位编号	
银行编号		外运公司编号	
合同(合约)号			

开证银行		开证日期		收到日期	
		金额		收汇方式	
经营单位（装船人)		货物性质		贸易国别	
收货人		中间商名称及地址			

提单或承运收据	抬头人		出口口岸		目的港	
	通知人		可否转运		可否分批	
	运费预付/到付		装运期限		有效期限	

货名规格及货号	H.S. 编码	件数及包装样式	数量/尺码	毛重(千克)	净重(千克)	价格(成交条件)总价

标记唛头	

注意事项		总体积	
		业务员	
		单证员	
		运输员	

PRACTICE 6

Execution of a Contract (III)

—Goods Inspection

履行合同(3)——货物报检

Example & Analysis 操作实例及解析

◆ Case Lead-in

Ningbo Xinxin Pets' Ware Factory fulfilled their commitment and finished the production of 2,400 pieces of Flocking Sweater on July 12th, 2008. It's time for Ningbo Sakai Pet Co., Ltd. to have the goods inspected by Ningbo Entry-Exit Inspection and Quarantine Bureau.

◆ 案例导入

宁波新新宠物用品厂根据国内购销合同要求，向宁波井通宠物用品有限公司提供 2400 件宠物用植绒毛衣，于 2008 年 7 月 12 日完成交货。宁波井通宠物用品有限公司开始着手向宁波出入境检验检疫局办理货物检验手续。

➢ **Procedure of inspection for export commodities 出口货物报检流程**

The inspection of export commodities is fulfilled by three steps: application, inspection and the issuance of the certificate.

出口货物的检验通常要经过：报检、检验检疫、出证放行三大环节。

(一) 报检

1. 检验时间的确定

出口货物的报检应在商检机构规定的期限内进行，最迟为出口报关或装运前 7 天报检。

但出境货物的报检时间不能太早，以免造成商检证书的失效。根据规定，经商检机构检验检疫合格发给检验证书或"出境货物通关单"的出口商品，一般应在证、单签发之日起两个月内装运出口；鲜活类商品，应在两周内装运出口。

2. 提供有关单证和资料

外贸企业办理出口货物报检，必须填写《出境货物报检单》；申请预检的，填写预检申请单；并随附以下单据：

(1) 销售合同或售货确认书；

(2) 商业发票；

(3) 信用证以及修改书；

(4) 装箱单或磅码单。

(二) 检验检疫

商检机构接受报检后，根据《出境货物报检单》和有关检验标准对出口货物进行检验。检验的标准是：

(1) 凡是法律法规定有强制性标准的，必须按法律法规规定的检验标准检验；

(2) 凡是法律法规定未有强制性标准的，则按合同中约定的检验标准检验。

商检机构对出口货物检验检疫或鉴定后，根据不同的项目签发各种检验检疫证书、鉴定证书和其他证明书。商检证书的作用为：

(1) 作为买卖双方交接货物的依据；

(2) 作为买卖双方结算货款的依据；

(3) 作为买卖双方进行索赔、理赔的依据。

检验证书份数由申请报验单位根据需要而定，一般为正本 1 份，副本 4 份。如需增加副本，则需提供需要副本的单位名称，并征得商检机构的同意。

(三) 签证与放行

出口货物经检验、检疫合格后，商检机构签发《出境货物通关单》，作为海关核放货物的依据；如果国外有要求签发有关检验检疫证书的，商检机构根据对外贸易联系人的申请，签发相应的检验检疫证书。经检验检疫不合格的，签发《出境货物不合格通知单》。

Directions 操作指南

《出境货物报检单》是商检机构进行出口货物检验检疫并出具商检证书的依据，在填写时，必须严格按照合同和信用证的要求。合同及信用证未作要求的项目，根据实际情况按通常的要求填写。各个项目的填写应注意以下问题：

(1) 报检单位：

必须加盖单位正式公章，不能使用其他印章代替。

(2) 报检单位登记号：

填写报检单位在检验检疫机构登记备案取得的报检单位代码。

(3) 报检日期：

填写实际报检日期。

(4) 发货人名称：

　　填写中英文全称，并注意与信用证的受益人名称完全一致。

(5) 收货人名称：

　　只需填写英文名称。

(6) 货物名称：

　　与合同或信用证一致。

(7) H.S. 编码：

　　填写该货物在《商品名称及编码协调制度》上查得的编号。

(8) 产地：

　　填写货物的原产地。

(9) 数量/重量：

　　填写货物的数量或重量，与商业发票上一致。

(10) 货物总值：

　　一般填写出口货物的总金额，它是商检部门计算检验费用的依据。

(11) 包装种类及数量：

　　填写包装材料和货物包装后的总件数。

(12) 运输工具名称号码：

　　如海运，填写船名、航次。

(13) 贸易方式：

　　填"一般贸易"、"三来一补"或"其他贸易"。

(14) 货物存放地点：

　　按实际情况填写，在工厂或在港区，以便商检机构进行检验。

(15) 合同、信用证号：

　　分别填入合同、信用证号码。

(16) 用途：

　　一般填"出口"。

(17) 发货日期：

　　因商检必须在货物装运前办理，所以发货日期填预计装运日期。

(18) 输往国家(地区)：

　　填写进口国国名。

(19) 许可证/审批号：

　　填写许可证或批准文件的号码。

(20) 启运地、到达口岸：

　　填写装运地(港)和目的地(港)名称。

(21) 生产单位注册号：

　　需要经卫生注册或生产许可的生产企业，应填写其注册号。

(22) 集装箱规格、数量及号码：

　　按实际装箱情况填写。

中华人民共和国出入境检验检疫
出境货物报验单

报检单位(加盖公章) *编号 __NQ1880__

报检单位登记号：33010111　　联系人：王立　　电话：13957476465　　报检日期：2008 年 7 月 16 日

发货人	(中文)宁波井通宠物用品有限公司				
	(外文)NINGBO SAKAI PET CO., LTD.				
收货人	(中文)ABF 国际贸易有限公司				
	(外文)ABF INTERNATIONAL CO., LTD.				
货物名称(中外文)	H.S. 编码	产地	数/重量	货物总值	包装种类及数量
FLOCKING SWEATERS 植绒毛衣(宠物用)	6200.1300	宁波	2,400PCS	USD7,122.00	100CTNS

运输工具名称号码 WUYING V.198	贸易方式 一般贸易		货物存放地点 宁波新新宠物用品厂
合同号 ST08020	信用证号 BOC070325		用途　　出口
发货日期 JULY 30TH, 2008	输往国家(地区)	美国	许可证/审批号
启运地　　宁波	到达口岸	迈阿密	生产单位注册号
集装箱规格、数量及号码	1×20'		

合同、信用证订立的检验检疫条款或特殊要求	标记及号码	随附单据(画√或补填)	
	ABF ST08020 MIAMI C/NO.:1-UP	☑合同 ☑信用证 ☑发票 □换证凭单 ☑装箱单 □厂检单	□包装性能结果单 □许可/审批文件 □ □ □ □

需要证单名称(画√或补填)		检验检疫费	
□品质证书　　__正__副	□植物检疫证书　　__正__副	总金额 (人民币元)	
□重量证书　　__正__副	□熏蒸/消毒证书　　__正__副		
□数量证书　　__正__副	□出境货物换证凭单　　__正__副		
□兽医卫生证书　　__正__副	☑出境货物通关单　1正 2副	计费人	
□健康证书　　__正__副			
□卫生证书　　__正__副		收费人	
□动物卫生证书　　__正__副			

报检人郑重声明：	领取证单
1. 本人被授权报检。 2. 上列填写内容正确属实，货物无伪造或冒用他人的厂名、标志、认证标志，并承担货物质量责任。	
	日期
签名：　　王立	签名

注：有"*"号栏由出入境检验检疫机构填写。

(23) 合同、信用证订立的检验检疫条款或特殊要求:

详细填写合同或信用证规定的检验证书的文字要求以及其他特殊加注条款。

(24) 标记及号码:

填货物的运输标志,应与信用证指定的唛头以及其他单据上的唛头一致。

(25) 随附单据:

在小方格内打"√",或不填。

(26) 需要单证名称:

根据实际情况在小方格内打"√",或不填。

(27) 检验检疫费:

由商检机构填写。

(28) 领取证单的日期、签名:

由出口企业报检员填写。

注意:出口企业的报检,一份报检单只能用于一种商品,且为一次出货和一个收货人的出口商品。

中华人民共和国出入境检验检疫
出境货物通关单

编号: **NQ1880**

1. 发货人 NINGBO SAKAI PET CO., LTD. 宁波井通宠物用品有限公司			5. 标记及号码 ABF ST08020 MIAMI C/NO.: 1-UP
2. 收货人 ABF INTERNATIONAL CO., LTD.			
3. 合同号/信用证号 ST08020/ **BOC070325**		4. 输往国家或地区 美国	
6. 运输工具名称及号码 WUYING V.198		7. 发货日期 2008-07-30	8. 集装箱规格及日期 1X20′
9. 货物名称及规格 FLOCKING SWEATERS 植绒毛衣(宠物用)	10. H.S.编码 6200.1300	11. 申报总值 USD7,122.00	12. 数/重量,包装数量及种类 2,400PCS 100CTNS
13. 证明 上述货物业经检验检疫,请海关予以放行 本通关单有效期至　2008　年　9　月　20　日 签字:　　　　　　　　　　日期:2008　年　7　月　20　日			
14. 备注			

Practice 操作练习

1. 操作信息

(1) 售货确认书

1. 售货确认书
SALES CONFIRMATION

2. 编号

Contract No.: ___06-234___

日期

Date: ___JUNE 30TH, 2008___

地点

Place: ___HANGZHOU, CHINA___

The Sellers:

ZHEJIANG GARMENTS IMP. & EXP. CORP.

The Buyers:

NEW YORK TRADING COMPANY

3. 下列签字双方同意按以下条款达成交易

The undersigned Sellers and Buyers have agreed to close the transaction according to the following terms and conditions.

4. 品名及规格 COMMODITY AND SPECIFICATIONS	5. 数 量 QUANTITY	6. 单 价 UNIT PRICE	7. 金 额 AMOUNT
LADIES' SILK BLOUSES PINK, BLUE AND WHITE EQUALLY ASSORTED; SIZE ASSORTMENT: S2,M6, L4 PER DOZEN; QUALITY AS PER SAMPLE	1,000.00DOZ	CIFC5% NEW YORK @USD52.00/DZ	USD52,000.00
8. PACKING: EACH BLOUSE IN A PLASTIC BAG, ONE DOZEN TO A PAPER BOX. 20 DOZEN TO A SEAWORTHY CARTON LINED WITH POLYTHENE SHEET			
			USD52,000.00

9. 总值

TOTAL VALUE: SAY U.S. DOLLARS FIFTY-TWO THOUSAND ONLY.

10. 目的地

DESTINATION: FROM SHANGHAI TO NEW YORK BY SEA.

11. 装运期限

SHIPMENT: IN AUGUST, 2008 WITH TRANSSHIPMENT ALLOWED, PARTIAL SHIPMENTS PROHIBITED.

12. 保险

INSURANCE: TO BE EFFECTED BY THE SELLERS AGAINST ALL RISKS AND WAR RISKS FOR 110% OF THE INVOICE VALUE AS PER CIC.

13. 付款方式

<u>PAYMENT:</u> BY IRREVOCABLE, TRANSFERABLE, SIGHT L/C TO REACH THE SELLERS 30 DAYS BEFORE THE TIME OF SHIPMENT AND REMAIN VALID FOR NEGOTIATION IN CHINA UNTIL THE 15TH DAY AFTER THE DATE OF SHIPMENT.

(2) 信用证

AMANDA BANK OF NEW YORK

IRREVOCABLE LETTER OF CREDIT NO. 609/23262

NEW YORK, DATE: JULY 25TH, 2008

BENEFICIARY: ZHEJIANG GARMENTS IMP./EXP. CORP.

NO.100 WENYI ROAD,

HANGZHOU, CHINA

ADVISING BANK: BANK OF CHINA, ZHEJIANG BRANCH, HANGZHOU, CHINA

AMOUNT: USD52,000.00 (U.S. DOLLARS FIFTY-TWO THOUSAND ONLY)

APPLICANT: NEW YORK TRADING COMPANY

P.O. BOX 299934, NEW YORK, U.S.A.

VALID IN: CHINA

AVAILABLE AT: SIGHT

VALID UNTIL: SEPT. 15TH, 2008

SHIPPING TERMS: CIFC5% NEW YORK

TRANSSHIPMENT: PERMITTED

PARTIAL SHIPMENT: PROHIBITED

LOADING IN CHARGE: CHINA

FOR TRANSPORT TO: NEW YORK

LATEST SHIP DATE: AUGUST 30TH, 2008

NEGOTIATION RESTRICTED TO ADVISING BANK ONLY

SHIPPING MARKS: A.V./NEW YORK

(3) 其他信息

发票号码	06YS018	发票日期	AUG. 20TH, 2008	产地证号码	CNUS71101811
许可证号码	CNUS01826	装运港	上海	货物存放地点	杭州半山仓库
船名	MARIE V. 275	商品编码	6200.1200	集装箱号码	MSK27868 1×20′
报检日期	AUG. 20TH, 2008	提单日期	AUG. 30TH, 2008	报检单位登记号	330191077

生产厂家：杭州新华服装厂，2008 年 8 月 20 日由报检员王林向浙江省出入境检验检疫局报检。

2. 操作要求

根据所给的资料填制出境货物报验单和出境货物通关单。

中华人民共和国出入境检验检疫
出境货物报验单

报检单位(加盖公章)　　　　　　　　　　　　　　　*编号＿＿＿＿＿＿＿＿

报检单位登记号：　　　　联系人：　　　电话：　　　　报检日期：　　年　月　日

发货人	(中文)				
	(外文)				
收货人	(中文)				
	(外文)				
货物名称(中外文)	H.S. 编码	产地	数/重量	货物总值	包装种类及数量

运输工具名称号码	贸易方式		货物存放地点
合同号	信用证号		用途
发货日期	输往国家(地区)		许可证/审批号
启运地	到达口岸		生产单位注册号
集装箱规格、数量及号码			

合同、信用证订立的检验检疫条款或特殊要求	标记及号码	随附单据(画√或补填)	
		□合同	□包装性能结果单
		□信用证	□许可/审批文件
		□发票	□
		□换证凭单	□
		□装箱单	□
		□厂检单	□

需要证单名称(画√或补填)		检验检疫费	
□品质证书　　　＿正＿副	□植物检疫证书　　＿正＿副	总金额	
□重量证书　　　＿正＿副	□熏蒸/消毒证书　　＿正＿副	(人民币元)	
□数量证书　　　＿正＿副	□出境货物换证凭单　＿正＿副		
□兽医卫生证书　＿正＿副	□出境货物通关单　　＿正＿副	计费人	
□健康证书　　　＿正＿副			
□卫生证书　　　＿正＿副		收费人	
□动物卫生证书　＿正＿副			

报检人郑重声明：	领取证单
1. 本人被授权报检。	
2. 上列填写内容正确属实，货物无伪造或冒用他人的厂名、标志、认证标志，并承担货物质量责任。	日期
签名：＿＿＿＿＿＿＿	签名

注：有"*"号栏由出入境检验检疫机构填写。

中华人民共和国出入境检验检疫
出境货物通关单

编号：

1. 发货人			5. 标记及号码
2. 收货人			
3. 合同号/信用证号		4. 输往国家或地区	
6. 运输工具名称及号码		7. 发货日期	8. 集装箱规格及日期
9. 货物名称及规格	10. H.S. 编码	11. 申报总值	12. 数/重量，包装数量及种类

13. 证明

上述货物业经检验检疫，请海关予以放行

本通关单有效期至　　　年　　月　　日

签字：　　　　　　　　　　　日期：　　　年　　月　　日

14. 备注

PRACTICE 7

Execution of a Contract (IV)

—Goods Insurance

履行合同（4）——货物投保

Learning Objectives 学习目标

◇ To be familiar with the procedure of effecting insurance 熟悉出口货物保险流程
◇ To be able to fill in the application form for goods insurance 填制投保单
◇ To be able to make out an insurance policy 保险单的缮制

Example & Analysis 操作实例及解析

◆ Case Lead-in

The 2,400pcs of Flocking Sweaters under S/C No. ST08020 manufactured by Ningbo Xinxin Pets' Ware factory have been inspected by Ningbo Entry-Exit Inspection and Quarantine Bureau and are going to be shipped via S.S. WUYING V.198 due to sail for Miami on or about July 30TH, 2008. The next thing Ningbo Sakai Pet Co., Ltd. should do is to effect insurance on the goods before shipment.

◆ 案例导入

ST08020 合同项下的 2400 件宠物用植绒毛衣，经宁波出入境检验检疫局检验合格后，即将于 2008 年 7 月 30 日前后出口装运至美国迈阿密。在货物出运前，宁波井通宠物用品有限公司还需办理货物投保手续。

> **The procedure of effecting insurance 国际货物运输保险程序**

在国际货物买卖过程中，由哪一方负责办理投保，应根据买卖双方商订的价格条件来确定。例如：按 FOB 条件和 CFR 条件成交，保险即应由买方办理；如按 CIF 条件成交，保险就应由卖方办理。办理货运保险的一般程序是：

1. 选定保险方式

　　— 逐笔投保；

　　— 预约保险：专门从事进出口业务的外贸公司，为了简化手续，可与保险公司事先签订"预约保险合同""Open Policy"，在合同中，对出口货物投保的险别、保险费率等作出规定。预约保险合同是出口企业与保险公司之间的正式的保险契约，凡属预约保险合同范围内的出口货物，一经启运，保险公司既自动按预约保单所订立的条件承保。

2. 确定投保的金额

　　保险金额是被保险人对保险货物的实际投保金额，也是保险公司承担保险责任和计收保险费的依据。在保险货物发生保险责任范围内的货损货差时，保险金额就是保险公司赔偿的最高限额。

　　海运出口货物运输保险的保险金额一般是以 CIF 价格为基础，再加上一定百分比的"加成"(一成为 10%；二成为 20%；以此类推)，即：

　　保险金额=CIF(1+投保加成率)

　　关于投保加成，如合同或信用证未作规定，按 INCOTERMS 2000 和 UCP500 的规定，保险单据上必须表明投保最低金额为货物的 CIF 或 CIP 货值加 10%，即 110%。

3. 填写投保单

　　投保单是投保人向保险人提出投保的书面申请，其主要内容包括被保险人的姓名、被保险货物的品名、标记、数量及包装、保险金额、运输工具名称、开航日期及起讫地点、投保险别、投保日期及签章等。投保单一式两份，一份由保险公司签署后交卖方作为接受承保的凭证，另一份则由保险公司留存，作为缮制、签发保险单的依据。

4. 支付保险费，取得保险单

　　保险费按投保险别的保险费率计算。保险费率是根据不同的险别、不同的商品、不同的运输方式、不同的目的地，并参照国际上的费率水平而制订的。它分为"一般货物费率"和"指明货物加费费率"两种。前者是一般商品的费率，后者系指特别列明的货物(如某些易碎、易损商品)在一般费率的基础上另行加收的费率。

　　交付保险费后，投保人即可取得保险单(Insurance Policy)。保险单实际上已构成保险人与被保险人之间的保险契约，是保险人给被保险人的承保证明。在发生保险范围内的损失或灭失时，投保人可凭保险单要求赔偿。

中国人民保险公司宁波分公司
国外运输险投保单

兹将我处出口物资依照信用证规定拟向你处投保国外运输险计开：

被保险人	(中文)宁波井通宠物用品有限公司 (英文)NINGBO SAKAI PET CO., LTD.		过户
标记或发票号码	件 数	物 资 名 称	保险金额
ABF ST08020 MIAMI C/NO.: 1-UP	100CTNS	FLOCKING SWEATERS	USD7,834.00
运输工具 (及运载工具)	WUYING V.198	约 于 2008 年 7 月 30 日启运	赔款偿付 地点　　　MIAMI
运输路程	自 NINGBO 经　　到 MIAMI	转载 地点	
要保险别： ALL RISKS			投保单位签章 2008 年 7 月 15 日

Directions 操作指南

➢ 保险单的缮制

1. 被保险人(THE INSURED)

　　被保险人的名称，该栏为保险单的抬头，如信用证无特别规定，一般填受益人。如信用证另有规定，则按信用证规定填写。如国外来证规定："…issued to the order of xxx bank."，则保险单的抬头必须做成"To order of xxx bank"。

2. 标记(MARKS & NOS.)

　　一般参照发票上的货物标记，目前保险公司采取打上"As per Invoice No. …"的做法，因为在索赔时，必须提供商业发票，可以参照发票进行核对。如果信用证规定所有单据都要显示装运唛头，则应按实际唛头缮制。

3. 包装和数量(QUANTITY)

　　与提单相同，填写最大包装的总件数。裸装货物填写货物本身的件数，散装货物填写货物净重，有包装但以重量计价的应同时填写总件数和计价总重量。

4. 货物名称(DESCRIPTION OF GOODS)

　　与提单、产地证上的描述一致，允许填写货物的统称。

中国人民保险公司宁波市分公司
The People's Insurance Company of China Ningbo Branch

总公司设于北京   一九四九年创立

Head Office Beijing   Established in 1949

货物运输保险单
CARGO TRANSPORTATION INSURANCE POLICY

保单号次

POLICY NO.

被保险人：

INSURED:

中国人民保险公司(以下简称本公司)根据被保险人的要求，由被保险人向本公司缴付约定的保险费，按照本保险单承保险别和背面所载条款与下列特款承保下述货物运输保险，特立本保险单。

THIS POLICY OF INSURANCE WITNESSES THAT THE PEOPLE'S INSURANCE COMPANY OF CHINA (HEREINAFTER CALLED "THE COMPANY") AT THE REQUEST OF THE INSURED AND IN CONSIDERATION OF THE AGREED PREMIUM PAID TO THE COMPANY BY THE INSURED, UNDERTAKES TO INSURE THE UNDERMENTIONED GOODS IN TRANSPORTATION SUBJECT TO THE CONDITIONS OF THIS POLICY AS PER THE CLAUSES PRINTED OVERLEAF AND OTHER SPECIAL CLAUSES ATTACHED HEREON.

标 记 MARKS & NOS.	包装及数量 QUANTITY	保险货物项目 DESCRIPTION OF GOODS	保险金额 AMOUNT INSURED
ABF ST08020 MIAMI C/NO.: 1-UP	100CTNS	FLOCKING SWEATERS	USD7,834.00

总保险金额

TOTAL AMOUNT INSURED: SAY U.S. DOLLARS SEVEN THOUSAND EIGHT HUNDRED AND THIRTY-FOUR ONLY.

保费   启运日期   装载运输工具：

RATE AS ARRANGED   SLG. ON OR ABT.: JULY 30TH, 2008 PER CONVEYANCE S. S. WUYING V.198

自   经   至

FROM: NINGBO   VIA   TO   MIAMI

承保险别：

CONDITIONS:

COVERING ALL RISKS AS PER OCEAN MARINE CARGO CLAUSES (WAREHOUSE TO WARE- CLAUSE IS INCLUDED) OF THE PEOPLE'S INSURANCE COMPANY OF CHINA DATED 01/01/1981.

所保货物，如发生保险单项下可能引起索赔的损失或损坏，应立即通知本公司下述代理人查勘。如有索赔，应向本公司提交保单正本(本保险单共有 2 份正本)及有关文件。如一份正本已用于索赔，其余正本自动失效。

IN THE EVENT OF LOSS OR DAMAGE WHICH MAY RESULT IN A CLAIM UNDER THIS POLICY, IMMEDIATE NOTICE MUST BE GIVEN TO THE COMPANY'S AGENT AS MENTIONED HEREUNDER. CLAIMS, IF ANY, ONE OF THE ORIGINAL POLICY WHICH HAS BEEN ISSUED IN ___TWO___ ORIGINAL(S) TOGETHER WITH THE RELEVANT DOCUMENTS SHALL BE SURRENDERED TO THE COMPANY. IF ONE OF THE ORIGINAL POLICY HAS BEEN ACCOMPLISHED, THE OTHERS TO BE VOID.

中国人民保险公司宁波市分公司

The People's Insurance Company of China Ningbo Branch

赔款偿付地点

CLAIM PAYABLE AT: MIAMI

出单日期   宁波   ___Authorized Signature___

ISSUING DATE: JULY 16TH, 2008   NINGBO

5. 保险金额(AMOUNT INSURED)

应在 CIF 基础上按信用证规定的加成计算，小数点后的尾数一律进为整数，使用的币制与信用证的货币相同。如发票已扣佣金或折扣，应按扣佣和折扣前的毛值投保；大写与小写金额必须一致。

6. 保险费和费率(PREMIUM & RATE)

一般填写"As arranged"，如信用证要求注明保险费和费率的，则应按要求注上具体的金额和费率。

7. 运输工具(PER CONVEYANCE S.S.)

海运注明船名、航次。如果转运的，并已知二程船名，则在一程船名后打上二程船名，如果还未知二程船名，则打上"&/or steamers"。使用其他运输方式的，则分别打上"By Train"，"By Air"等。如转运到内陆加打"Other Conveyance"。

8. 开航日期(SLG. ON OR ABT.)

有确切日期的，填确切日期，如无，则填写"As per B/L"。

9. 运输起讫地(FROM...TO)

一份保险单只能有一个装运港和一个目的港，如中途转运的，必须注明转运港名称，如到达纽约港后转运到芝加哥，可填写"New York and thence to Chicago"或"New York in transit to Chicago"。

10. 承保险别(CONDITIONS)

按信用证上保险条款所列的险别、加成填写。注意：

● 应严格按信用证规定的险别投保。为了避免混乱和误解，最好按信用证规定的顺序填写。

● 如信用证没有规定具体险别，则可投保一切险、水渍险、平安险三个基本险中的任何一种。

● 如信用证规定使用伦敦协会条款，包括修订前的或修订后的，根据中国人民保险公司的现行做法，可以承保，保险单应按要求填制。

● 如果信用证没有规定"不计免赔率"(Irrespective of Percentage)，保险单可以加注免赔率条款。

● 投保的险别除注明险别名称外，还应注明险别适用的文本和日期。例如：Covering All Risks and War Risks as per Ocean Marine Cargo and War Risks Clauses (CIC) of the People's Insurance Company of China dated 01/01/1981. (按照中国人民保险公司 1981 年 1 月 1 日海运货物条款和海运货物战争险条款承保一切险和战争险。)

在实际业务中，有些文句可采用缩略写，如 OMCC 代表 Ocean Marine Cargo Clauses，OMCWRC 代表 Ocean Marine Cargo War Clauses，PICC 代表 People's Insurance Company of China，DD 代表 dated，CIC 代表 Institute Cargo Clause(伦敦协会条款)。

11. 保险公司在目的地的代理人(INSURANCE AGENT)

应列明代理人名称、详细地址，以便收货人出险后索赔。

12. 赔付地点和赔付货币名称(CLAIMS PAYABLE AT/IN)

按信用证规定填写，一般将目的地作为赔付地点，将目的地的名称填入该栏。赔付货币一般与汇票货币相同。

13. 保险单签发日期和地点(DATE AND PLACE)

保险单日期应在货物装上运输工具之前。根据 UCP500 的规定，银行不接受出单日期迟于装船或发运或接受监管日的保险单据。

Practice 操作练习

Case No. 1

根据所给资料填制一张投保单和保险单。

MIDLAND BANK PLC., LONDON

IRREVOCABLE LETTER OF CREDIT NO. 044/3075989

LONDON, DATE: NOV. 15TH, 2008

BENEFICIARY:	HANGZHOU TRADING IMPORT & EXPORT CORPORATION, 60, HUAHAI ROAD, HANGZHOU, CHINA
ADVISING BANK:	BANK OF CHINA, HANGZHOU BRANCH, HANGZHOU, CHINA
AMOUNT:	USD3,180.00 (U.S. DOLLARS THREE THOUSAND ONE HUNDRED AND EIGHTY ONLY)
APPLICANT:	W W TEXTILES
	P.O. BOX 9, CEMEERY ROAD
	PUDSET WEST YORKS LS8 7XD
EXPIRY:	DATE JAN. 15TH, 2008 PLACE CHINA
AVAILABLE WITH/BY:	FREELY NEGOTIABLE AT ANY BANK BY NEGOTIATION AT SIGHT
DRAWEE:	DRAWN ON US FOR FULL INVOICE VALUE
TRANSSHIPMENT:	PERMITTED
PARTIAL SHIPMENT:	PERMITTED
LOADING IN CHARGE:	CHINA
FOR TRANSPORT TO:	SOUTHAMPTON IN TRANSIT TO LEEDS
LATEST SHIP DATE:	DEC. 25TH, 2008
DESCRIP. OF GOODS:	10,000 DOZEN COTTON TOWELS AT USD 0.318 PER DOZ

COLOUR ASSORTMENT AS PER CONTRACT NO. 001131 CIF SOUTHAMPTON

DOCUMENTS REQUIRED:

- SIGNED COMMERCIAL INVOICE IN QUINTUPLICATES SHOWING ORDER NO. WW65-3.
- PACKING LIST IN TRIPLICATE SHOWING DESCRIPTION OF GOODS.
- FULL SET OF CLEAN "ON BOARD" MARINE BILLS OF LADING MADE OUT TO THE ORDER OF MIDLAND BANK PLC, LONDON. MARKED "FREIGHT PREPAID" NOTIFYING ACCOUNTEE.

- INSURANCE MARINE INSURANCE POLICY OR CERTIFICATE IN DUPLICATE, ENDORSED IN BLANK, FOR 110% OF THE INVOICE VALUE INCLUDING: OCEAN MARINE CARGO CLAUSES (ALL RISKS), OCEAN MARINE CARGO WAR RISKS CLAUSES OF THE PEOPLE'S INSURANCE COMPANY OF CHINA INCLUDING WAREHOUSE TO WAREHOUSE CLAUSE, CLAIMS PAYABLE IN ENGLAND IN CURRENCY OF DRAFTS...

SUPPLEMENTS:

1. Commodity: Cotton Towels

2. S/C No. ST88 dated Oct. 5th, 2008

3. Price: USD0.318 per dozen CIF Southampton

4. Total value: USD3,180.00

5. Packing: One dozen in a plastic bag, ten dozen to a carton

6. Shipped per S/S "East Wind" V.24

7. Invoice No.: 254

8. B/L NO.: 165

9. Measurement: 25CBM

   Gross weight: 680kgs

   Net weight: 600kgs

10. Container/Seal No.: MSKU123456/6789

中国人民保险公司杭州分公司
国外运输险投保单

兹将我处出口物资依照信用证规定拟向你处投保国外运输险计开:

被保险人	(中文) (英文)		过户	
标记或发票号码	件　数	物　资　名　称		保险金额
运输工具 (及运载工具)		约 于　　年　　月　　日启运		赔款偿 付地点
运输路程	自　　经　　到	转载 地点		
要保险别:				投保单位签章 年　　月　　日

中国人民保险公司杭州市分公司
The People's Insurance Company of China Hangzhou Branch

总公司设于北京　　　一九四九年创立
Head Office Beijing　　　Established in 1949

货物运输保险单
CARGO TRANSPORTATION INSURANCE POLICY

保单号次
POLICY NO.

被保险人：
INSURED:

中国人民保险公司(以下简称本公司)根据被保险人的要求，由被保险人向本公司缴付约定的保险费，按照本保险单承保险别和背面所载条款与下列特款承保下述货物运输保险，特立本保险单。

THIS POLICY OF INSURANCE WITNESSES THAT THE PEOPLE'S INSURANCE COMPANY OF CHINA (HEREINAFTER CALLED "THE COMPANY") AT THE REQUEST OF THE INSURED AND IN CONSIDERATION OF THE AGREED PREMIUM PAID TO THE COMPANY BY THE INSURED, UNDERTAKES TO INSURE THE UNDERMENTIONED GOODS IN TRANSPORTATION SUBJECT TO THE CONDITIONS OF THIS POLICY AS PER THE CLAUSES PRINTED OVERLEAF AND OTHER SPECIAL CLAUSES ATTACHED HEREON.

标 记 MARKS&NOS	包装及数量 QUANTITY	保险货物项目 DESCRIPTION OF GOODS	保险金额 AMOUNT INSURED

总保险金额
TOTAL AMOUNT INSURED: _____

保费　　　　　　启运日期　　　　　　装载运输工具：
RATE _____　SLG. ON OR ABT.:_____　PER CONVEYANCE S. S. _____
自　　　　　经　　　　　　　　　至
FROM:_____ VIA_____　TO_____
承保险别：
CONDITIONS:

所保货物，如发生保险单项下可能引起索赔的损失或损坏，应立即通知本公司下述代理人查勘。如有索赔，应向本公司提交保单正本(本保险单共有____份正本)及有关文件。如一份正本已用于索赔，其余正本自动失效。

IN THE EVENT OF LOSS OR DAMAGE WHICH MAY RESULT IN A CLAIM UNDER THIS POLICY, IMMEDIATE NOTICE MUST BE GIVEN TO THE COMPANY'S AGENT AS MENTIONED HEREUNDER. CLAIMS, IF ANYONE OF THE ORIGINAL POLICY WHICH HAS BEEN ISSUED IN _____ ORIGINAL(S) TOGETHER WITH THE RELEVANT DOCUMENTS SHALL BE SURRENDERED TO THE COMPANY. IF ONE OF THE ORIGINAL POLICY HAS BEEN ACCOMPLISHED, THE OTHERS TO BE VOID.

中国人民保险公司杭州市分公司
The People's Insurance Company of China Hangzhou Branch

赔款偿付地点
CLAIM PAYABLE AT: _____
出单日期　　　　　　杭州
ISSUING DATE:_____　HANGZHOU

_____
Authorized Signature

Case No. 2

根据所给资料填制一张投保单和保险单。

信用证中关于保险单的要求:

MARINE INSURANCE POLICY OR CERTIFICATE IN DUPLICATE, ENDORSED IN BLANK, FOR 110% OF THE INVOICE VALUE INCLUDING: OCEAN MARINE CARGO CLAUSES (ALL RISKS), OCEAN MARINE CARGO WAR RISKS CLAUSES AND OCEAN MARINE CARGO STRIKES RISKS AND CIVIL COMMOTIONS CLAUSES OF THE PEOPLE'S INSURANCE COMPANY OF CHINA INCLUDING WAREHOUSE TO WAREHOUSE CLAUSE, CLAIMS PAYABLE IN JAPAN IN CURRENCY OF DRAFTS.

SUPPLEMENTS:

BENEFICIARY:	HANGZHOU ZHONGHUA TEXTILES I/E CORP.
APPLICANT:	TOYOHAMM AND CO., LTD.
COMMODITY:	100% COTTON PIECE GOODS
LATEST SHIPMENT DATE:	MAY 31TH, 2007
NAME OF THE VESSEL:	YIFENG V.226
PORT OF LOADING:	SHANGHAI
PORT OF DESTINATION:	KOBE
PRICE TERM:	CIFC5% KOBE
AMOUNT:	USD66,500.00
S/C NO.:	06YS88
SHIPPING MARK:	T.C./KOBE/NO.1-UP
QUANTITY:	50,000YDS
PACKING:	IN BALES OF 50 YARDS EACH

中国人民保险公司杭州分公司
国外运输险投保单

兹将我处出口物资依照信用证规定拟向你处投保国外运输险计开:

被保险人 （中文）（英文）			过户	
标记或发票号码	件 数	物 资 名 称		保险金额
运输工具（及运载工具）		约 于 年 月 日启运		赔款偿付地点
运输路程	自 经 到	转载地点		
要保险别:				投保单位签章 年 月 日

中国人民保险公司杭州市分公司
The People's Insurance Company of China Hangzhou Branch

总公司设于北京　　　一九四九年创立
Head Office Beijing　　Established in 1949

货物运输保险单
CARGO TRANSPORTATION INSURANCE POLICY

保单号次
POLICY NO.:

被保险人：

INSURED:

中国人民保险公司(以下简称本公司)根据被保险人的要求，由被保险人向本公司缴付约定的保险费，按照本保险单承保险别和背面所载条款与下列特款承保下述货物运输保险，特立本保险单。

THIS POLICY OF INSURANCE WITNESSES THAT THE PEOPLE'S INSURANCE COMPANY OF CHINA (HEREINAFTER CALLED "THE COMPANY") AT THE REQUEST OF THE INSURED AND IN CONSIDERATION OF THE AGREED PREMIUM PAID TO THE COMPANY BY THE INSURED, UNDERTAKES TO INSURE THE UNDERMENTIONED GOODS IN TRANSPORTATION SUBJECT TO THE CONDITIONS OF THIS POLICY AS PER THE CLAUSES PRINTED OVERLEAF AND OTHER SPECIAL CLAUSES ATTACHED HEREON.

标　记 MARKS&NOS	包装及数量 QUANTITY	保险货物项目 DESCRIPTION OF GOODS	保险金额 AMOUNT INSURED

总保险金额
TOTAL AMOUNT INSURED: _____

保费　　　　　　启运日期　　　　　装载运输工具：
RATE _____ SLG. ON OR ABT.:_____ PER CONVEYANCE S. S. _____
自　　　　　　　经　　　　　　　　　至
FROM:_____ VIA_____ TO_____
承保险别：
CONDITIONS:

所保货物，如发生保险单项下可能引起索赔的损失或损坏，应立即通知本公司下述代理人查勘。如有索赔，应向本公司提交保单正本(本保险单共有____份正本)及有关文件。如一份正本已用于索赔，其余正本自动失效。

IN THE EVENT OF LOSS OR DAMAGE WHICH MAY RESULT IN A CLAIM UNDER THIS POLICY, IMMEDIATE NOTICE MUST BE GIVEN TO THE COMPANY'S AGENT AS MENTIONED HEREUNDER. CLAIMS, IF ANYONE OF THE ORIGINAL POLICY WHICH HAS BEEN ISSUED IN _____ ORIGINAL(S) TOGETHER WITH THE RELEVANT DOCUMENTS SHALL BE SURRENDERED TO THE COMPANY. IF ONE OF THE ORIGINAL POLICY HAS BEEN ACCOMPLISHED, THE OTHERS TO BE VOID.

中国人民保险公司杭州市分公司
The People's Insurance Company of China Hangzhou Branch

赔款偿付地点
CLAIM PAYABLE AT: _____
出单日期　　　　　杭州
ISSUING DATE:_____HANGZHOU

_____ Authorized Signature _____

*P*RACTICE *8*

Execution of a Contract (V)

—Customs Declaration for Exports

履行合同(5)——出口报关

✧ To be familiar with the procedure of the customs declaration for exports 熟悉一般出口货物的报关流程

✧ To be able to fill in declaration form to the customs 掌握出口报关单的缮制方法及技巧

Example & Analysis 操作实例及解析

◆ Case Lead-in

As required, completed forms including Customs Declaration Form together with Sales Contract, Commercial Invoice, Packing List, Inspecting Certificate, Authority to Customs Declaration and other relevant documents should be submitted to the customs agency. The release is effected by the customs after the relevant goods have been checked and examined with satisfaction.

◆ 案例导入

在着手办理货物出口运输手续的同时，宁波井通宠物用品有限公司委托报关企业办理出口货物的报关，公司业务员将出口货物报关单、商业发票、装箱单、销售合同、商检证明、报关委托书等一系列单证与资料整理好提交给报关企业。报关企业向海关报关后，经海关查验货物合格后予以放行。

➢ **Procedure of customs declaration for export commodities** 出口货物报关流程

The customs declaration of export commodities is fulfilled by four steps: application, examine, pay duty and release.

一般出口货物的报关程序通常要经过：申报、查验、征税、放行等四大环节。

（一）出口货物申报

1. 申报地点

出口货物应当在出境地海关申报；经发货人申请，海关同意，出口货物可以在启运地海关申报。

2. 申报的期限

出口货物运抵海关监管区后、装货的 24 小时以前向海关申报。

3. 提供有关单证和资料

出口货物报关时，必须由报关员填制或由自动化报关预录入人员录入打印的报关单一式多份；其次出口货物属于国家限制出口或配额出口的应提供许可证件或其他证明文件；并随附其他单证包括：

(1) 货物的发票、装箱清单、销售合同等；

(2) 商检证明；

(3) 对方要求的产地证明；

(4) 出口收汇核销单；

(5) 其他有关文件。

出口货物发货人委托报关企业向海关报关的，必须同时提供出口货物报关委托书。

（二）查验

海关对报关数据或报关单证进行审核后，发出书面或电子形式的查验通知。

1. 货物查验

海关根据国家的法律规定确定进出境货物的性质、价格、数量、原产地、货物状况等是否与报关填报内容一致的行为。

2. 海关查验

(1) 查验地点：海关监管区或装卸现场；特殊情况下海关可以派人员到监管区外进行查验。

(2) 查验时间：正常工作日内海关以书面形式提前通知；特殊情况下经申请也可以在其他时间查验。

3. 配合查验

海关查验货物时，要求货物的收发货人或其代理人必须到场。在海关认为有必要的情况下，报关人员要配合海关进行货物的查验。

(1) 负责搬运货物、开箱、封箱；

(2) 回答提问，提供有关单证；

(3) 需要做进一步检验、化验或鉴定的货样，收取海关开具的取样清单；

(4) 确认查验结果，在《海关进出境货物查验记录单》上签字。

（三）征税

属于应纳税缴费范围的出口货物，由出口货物发货人或其代理人在规定时间内，持海关开具的税款缴款书或收费票据向指定银行办理税费缴纳手续。收到银行缴款成功的信息，即可报请海关办理货物放行手续。

(四) 放行

出口货物在办完向海关申报、接受查验、缴纳税款等手续后，由海关在货运单据上签印放行。货物收发货人或其代理人必须凭海关签印放行的货运单据才能提取或发运进出口货物。

进出口货物代理报关委托书

编号：

委托单位	宁波井通宠物用品有限公司	十位编码	3800912061
地　　址	宁波市中山路 118 号	联系电话	0574-88762018
经 办 人		身份证号	

我单位委托宁波永达报关有限公司代理以下进出口货物的报关手续，保证提供的报关资料真实、合法，与实际货物相符，并愿承担由此产生的法律责任。

货物名称	植绒毛衣	商品编号	6200.1300	件　　数	100 箱
重　　量	1,100KGS	价　　值	USD7,122.00	币　　制	美元
贸易性质	一般贸易	货物产地	宁波	合 同 号	ST08020
是否退税	是	船名/航次	WUYING V.198		
委托单位 开户银行	中国银行宁波市分行			账　　号	

随附单证名称、份数及编号：

1. 合同　　　壹　份：ST08020		6. 机电证明　　份、编号：
2. 发票　　　壹　份：08NSP168		7. 商检证　　　份：
3. 装箱清单　壹　份：08NSP168		8. 外汇核销单 壹 份：435849673
4. 登记手册　　本、编号：		9.
5. 许可证　　　份、编号：		10.

(以上内容由被委托单位填写)

被 委 托 单 　 位		十位编码	
地　　址		联系电话	
经 办 人		身份证号	

(以上内容由被委托单位填写)

代理(专业) 报关企业 章及法人 代 表 章		委托单位 章及法人 代 表 章	

年　　月　　日

Directions 操作指南

出口货物报关单的主要内容及填制如下所述：

(1) 预录入编号：预录入编号非报关员填写，由接受申报的海关决定编号规则，由计算机自动打印，无须填写。

(2) 海关编号：海关编号同样非报关员填写，是指海关接受申报时给予报关单的编码，一般由 18 位数字组成，其中第 1—4 位为接受申报海关的编号，第 5—8 位为海关接受申报的公历年份，第 9 位为进出口标志，后 9 位为顺序编号。

(3) 出口口岸：指货物实际出口我国关境的口岸海关名称。本栏根据《关区代码表》填报货物实际出口我国关境的口岸海关的名称及相应代码，注意填写时口岸海关的名称和代码都不能缺少，并且填写的是口岸海关的名称而不是港口的名称。

(4) 备案号：指出口企业在海关申请办理加工贸易货物合同备案、特定减免税货物审批备案等手续时，经海关批准后发给加工贸易手册、征免税证明等备案审批文件的编号。一份报关单只允许填报一个备案号。备案号长度为 12 位，第 1 位是标记代码，表示的是何种性质的备案，用不同的英文字母表示；第 2—5 位是备案地海关的关区代码；第 6 位表示的是年份；第 7—12 位是序列号。无备案审批文件的报关单此栏免予填报。

(5) 出口日期：指运载所申报货物的运输工具申报出境的日期。本栏应为 8 位数，顺序为年(4 位)、月(2 位)、日(2 位)。

(6) 申报日期：指海关接受出口货物的收发货人或其代理人申请办理货物出口手续的日期。本栏填报为 8 位数，顺序为年(4 位)、月(2 位)、日(2 位)。除特殊情况外，出口货物的申报日期不能晚于出口日期。

(7) 经营单位：经营单位指已在海关注册登记对外签订并执行出口贸易合同的中国境内企业、单位或个人(个体工商户)。经营单位编码为 10 位数字，是出口企业在所在地主管海关办理注册登记手续时，海关给企业设置的注册登记编码。10 位编码结构设置是有规则的，第 1—4 位表示经营单位属地的行政区划代码；第 5 位表示市内经济区域；第 6 位表示企业经济类型的代码；第 7—10 位顺序号。本栏填报经营单位名称及经营单位编码。

(8) 运输方式：指载运货物出关境所使用的运输工具的分类。本栏应根据实际运输方式，按海关规定的《运输方式代码表》，填报相应的运输方式名称或代码。与运输工具相对应，海关规定了如下的运输方式并对应有代码：江海运输(2)；铁路运输(3)；汽车运输(4)；航空运输(5)；邮件运输(6)；其他运输(9)。

(9) 运输工具名称：指载运货物进出境的运输工具的名称或运输工具编号。一份报关单只允许填报一个运输工具名称。直接在出境地办理报关手续的报关单具体填报要求如下：

　　1) 江海运输填报船舶英文名称或船舶编号+"/"+航次号。

　　2) 航空运输填报航班号。

　　3) 汽车运输填报国内行驶的车牌号+"/"+出境日期。

　　4) 铁路运输填报车厢编号或交接单号+"/"+出境日期。

(10) 提运单号：指出口货物提单或运单的编号。一份报关单只允许填报一个提运单号，当一票货物对应多个提运单时，应分单填报。直接在出境地办理报关手续的报关单具体填报要求如下：

1) 江海运输填报出口提单号。

2) 航空运输填报总运单号+"＿＿＿"+分运单号。无分运单的填报总运单号。

3) 汽车运输免于填报。

4) 铁路运输填报运单号。

(11) 发货单位：指自行出口货物的单位，或者委托有外贸进出口经营权的企业出口货物的单位。发货单位有海关注册编码的应填报编号(有编码时不填中文名称)，没有海关编码的填报中文名称。

(12) 贸易方式：本栏应根据实际情况，按海关规定的《贸易方式代码表》选择填报相应的贸易方式简称或代码。一份报关单只允许填报一种贸易方式。常用的贸易方式有：一般贸易(0110)、来料加工(0214)、进料对口(0615)、外资设备物品(2225)、合资合作设备(2025)、不作价设备(0320)、无代价抵偿(3100)。

(13) 征免性质：指海关根据《海关法》、《关税条例》及国家有关政策对进出口货物实施征、减、免税管理的性质类别。一份报关单只允许填报一种征免性质。本栏应按照海关核发的《征免税证明》中批注的征免性质填报，或根据实际情况按海关规定的《征免性质代码表》选择填报相应的征免性质简称或代码。

(14) 结汇方式：指出口货物的发货人或其代理人收结外汇的方式，也就是国际贸易中的汇款支付、结算的方式。本栏应按海关规定的《结汇方式代码表》选择填报相应的结汇方式名称、缩写或代码。

(15) 许可证号：指国务院商务主管部门及其授权发证机关签发的出口货物许可证的编号。应申领出口许可证的货物，必须在此栏填报。

(16) 运抵国(地区)：指出口货物直接运抵的国家(地区)。本栏应按海关规定的《国别(地区)代码表》选择填报相应的运抵国(地区)中文名称或代码。

(17) 指运港：指出口货物运往境外的最终目的港。本栏填报指运港的中文名称，最终目的港是不可预知的，可按尽可能预知的目的港填报。

(18) 境内货源地：指出口货物在国内的产地或原始发货地。本栏按海关规定的《国内地区代码表》选择填报相应的国内地区名称或代码。

(19) 批准文号：出口报关单本栏直接填写出口收汇核销单编号。

(20) 成交方式：指国际贸易中的贸易术语，是买卖双方就成交的商品在价格构成、责任、费用和风险的分担，以及货物所有权转移界线的约定。本栏应根据实际成交价格条款按海关规定的《成交方式代码表》选择填报相应的成交方式名称或代码。

(21) 运费：本栏用于填报成交价格中含有运费的出口货物。可按运费单价、总价或运费率三种方式之一填报，同时注明运费标记，并按海关规定的《货币代码表》选择填报相应的币种代码。运费标记中"1"表示运费率，"2"表示每吨货物的运费单价，"3"表示运费总价。三种方式的填报形式分别是：

1) 运费率方式直接填报运费率的数值。

  2) 运费单价方式填报"币制代码／运费的单价数值／运费单价标记"。

  3) 运费总价方式填报"币制代码／运费的总价数值／运费总价标记"。

(22) 保费：本栏用于填报成交价格中含有保险费的出口货物。可按保险费总价和保险费率两种方式之一填报，同时注明保险费标记，并按海关规定的《货币代码表》选择填报相应的币种代码。保险费标记"1"表示保险费率，"3"表示保险费总价，填报形式分别是：

  1) 保费率方式直接填报保费率的数值。

  2) 保费总价方式填报"币制代码／保费的总价数值／保费总价标记"。

(23) 杂费：指成交价格以外的，应计入完税价格的费用或计算完税价格时应扣除的费用。填报成交方式总价以外的、应计入完税价格的费用，如佣金、经济费、回扣、包装费、特许权使用费等，或填成交方式总价以内的，计算完税价格时应该扣除的费用，如回扣、折扣、安装费等。可按杂费总价或杂费率两种方式之一填报，同时注明杂费标记，并按海关规定的《货币代码表》选择填报相应的币种代码。杂费标记"1"表示杂费率，"3"表示杂费总价。应计入完税价格的杂费填报为正值或正率，不应包含在完税价格中的，应该扣除的杂费填报为负值或负率。

(24) 合同协议号：指买卖双方就买卖的商品所签订的合同或者协议的编号。本栏应填报出口货物合同(协议)编号的全部字头和号码。

(25) 件数：本栏应填报有外包装的出口货物的实际件数。

(26) 包装种类：本栏应根据出口货物的实际外包装种类填报。

(27) 毛重：指货物及其包装材料的重量之和。本栏填报所申报的出口货物实际毛重，计量单位为千克(公斤)，不足 1 千克的填报为"1"。

(28) 净重：指货物的毛重减去外包装材料后的重量，即商品本身的实际重量。本栏填报所申报的出口货物实际净重，计量单位为千克(公斤)，不足 1 千克的填报为"1"。

(29) 集装箱号：集装箱两侧标示的全球唯一的编号，通常前 4 位是字母，后跟一串数字。本栏应该填写"集装箱号"＋"/"＋"规格"＋"/"＋"自重"。多个集装箱的，第一个集装箱号等信息填报在"集装箱号"栏，其他依次按相同的格式填在"标记唛码及备注"栏中。非集装箱货物填报为"0"。

(30) 随附单据：指出口货物报关单一并向海关递交的单证或文件。合同、装箱单、发票、许可证等必备的随附单据不在本栏填报，只填报监管证件代码表中的除去许可证以外的监管证件代码及编号。

(31) 生产厂家：指出口货物的境内生产企业，本栏供必要时手工填写。

(32) 标记唛码及备注：标记唛码指运输的标志，填报货物运输包装上的标记唛码中除图形以外的所有文字、数字，无标记唛码的免于填报。备注栏内容包括：

  1) 受外商投资企业委托代理其在投资总额内出口投资设备、物品的外贸企业名称填写在本栏。

  2) 一票货物有多个集装箱需要填报的，本栏中填写其余集装箱的信息。

  3) 一个以上监管证件的，本栏填写其余的监管证件的代码及编号。

(33) 项号：指同一票货物在报关单中的商品排列序号和在备案文件上的商品序号。每一栏项号下都分两行填报，第一行填报报关单中的商品排列序号，第二行要填写该项商品对应在加工贸易手册中或原产地证书中的项号，非备案商品免填。

(34) 商品编号：指按海关规定的商品归类编码规则确定的出口货物的商品编号。

(35) 商品名称、规格型号：本栏分两行填报，第一行填报出口货物规范的中文商品名称，第二行填报规格型号，规格型号应足够详细，并与所提供的商品发票相符，填报内容应包括品名、牌名、规格、型号、成分、含量、等级等。

(36) 数量及单位：本栏分三行填报，具体填报要求如下：

    1) 出口货物必须按海关法定计量单位和成交计量单位填报，法定第一计量单位及数量填报在本栏第一栏。

    2) 凡海关列明法定第二计量单位的，必须报明该商品法定第二计量单位及数量，填报在本栏第二行，无第二计量单位的，本栏第二行为空。

    3) 成交计量单位与海关法定计量单位不一致时，还需填报成交计量单位及数量，填报在数量及单位栏的第三行。成交计量单位与海关法定计量单位一致时，本栏第三行为空。

(37) 最终目的国(地区)：指已知的出口货物的最终实际消费、使用或进一步加工制造的国家(地区)。本栏按海关规定的《国别(地区)代码表》中的国别(地区)的中文名称或代码填写。

(38) 单价：本栏应填报同一项号下出口货物实际成交的商品单位价格的金额。单价填报到小数点后4位，第5位及其后略去。

(39) 总价：本栏应填报同一项号下出口货物实际成交的商品总价。总价填报到小数点后4位，第5位及其后略去。

(40) 币制：本栏应根据实际成交情况按海关规定的《货币代码表》选择填报相应的货币名称或代码。

(41) 征免：指海关对出口货物进行征税、减税、免税或特案处理的实际操作方式。本栏应按照海关核发的《征免税证明》或有关政策规定，对报关单所列每项商品选择填报海关规定的《征减免税方式代码表》中相应的征、减、免税方式的名称。

(42) 税费征收情况：本栏供海关批注出口货物税费征收及减免情况。

(43) 录入员：本栏用于记录并打印录入人员的姓名。

(44) 录入单位：本栏用于记录并打印录入单位的名称。

(45) 申报单位：本栏用于填报申报单位有关情况的总栏。

(46) 填制日期：指报关单的填制日期。

(47) 海关审单批注栏：本栏指供海关内部作业时签注的总栏，由海关关员手工填写在预录入报关单上，其中"放行"栏填写海关对接受申报的出口货物做出放行决定的日期。

中华人民共和国海关出口货物报关单

预录入编号：　　　　　　　　　　　　　　　海关编号：

出口口岸　宁波海关 3102		备案号	出口日期 2008.07.20	申报日期 2008.07.13
经营单位	宁波井通宠物用品有限公司 3800912061	运输方式 江海运输	运输工具名称 WUYING/V198	提运单号 Cosco8867980
发货单位	宁波井通宠物用品有限公司	贸易方式 一般贸易	征免性质 一般征税	结汇方式 L/C
许可证号	运抵国(地区) 美国		指运港 迈阿密	境内货源地 宁波
批准文号	成交方式 CIF	运费 USD7,400.00	保费 USD68.94	杂费
合同协议号　STO8020	件数 100	包装种类 纸箱	毛重(千克) 1,100	净重(千克) 1,000
集装箱号　COSCO123 456/98765	随附单据			生产厂家

标记唛码及备注
　ABF
　ST08020
　MIAMI
　C/NO.: 1-UP

项目	商品编号	商品名称、规格型号	数量及单位	最终目的国(地区)	单价	总价	币制	征免
01	6200.1300	FLOCKING SWEATERS	2,400 PCS	美国	3.09	1,545.00	USD	照章

税费征收情况

录入员　录入单位	兹声明以上申报无讹并承担法律责任	海关审单批注及放行日期(签章)	
		审单	审价
报关员			
单位地址	申报单位(签章)	征税	统计
		查验	放行
邮编　　　电话　　　填制日期			

Practice 操作练习

1. 操作信息

宁波格然得国际贸易有限公司(经营单位编码：3800910028)于 2008 年 7 月 2 日向宁波海关(关区代码：3102)申报货物出口。商品编码为 5786.2000；法定计量单位：只。船公司核定的运费率为 8%，保险公司收取保费 100 美元。

格然得国际贸易有限公司

GRAND POWER INTERNATIONAL CO., LTD.

ROOM 307, JIAHUI BUILDING, NO. 80, YINHE ROAD,

NINGBO, P.R.CHINA

COMMERCIAL INVOICE

To: WALTS UNITED CORP.

ALEKSANTER INKATU 70, 01510 HELSINKI,FINLAND

Invoice No: GP2008I05

Date: JUNE. 22ND, 2008

S/C No: GP2008X05

L/C No: LRT0802110

Shipped per   DONGFANGHAI615   From   NINGBO   To   FINLAND

Shipping Mark	Description of Goods	Quantity	Unit Price	Amount
			CIF FINLAND	
N/M	HALOGEN LAMP	6,000PCS	USD 6.50/PC	USD39,000.00

TOTAL VALUE: USD39,000.00

SUPPLEMENTS:

1. B/L NO.: BL602

2. PACKING: ONE DOZEN IN A CARTON, TOTALLY 500 CARTONS.

3. GROSS WEIGHT: 12,000KG

4. NET WEIGHT: 11,800KG

5. CONTAINER/SEAL NO.: MSKC54782300

6. DATE OF CUSTOMS DECLARATION: JULY 2ND, 2008

7. TIME OF SHIPMENT: JULY 7TH, 2008

2. 操作要求

根据上述所给资料填制一份出口货物报关单。

中华人民共和国海关出口货物报关单

预录入编号：　　　　　　　　　　　　　　　海关编号：

出口口岸		备案号	出口日期	申报日期
经营单位		运输方式	运输工具名称	提运单号
发货单位		贸易方式	征免性质	结汇方式
许可证号	运抵国(地区)		指运港	境内货源地
批准文号	成交方式	运费	保费	杂费
合同协议号	件数	包装种类	毛重(千克)	净重(千克)
集装箱号	随附单据			生产厂家

标记唛码及备注

项目	商品编号	商品名称、规格型号	数量及单位	最终目的国(地区)	单价	总价	币制	征免

税费征收情况

录入员　　　录入单位	兹声明以上申报无讹并承担法律责任	海关审单批注及放行日期(签章)
		审单　　　　　　　审价
报关员		
单位地址	申报单位(签章)	征税　　　　　　　统计
		查验　　　　　　　放行
邮编　　　电话　　　填制日期		

PRACTICE 9

Making out Documents and Settlement of Foreign Exchange
出口制单结汇

Learning Objectives 学习目标

◇ To be familiar with procedure of settlement of foreign exchange in international trade 熟悉国际贸易出口收汇的主要流程

◇ To make out the main documents for settlement of foreign exchange in international trade 掌握主要出口结汇单证的缮制

Example & Analysis 操作实例及解析

◆ Case Lead-in

The 2,400 pcs of Flocking Sweaters under S/C No. ST08020 manufactured by Ningbo Xinxin Pets' Ware factory have been shipped via S.S. WUYING V.198 due to sail for Miami on July 30th, 2008. At last Ningbo Sakai Pet Co., Ltd. should make out all the necessary documents stipulated in the L/C. The documents include Commercial Invoice, Packing List, Marine Bill of Loading, Certificate of Origin, Insurance policy, Shipping Advice, Beneficiary's Certificate and Shipping Company's Certificate.

◆ 案例导入

ST08020 合同项下的 2400 件宠物用植绒毛衣已由宁波新新宠物用品厂备货完成，并于 2008 年 7 月 30 日装船出运前往美国迈阿密。最后，出口商宁波井通宠物用品有限公司应按照信用证条款规定，及时缮制单据，包括商业发票、装箱单、海运提单、原产地证、保险单、装船通知、受益人证明与船公司证明。

> ➤ **Basic requirements for making out documents** 制单基本要求

1. Contents and requirements 内容和要求

Making out documents for settlement of foreign exchange, which is the last and most important procedure in export, can be divided into three steps including document-making, presentation of documents and settlement of foreign exchange.

When the terms of payment is by L/C, the exporter should make out the documents as stipulated in the L/C after the shipment is effected. All the documents should be presented to the bank for negotiation within the presentation of documents and validity of the L/C.

When the terms of payment is by collection (D/P, D/A), the exporter should make out the documents as stipulated clauses in the contract and present all the documents to the bank for settlement after the shipment of the goods.

When the terms of the payment is by T/T, M/T or D/D, the exporter should make out the documents as stipulated clauses in the contract and send all the documents to the importer after the shipment of the goods. Thereafter, settlement of the foreign exchange can be made by the bank.

制单结汇分为制单、交单和结汇三个步骤。这是出口方面业务流程最后，也是最重要的环节之一。

按信用证(L/C)方式成交时，货物在装船出运之后，出口商应按照信用证规定，及时备妥缮制单证，并在信用证规定的交单有效期内交银行办理议付、结汇手续。

按托收(D/A、D/P)方式成交时，出口商应按照合同条款规定备妥缮制单证，交银行办理结汇手续。

按汇付(T/T、M/T、D/D)方式成交时，出口商应按照合同条款规定备妥缮制单证，交寄给进口商，最后到银行办理结汇手续。

2. Requirements for making out documents 制单的要求

The quality of the whole set of the documents plays a crucial role in prompt and safe settlement of foreign exchange, especially when the terms of payment is by L/C. Therefore, if the terms of payment are by L/C, the exporter should make out the documents strictly in compliance with the stipulations of L/C and with each other. In case there were any discrepancy, the bank would dishonor the draft, causing great loss or trouble for the exporter. So special attention should be paid to when the documents are being made out. The following are the basic requirements:

Correct. All the contents in the documents should be correct, which are in compliance with each other, with the requirements of the L/C and with the goods themselves.

Complete. The copies of the documents should be prepared as stipulated in the L/C. All the necessary information should be provided.

Prompt. Documents should be made out immediately after the shipment of the goods and presented before the period of the presentation and validity of the relevant L/C.

Concise. All the information should be written in accordance with international uniform practice. Don't add any information at one's own will.

Clean. All the documents should be clearly typed without being altered.

提高单证质量，对保证安全迅速收汇有着十分重要的意义，特别是在信用证付款条件下，实行的是单据和货款对流的原则，单证不相符，单单不一致，银行和进口商就可能拒收单据和拒付货款，出口商就会有很大的麻烦或损失，因此，缮制结汇单据时，要求做到以下几点：

正确：单据内容必须正确，既要符合信用证的要求，又要能真实反映货物的实际情况，且各单据的内容不能相互矛盾。

完整：单据份数应符合信用证的规定，不能短少，单据本身的内容，应当完备，不能出现项目短缺情况。

及时：制单应及时，以免错过交单日期或信用证有效期。

简明：单据内容应按信用证要求和国际惯例填写，力求简明，切勿加列不必要的内容。

整洁：单据的布局要美观大方，缮写或打印的字迹要清楚醒目，不宜轻易列改，尤其对金额、件数和重量等，更不宜改动。

> **Procedures of making out documents and settlement of exchange 制单结汇流程**

1. Making out documents 制单

The exporter should make out the documents according to the regarding L/C or contract immediately before or after the shipment of the goods.

出口商应在货物装运前后根据相关信用证缮制整套交单议付的单据。

2. Presentation of the documents 交单

Presentation of the documents means that the exporter (the beneficiary under the L/C) present the full set of the documents under the relevant L/C to the bank for negotiation. The period of the presentation should be before or on the date of presentation and the validity of the L/C.

单证的交付是指出口商（即信用证付款方式下的受益人）在规定时间内向议付银行送交信用证条款规定的全套议付单证。出口商需要控制交单的时间，一般来讲交单日期主要取决于信用证的有效期和信用证规定的交单日期。

3. Settlement of foreign exchange 结汇

The negotiating bank will check the full set of the documents under the L/C after receipt of them. If there are no discrepancies under the clauses of the L/C, the negotiating bank will send the documents to the opening bank or the appointed bank and ask for remittance of foreign exchange.

议付行收到出口商的议付单证后，会按照信用证规定进行严格审核。如果审核无误，议付行即向信用证的开证行或被指定的其他付款银行寄单索汇，同时按照与出口商约定的方法进行结汇。

Task 1　Commercial Invoice 商业发票

Commercial invoice is a bill for the goods from the seller to the buyer. These invoices are often used by governments to determine the true value of goods when assessing customs duties. It is also the necessary documents in import customs clearance. According to the L/C, the seller made out the commercial invoice as follows:

宁波井通宠物用品有限公司

NINGBO SAKAI PET CO., LTD.

118 ZHONGSHAN ROAD, NINGBO, CHINA

商业发票

COMMERCIAL INVOICE

To:　　　　　　　　　　　　　　　　INVOICE NO.: __08NSP168__

ABF INTERNATIONAL CO., LTD.　　　INVOICE DATE: __JULY 15TH, 2008__

USA　　　　　　　　　　　　　　　　L/C NO.: __BOC070325__

　　　　　　　　　　　　　　　　　　S/C NO.: __ST08020__

Transport details:

SHIPMENT FROM NINGBO

TO MIAMI BY SEA

Marks & Nos.	Description of Goods	Quantity	Unit Price	Amount
ABF	FLOCKING SWEATERS		CIF MIAMI	
ST08020		2,400 PCS		USD7,122.00
MIAMI				
C/NO.: 1-UP				

　　　　AS PER S/C NO. ST08020 DD MAY 26TH, 2008

　　　　PACKED IN (100) CARTONS ONLY.

　　　　G.W.: 1,100KGS

　　　　TOTAL SAY U.S.DOLLARS SEVEN THOUSAND AND ONE HUNDRED

　　　　TWENTY-TWO ONLY.

　　　　　　　　　　　　　　　　宁波井通宠物用品有限公司

　　　　　　　　　　　　　　　　NINGBO SAKAI PET CO., LTD.

　　　　　　　　　　　　　　　　　　　王立

Directions 操作指南

➤　发票的种类主要包括：商业发票、银行发票、海关发票、领事发票、形式发票等。

(1) 商业发票(Commercial Invoice)，是出口商于货物运出时开给进口商作为进货记账或结算货款和报关缴税的凭证。

(2) 银行发票(Banker's Invoice)，是出口商为办理议付和结汇，以适应议付行和开证行需要而提供的发票。

(3) 海关发票(Customs Invoice)，是某些国家规定在进口货物时，必须提供其海关规定的一种固定格式和内容的发票。

(4) 领事发票(Consular Invoice)，又称签证发票。　是按某些国家法令规定，出口商对其国家输入货物时必须取得进口国在出口国或其邻近地区的领事签证的、作为装运单据一部分和货物进口报关的前提条件之一的特殊发票。

(5) 形式发票(Proforma Invoice)，也称预开发票或估价发票，是进口商为了向其本国当局申请进口许可证或请求核批外汇，在未成交之前，要求出口商将拟出售成交的商品名称、单价、规格等条件开立的一份参考性发票。

➤　商业发票各项内容的填制所示如下：

1. 发票抬头人名称与地址(MESSRS)

　　如果是信用证项下结算的发票，发票必须做成以信用证申请人名称为抬头。当采用托收或其他方式支付货款时，填写合同买方的名称和地址。

2. 发票出票人的名称和地址(EXPORTER)

　　发票出票人的名称和地址应与信用证受益人的名称和地址相一致，一般为出口商，填写出票人的英文名称及地址。

3. 运输资料(TRANSPORT DETAILS)

　　运输资料(TRANSPORT DETAILS)的填写应与货物的实际起运港(地)、目的港(地)以及运输方式，如果货物需经转运，应把转运港的名称打上。例如：Shipment from Shanghai to Hamburg with transshipment (W/T) at Hong Kong by sea/vessel (装运自上海到汉堡，在香港转运)。

4. 发票号码和日期(INVOICE NUMBER AND DATE)

　　发票号码和日期(INVOICE NUMBER AND DATE)由出口公司自行编制，一般在编制时可附加部门、年份等信息，发票日期一般不早与信用证的开证日，不迟于信用证的有效期限。

5. 信用证号码(L/C NUMBER)

　　当采用信用证结算方式时，填写信用证号码。当采用其他支付方式时，此项也可不填。

6. 合同号码(S/C NUMBER)

　　合同号码应与信用证上所列的相一致，如果一笔交易牵涉到几个合同时，应在发票上全部表示出来。

7. 支付方式(TERMS OF PAYMENT)

　　支付方式应填写该笔业务的付款方式，是电汇(T/T)、托收(D/P 或 D/A)或者信用证(L/C)

结算方式等。

8. 唛头及件数编号(SHIPPING MARK AND NUMBERS)

　　唛头及件数编号，应按信用证或合同的规定填写，并与提单、托运单等单据严格一致。如果无唛头，则应填写"NO MARK"(缩写 N/M)。如信用证或合同中没有规定唛头，出口商可自行设计唛头。唛头的内容可以包括客户名称缩写、合同号、目的港、件数号等部分，如货物还要转运到内陆目的地，可打上"IN TRANSIT TO 某地"等字样。

9. 商品描述(DESCRIPTION OF GOODS)

　　商品描述应先打上货物名称和总数量，然后根据信用证或合同的规定打出详细规格、单位及有关订单或合约号码等。信用证中此栏所用的词汇或词组一般有：

COVERING;

COVERING VALUE OF DESCRIPTION OF GOODS;

COVERING SHIPMENT OF;

DESCRIPTION OF GOODS;

SHIPMENT COVERING FOLLOWING GOODS;

SHIPMENT OF GOODS AS THE FOLLOWING.

10. 商品包装及件数(PACKING AND QUANTITY)

　　商品的包装及件数填写应与实际装运的数量包装单位，并与其他单据相一致。同时标出货物的毛、净重及包装尺码等。

11. 单价(UNIT PRICE)

　　单价必须显示计价货币、计量单位、单位金额。

12. 总值(TOTAL AMOUNT)

　　发票的总值不能超过信用证规定的最高金额。但是信用证总值前有"约"、"大概"、"大约"或类似词语的，允许有 10%的增减幅度。

13. 价格术语(TRADE TERMS)

　　价格术语必须根据信用证或合同的规定照打，不能遗漏。

14. 声明文句(STATEMENT)

　　此项是根据不同(国家)地区及不同信用证的要求缮打的。声明文句中词语要求内容确切、通顺、简洁。信用证里的有些条款，不能原文照抄，而要视具体情况重新组织。常用的声明文字有：

● This is to certify that the goods named herein are of Chinese Origin. 兹证明所列商品系中国产。

● We certify that the goods named above have been supplied in conformity with Order No. 8970. 兹证明本发票所列货物与合同号 8970 相符。

● We hereby certify that the abovementioned goods are of Chinese origin. 兹证明上述产品在中国制造。

● We hereby certify that we are the actually manufacturer of the goods invoiced. 兹证明发票所列产品确为本厂制造。

● We hereby certify that the above-mentioned particulars and figures are true and correct. 我们

仅此证明发票所述详细内容真实无误。

- We certify that the goods mentioned in this invoice have not been shipped on board of any vessel flying Israeli flag or due to call at any Israeli port. 兹证明本发票所列货物不装载于悬挂以色列国旗或驶靠任何以色列港口的船只。

- This is to certify that two copies of Invoice, Packing List and N/N Bill of Lading have been airmailed direct to applicant immediately after shipment effected. 兹证明发票、箱单和提单各两份副本，已于装运后立即直接航空快邮寄开证人。

- It is hereby certified that this invoice shows the actual price of the goods described, that no other invoice has been or will be issued and that all particulars are true and correct. 兹证明本发票的价格系所述商品的真实价格，并未签发其他发票。

15. 出票人签章(SIGNATURE)

　　发票的出票人即受益人、出口商，其名称必须与信用证规定的受益人名址相一致。根据规定，发票可无须签字，但须表示出具人。如果信用证有"SIGNED COMMERCIAL INVOICE"字样，则此发票必须签字；若信用证中有"MANUALLY SIGNED INVOICE"字样，则必须要有出票人的手签。

➢ 信用证中有关商业发票条款举例如下：

- Signed Commercial Invoice in duplicate showing a deduction of USD200.00 being commission. 签字商业发票一式两份，显示扣除 200 美元作为佣金。

- Signed Commercial Invoice, one original and two copies. 签字商业发票，一正两副。

- Manually Signed Invoice in five folds certifying that goods are as per Indent No. ABC567 of March 10th, 2008 quoting L/C No. 手签发票一式五份，并在发票上显示根据 2008 年 3 月 10 日合同号 ABC567 订立，注明信用证号码。

- Signed Commercial Invoice combined with certificate of origin and value in triplicate as required for imports into Nigeria. 已签字商业发票一式三份，发票须连同产地证明和货物价值声明为输入尼日利亚所需。

- Signed Commercial in quintuplicate, certifying merchandise to be of Chinese origin. 签字商业发票一式五份，证明产品的原产地为中国。

- 5% Discount should be deducted from total amount of the commercial invoice. 商业发票的总金额须扣除 5%折扣。

- Signed commercial invoice in five fold certifying that goods are as per Contract No. 12345 of March 11th, 2004 quoting L/C Number BTN/HS NO. and showing original invoice and a copy to accompany original set of documents. 签字发票一式五份，证明货物是根据 2004 年 3 月 11 日号码为 12345 的合同，并注明信用证号码和布鲁塞尔税则分类号码，显示正本发票和一份副本随附原套单证。

- Commercial Invoice in triplicate showing separately FOB. Value, Freight Charges, Insurance Premium, CIF Value and Country of Origin. 商业发票一式三份，分别显示 FOB 价值、运费、保险费，CIF 总值和原产地国。

Task 2　Bill of Exchange 汇票

Bill of Exchange is the financial documents in the trade. The following Bill of Exchange was made out by the seller according to the L/C.

BILL OF EXCHANGE

Drawn under STANDARD BANK LTD., USA

L/C No.　BOC070325　　　　　　Dated　　　080628

Payable with interest at　　　　　%

No.　08NSP168

Exchange for USD7,122.00 　　　NINGBO　China　Dated　AUG. 5TH, 2008

At　30 DAYS　sight of this FIRST of Exchange (Second of Exchange being unpaid) pay to the order of 　BANK OF CHINA, NINGBO BRANCH

The sum of 　U.S.DOLLARS SEVEN THOUSAND ONE HUNDRED AND TWENTY-TWO ONLY.

Value received

To　STANDARD BANK LTD., USA　　　　　宁波井通宠物用品有限公司

　　　　　　　　　　　　　　　　　　　NINGBO SAKAI PET CO., LTD.

　　　　　　　　　　　　　　　　　　　　　王立

Directions 操作指南

> 汇票各项内容的填制所示如下：

1. 汇票当事人(PARTIES TO A BILL)

一张汇票通常涉及出/开票人(issuer/drawer)、受票人/付款人(drawee/payer)和收/受款人(payee)三方。

出票人即出具汇票的人，一般填在汇票右下角的空白处，由出口单位填写，除非信用证上有特别说明要求手签汇票，通常都是盖一个章，包括出口公司的全称和法人代表或经办人的名字。

受票人/付款人是指接受命令付款的人，但他可以拒付或指定担当付款人付款。按规定，信用证支付方式下汇票的付款人为开证行，或其指定的另一家银行。信用证中常见的语句为：draft drawn on XX bank, issued on us, value on ourselves 等。

收/受款人又称汇票的抬头人，一般以银行(议付行)作为指示抬头人。

来证规定"限制议付"，则填限制银行。例如：negotiations are restricted to Bank of China only 则填写: pay to the order of Bank of China。

来证没有规定"限制议付"，则填任何议付银行。

汇票当事人还可能包括承兑人(acceptor)、背书人(indorser/endorser)、被背书人(indorsee/endorsee)、保证人(guarantor)和持票人(holder)等。

2. 汇票中的时间/期限(DATE AND PERIOD)

主要包括出票日期、付款期限和 L/C 方式下的开证日期。

出票日期通常在提单签发日期之后；付款期限的填写：即期 L/C 条件下，在汇票中的 At 和 sight 之间打上"XXX"或"***"或"---"等符号，远期则在 At 后根据实际情况打上具体期限(例如：L/C 要求汇票为 at 30 days after sight，则在 At 和 sight 之间打上"30 days after"字样，托收时在汇票中的 At 之前打上 D/P 或 D/A，余下内容的填写与 L/C 条件下的要求相同；开证日期则只出现在 L/C 方式下的汇票中。

3. 金额(AMOUNT)

大小写金额要一致，注意货币符号和数字的顺序，习惯在大写数字前加"Say"或"Total"，在数字后加"Only"，大写写法应注意小数部分的表达。例如: United States Dollars Two Thousand Five Hundred and Thirty-One Cents Ninety Only. (USD2,531.90)

表示金额 USD2,587.87 中的 0.87 有以下几种写法：

(1) cents eighty-seven

(2) point eighty-seven

(3) 87% or 87/100

4. 出票依据(DRAWN UNDER)

表明根据什么填写制作汇票。L/C 条件下有三项: 开证行名称、信用证号和开证日期，这是开证行在一定的期限内对汇票的金额保证履行付款责任的法律根据；托收项下可填写 Inv. No.(发票号码)，B/L No.(提单号码)，S/C No.(合同号码)或合同中的货物名称等。信用证一般为：

Drawn under + name of the opening bank + L/C No. + opening date

例如: Drawn under Bank of China, Hong Kong an irrevocable letter of credit No. 89705, dated Aug. 21st, 2007.

5. 出票地和付款地(PLACE OF ISSUE AND PLACE OF NEGOTIATION)

出票地在出口方所在地；付款地为付款人的地点。

6. 汇票号码(NUMBER OF DRAFT)

通常使用与发票号码相同的号码。

➢　信用证中有关汇票条款列举如下：

● We hereby issue our irrevocable documentary Letter of Credit No. XXX available at sight for full value of invoice. 我行在此开出不可撤销跟单信用证，号码为 XXX，即期汇票，金额为发票金额的 100%。

● This L/C is available with us by payment at 60 days after receipt of full set of documents at out counter. 此信用证在收到整套单据后 60 天在我行付款有效。

● Draft for negotiation with any bank in the Beneficiary's country. 汇票可在受益人国家任何银行议付。

- The L/C is available by negotiation of your drafts at sight for 100 percent of invoice value drawn on us. 此信用证议付须即期汇票，金额为发票金额的 100%，付款人为我行。

Task 3　Packing List 装箱单

Packing List is necessary for the buyer to know the packing details of the goods. The following Packing List was made out by the seller according to the requirement of the L/C.

宁波井通宠物用品有限公司

NINGBO SAKAI PET CO., LTD.

118 ZHONGSHAN ROAD, NINGBO, CHINA

装箱单

PACKING LIST

INV. NO.: 08NSP168

DATE: JULY 15TH, 2008

L/C NO.: BOC070325

S/C NO.: ST08020

To: ABF INTERNATIONAL CO., LTD. USA

Transport details:

SHIPMENT FROM NINGBO TO MIAMI

BY SEA

件号 C/Nos.	件数 Quantity	货名 Description of Goods	毛重 Gross Weight	净重 Net Weight	尺码 Measurement
		FLOCKING SWERTERS			
1—100	2,400PCS		11KGS/CTN	10KGS/CTN	0.24CBM/CTN
TOTAL: 2,400PCS			G.W.:1,100KGS	N.W.: 1,000KGS	MEAS: 24CBM

PACKED IN (100) CTNS ONLY.

L/C NO.: BOC070325

宁波井通宠物用品有限公司

NINGBO SAKAI PET CO., LTD.

王立

Directions 操作指南

➤ 常用的包装单据有以下几种：

(1) 装箱单(PACKING LIST 或 PACKING SLIP)；

(2) 重量单(WEIGHT LIST 或 WEIGHT NOTE)；

(3) 尺码单(MEASUREMENT LIST)；

(4) 详细装箱单(DETAILED PACKING LIST)；

(5) 包装明细单(PACKING SPECIFICATION)；

(6) 包装提要(PACKING SUMMARY)；

(7) 磅码单(WEIGHT MEMO)；

(8) 规格单(SPECIFICATION LIST)；

(9) 花色搭配单(ASSORTMENT LIST)。

包装单据并无统一固定的格式，制单时可以根据信用证或合同的要求和货物的特点自行设计，但包装单据应大致具备以下内容：

(1) 编号和日期(NUMBER AND DATE)；

(2) 合同号码或信用证号码(CONTRACT NUMBER or L/C NUMBER)；

(3) 唛头(SHIPPING MARK)；

(4) 货物名称、规格和数量(NAME OF COMMODITY, SPECIFICATIONS AND QUANTITIES)；

(5) 包装件数及件号、包装件尺码(NUMBERS AND MEASUREMENT)；

(6) 包装类别(KINDS OF PACKING)；

(7) 货物毛净重(GROSS AND NET WEIGHT)。

➤ 装箱单据的缮制

(1) Issuer: 出口公司名称及地址。

(2) To: 收货人名称、地址。

(3) No/Date: 装箱单据的号码、日期(一般填写发票号码、日期)。

(4) L/C No.: 填写信用证号码；S/C No.: 填写合同号码。

(5) Transport Details: 填写运输的装运港(地)、目的港或中转港(地)名称及运输方式和船名。

例如：From Shanghai To New York by sea。

(6) Marks & Nos.: 填写唛头，与发票一致。

(7) No. & Kind of Pkgs: 填写商品数量。该数量为运输包装单位的数量，而不是计价单位的数量。

(8) Description of Goods: 填写商品名称。

(9) Gross Weight: 填写商品的单位净重和总净重。

(10) Net Weight: 填写商品的单位毛重和总毛重。

(11) Measurement: 填写商品的单位尺码和总尺码。

(12) 下面空白处应填写包装数量的大写。

(13) 如有特别要求，应特别说明。如有的信用证规定"SEAWORTHY PACKING"(适用于海运包装)、"PACKING SUITABLE FOR LONG DISTANT"(适合于长途运输包装)或"STRONG WOODEN CASE PACKING"(坚固木箱装运)，等等。信用证中的这些表达方法，都应在发票及箱单中照抄。

(14) 出口公司落款、签字或盖章。

➤ 信用证中包装单据条款列举如下：

(1) Packing list in triplicate. 装箱单一式三份。

(2) Signed packing list, one original and one copy. 签字装箱单，一正一副。

(3) Manually signed packing list in triplicate detailing the complete inner packing specifications and contents of each package. 手签装箱单一式三份，详注每件货物内部包装的规格和内容。

(4) Detailed packing list in quadruplicate showing gross weight, net weight, net net weight, measurement, color, size and quantity breakdown for each package, if any applicable. 详细装箱单一式四份，如适用，请标明每个包装的毛重、净重、净净重、尺码、颜色、尺寸和数量。

(5) Packing list in triplicate issued by beneficiary indicating quantity, gross and net weight of each package or container. 受益人出具的装箱单一式三份，指出每一容器或集装箱的数量、毛重、净重。

Task 4　Bill of Lading 海运提单

When the goods have been shipped on board the vessel, the shipping company or its agent will issue a Bill of Lading to the shipper. Marine Bills of Lading performs a number of functions. Generally, it's a receipt for the goods shipped, a document of title to the goods and evidence of the terms of the contract between the shipper and the shipping line. The following is the B/L for the cargo issued by COSCO CONTAINER LINES.

中远集装箱运输有限公司
COSCO CONTAINER LINES

PAGE:　　　OF

ORIGINAL　　TLX: 33057 COSCO CN

FAX: +86(21)65458984

PORT TO PORT OR COMBINED TRANSPORT BILL OF LADING

1. Shipper　Insert Name Address and Phone/Fax **NINGBO SAKAI PET CO., LTD.** **118 ZHONGSHAN ROAD, NINGBO, CHINA**	Booking No.	Bill of Lading No. **COSCO8867980**
		Export References
2. Consignee　Insert Name Address and Phone/Fax **TO ORDER**	Forwarding Agent and References FMC/CHB No.	
	Point and Country of Origin	

3. Notify Party Insert Name Address and Phone/Fax (It is agreed that no responsibility shall attach to the Carrier or his agents for failure to notify) **ABF INTERNATIONAL CO., LTD.** **35 FOREST AVENUE, MIAMI, USA**		
4. Combined Transport* Pre-Carriage by	5. Combined Transport* Place of Receipt	
6. Ocean Vessel Voy. No. **WUYING V.198**	7. Port of Loading **NINGBO**	Service Contract No. Commodity Code
8. Port of Discharge **MIAMI**	9. Combined Transport* Place of Receipt	Type of Movement

Marks & Nos. Container/Seal No.	No. of Container or Packages	Description of Goods (If Dangerous Goods, See Clause 20)	Gross Weight	Measurement
ABF **ST08020** **MIAMI** **C/NO.: 1-UP**	**100CTNS**	**FLOCKING SWEATERS** **L/C NO.: BOC070325** **ON BOARD** **FREIGHT PREPAID** **SHIPPER'S LOAD, COUNT & SEAL** **CY-CY 1X20′** **COSCO123456/98765**	**1,100KGS**	**24CBM**
Declared Cargo Value USD		Description of Contents for Shipper's Use Only (Not part of this B/L Contract)		

10. Total Number of Containers and/or Packages (in words)   **SAY ONE HUNDRED CARTONS ONLY.**

   Subject to Clause 7 Limitation

11. Freight t& Charges	Revenue Tons	Rate	Per	Amount	Prepaid	Collect	Freight & Charges Payable at/by

Received in external apparent good order and condition except as otherwise noted. The total number of the packages or units stuffed in the container, the description of the goods and the weights shown in this Bill of Lading are furnished by the merchants, and which the carrier has no reasonable means of checking and is not a part of this Bill of Lading. The carrier has issued **3(THREE)** original Bills of Lading, all of this tenor and date, one of the original Bill of Lading must be surrendered and endorsed or signed against the delivery of the shipment and whereupon any other Original Bills of Lading shall be void. The merchants agree to be bound by the terms and conditions of this Bill of Lading as if each had personally signed this Bill of Lading.

*Applicable Only When Document Used as a Combined Transport Bill of Lading

Date Laden on Board: JULY 30TH, 2008

Signed by

COSCO CONTAINER

LINES

AS CARRIER

Date of Issue

JULY 30TH, 2008

COSCO CONTAINER LINES

Place of Issue

NINGBO, CHINA

Signed for the Carrier, COSCO CONTAINER LINES

Directions 操作指南

运输单据(Transport Documents)是国际贸易的基本单据之一，是指托运人将货物移交给承运人办理装运时，由承运人签发给托运人的书面文书，通常代表了运输中的货物已经装运的证明。运输单据按运输方式不同，可分为海运提单(Marine Bill of Lading)、航空运单(Air Waybill)、铁路运单(Rail Waybill)、邮包收据(Parcel Post Receipt)和联合运输单据(Multimodal Transport Document)等。在国际货物运输中，尽管空运、铁路运输发展很快，但是目前国际贸易运输仍然以海洋货运为主。

海运提单，简称"提单"(B/L)，是由船长或承运人或其代理人签发的，证明收到特定的货物，或已装船，并将约定的货物运至特定的目的地，并交付于收货人或提单持有人的物权凭证，也是承运人和托运人之间运输合同的证明。

1. 海运提单的作用

(1) 海运提单是承运人或其代理人签发的货物收据(receipt for the goods)，确认承运人已经按海运提单所列内容收到货物。

(2) 海运提单是托运人和承运人之间的运输合约(contract)。双方必须履行提单上所说明的权利和义务。

(3) 海运提单是物权凭证(document of title)。提单的持有人对提单上所说明的货物拥有所有权，并可以经过背书进行抵押、转让，受法律保护。

(4) 海运提单可以作为收取运费的证明，以及在运输过程中起到办理货物的装卸、发运和交付等方面的作用。

(5) 提单是向船公司或保险公司索赔的重要依据。

2. 海运提单的种类

(1) 根据货物是否装船分为"已装船提单"和"备运提单"。

已装船提单(On Board B/L)，是指轮船公司将货物已经装上指定船舶并经船长签收后才签发的提单。提单上载明货物"已由某轮装运"的字样和装运日期的提单。

备运海运提单(Received for Shipment B/L)，是指承运人在收到托运货物，等待装船期间，向托运人签发的提单。待运的货物一旦装运后，在备运提单上加"已装船"字样，这样备运提单就成了"已装船提单"。

(2) 根据货物表明状况有无附加批注，分为"清洁提单"和"不清洁提单"。

清洁提单(Clean B/L)，是指提单上并无承运人或其代理人附加条款，或对货物的外表状况或包装不作任何批注。

不清洁提单(Unclean B/L)，是指有承运人的批注(notation)或附加条款(superimposed clause)，表示货物或其包装有瑕疵状态的提单。例如，提单上批有："some rusty"(有生锈)或"one case broken, content exposed"(有一箱破损，内装货物裸露)等文字。

(3) 根据承运方式分为"直达提单"、"转船提单"和"联运提单"。

直达提单(Direct B/L)，是指同一船舶将货物直接从起运港运达目的港的提单。这种提单船方责任明确，权利和义务易于处理。

转船提单，是指从起运港载货的船舶不直接驶往托运货物的目的港，须在其他港口换船转运，并由签发提单的轮船公司负责代办转运手续的海运提单。

联运提单(Through B/L)，联运提单用于"海陆、海河、海海"联运。第一承运人在货物起运港签发运往最终目的地的提单，并收取全程运费。货物到达转运港后，由第一承运人代货主将货物交与下一航运的承运人，再运往目的港。各程承运人的责任，只限于其本身经营船舶所完成的运输。

(4) 根据收货人抬头，分为"记名提单"、"不记名提单"和"指示提单"。

记名提单(Straight B/L)又称"收货人抬头提单"，是指填明收货人姓名或名称地址的提单。

不记名提单(Blank B/L)，是指记载应向提单持有人交付货物的提单。这种提单不需背书就可转让，一旦遗失或被盗，货物就很容易被人提走，所以这种提单应避免使用。

指示提单(Order B/L)，是指按照记名人的指示或非记名人的指示交货的提单。这种提单在收货人一栏中填写"To Order"、"To Order of XXX"，可以通过背书转让。

(5) 根据轮船公司经营方式不同，分为"班轮提单"和"租船提单"。

班轮提单(Liner B/L or Regular Line B/L)，有固定航线，按照规定时间，停靠规定港口而航行的船舶叫做班轮，货物由班轮承运而签发的提单叫做"班轮提单"。班轮公司租给托运人的不是整船而是部分舱位，所以托运货物多少船方都可接受。班轮公司将预先规定的船期表(sailing schedule)印发给各地货主或登报招揽承运业务。班轮装运货物，船方负责装船、理舱、卸货，装卸费用计算在班轮费之内。

租船提单(Chart Party B/L)，是指承运人根据租船合同而签发的提单。在这种提单上注明"一切条款、条件和免责事项按某年某月某日的租船合同"或批注"根据 XXX 租船合同开立"字样。这种合同受租船合同条款的约束。银行或买方在接受这种提单时，通常要求卖方提供租船合同的副本。

(6) 集装箱提单(Container B/L)

集装箱提单，是指以集装箱装运货物所签发的提单。集装箱提单有两种形式：一种是在普通的海运提单上加注"用集装箱装运"(Containerized 或 Shipment Effected by Container Vessel)等字样；另一种是使用"多式联运提单"(Combined Transport B/L)，这种提单的内容增加了集装箱号码(Container No.)和"封号"(Seal No.)。货物从起运地(港)到最终目的地(港)的全程中需使用陆、海、空其中的两种以上运输方式。由联运人作为全程的总承运人签发的这种联运提单，作为对托运人的总负责人。使用多式联运提单，应在信用证上注明多式联运提单接受(Combined Transport B/L Acceptable)或类似的条款。

➢ 海运提单的缮制

1. 托运人(SHIPPER)

托运人，又叫发货人。托运人是指委托运输的人，在贸易中是合同的卖方。如信用证无特殊规定，都填写卖方的名称。根据规定，除非信用证另有规定，银行将接受以信用证受益人以外的一方作为发货人的运输单据。

2. 收货人(CONSIGNEE)

提单的收货人又称提单的抬头，它决定了海运提单的性质和货权，在进出口贸易中多使用指示式抬头。指示式又可分为"记名指示式"和"不记名指示式"两种。

(1) 记名指示式：一般有发货人指示式(To Order of Shipper)、银行指示式(To Order of XXX Bank)和收货人指示式(To Order of ABC Company Ltd.)，一般只要根据信用证的要求，制单时分别填入就行了。在信用证项下，"To Order of XXX Bank"，一般大多是指开证行(the issuing bank)。信用证上的词汇常常是："full set of B/L made out to our order"。这个"our"，指的就是开证行。

(2) 不记名指示式：即在收货人一栏填写"to order"，然后在提单背面由发货人签字盖章进行背书，以示转让物权。信用证上用的词汇常常是："full set of B/L made out to order"，凭指示抬头，即"空白抬头"。

3. 通知人(NOTIFY PARTY)

通知人一栏，在信用证结算方式下，按信用证规定填写。若信用证对此无规定，可将开证申请人作为通知人。如果信用证要求两个或两个以上的公司作为通知人，出口公司应把这两个或两个以上的公司名称及地址完整地填写在这一栏中。

4. 首程运输(PRE-CARRIAGE BY)

如果货物需转运，在这一栏目中填写第一程船的名称；如果货物不需要转运，此栏则空白不填。

5. 收货地点(PLACE OF RECEIPT)

如果货物需转运，填写收货的港口名称或地点；如果货物不需要转运，此栏则留空不填。

6. 海运船名及航次(OCEAN VESSEL & VOY NO.)

此栏填写该批货物的实际装运的船名和航次号；若货物需转运，则填写第二程船名及航次号。

7. 装运港(PORT OF LOADING)

此栏填写该批货物的实际起运港名称；需转运的货物，则填写中转港口的名称。

8. 卸货港(PORT OF DISCHARGE)

此栏填写信用证中的目的港名称。如果货物转运，可在目的港之后加注"with transshipment at..."例如，从上海港到汉堡，在香港转运。那么就打上：from Shanghai to Hamburg with transshipment at Hong Kong。如果货运目的港装运到内陆某地，或利用邻国港口过境，则须在目的港后加注"in transit to 某地"字样。如"Dubai in transit to Saudi Arabia"(目的港迪拜转运沙特阿拉伯)。

9. 交货地点(PLACE OF DELIVERY OR DESTINATION)

填写最终目的地名称。如果货物的目的地就是目的港的话，该栏可留空。

10. 唛头(MARKS AND NOS.)

填写实际的唛头。

11. 集装箱号和封号(CONTAINER NO. & SEAL NO.)

填写实际的集装箱号及铅封号等。

12. 商品描述及数量(NUMBER AND KIND OF PACKAGES & DESCRIPTION OF GOODS)

此栏填写件数和包装种类、货物名称。必须与发票、装箱单等单据一致，提单上的货物名称的描述可以只写总的名称，而不必如发票上描述的那么细致。

13. 毛量(GROSS WEIGHT)

　　填写总毛重，应与其他单据相一致。如果是裸装货物没有毛重，只有净重，则在净重千克数前加注"Net Weight"。

14. 尺码(MEASUREMENT)

　　填写总尺码(立方米)，即指货物的体积。

15. 运费条款(FREIGHT CLAUSE)

　　除非信用证有特别要求，一般的海运提单都不填写运费的数额，而只是表明运费是否已付清或什么时候付清。主要有：

(1) 运费已付(Freight paid)

(2) 运费预付(Freight prepaid)

(3) 运费到付(Freight collect)

16. 大写总件数(TOTAL PACKAGES IN WORDS)

　　此栏的大写总计件数与其他单据及提单的小写总计件数保持一致。

17. 签发地点和时间(PLACE AND DATE OF ISSUE)

　　海运提单签发的地点和时间，一般为承运人实际装运的地点和时间，货物装运的港口或接受有关方面监管的地方，海运提单必须经装载船只船长签字才能生效，在没有规定非船长签字不可的情况下，船方代理也可以代办。如果一批货物分几个装运港于同一艘船上运往同一目的港，签发几个不同日期的提单时，则以较迟的日期为装运日期。

18. 提单正本的签发份数(NUMBER OF ORIGINAL B/L)

　　海运提单正本的签发份数，承运人一般签发两份正本，也可应收货人的要求签发两份以上。签发的份数，应用大写数字来表示，如 two, three, four 等，在栏目内标明。信用证规定要求出口方提供"全套海运提单"(full set or complete set of bill of lading)，按国际惯例，一般是提供三份正本海运提单。这三份正本提单同时有效，如果持票人凭其中的一份提取货物，其他两份自动失效。

19. 承运人或其代理人签字(SIGNED FOR AND/OR ON BEHALF OF THE CARRIER)

　　承运人或其代理人签字，此处必须表示"承运人"或"代理人"的身份。代理人代表承运人或船长签字或证实时，也必须表明所代表的委托人的名称和身份，即注明代理人是代表承运人或船长签字或证实的。提单签字人应根据签字人的不同情况做出不同批注，例如：

(1) 承运人签署的提单

　　提单上部为：Cosco　　提单签字处：Cosco

　　　　(签字) as carrier 或 the carrier

(2) 代理人签字的提单

　　提单上部为：Cosco　　提单签字处：XXX Shipping Company

　　　　(签字) as agent for and/or on behalf of the carrier Cosco 或 as agent for and/or on behalf of Cosco as carrier (或 the carrier)

(3) 船长签字的提单

　　提单上部为：Cosco　　提单签字处：Cosco

　　　　(签字) as master 或 the master

(4) 代理人签字的提单

提单上部：Cosco　　　　　　　　　　　　　提单签字处：XXX Shipping Company

(签字) as agent for and/or on behalf of the master xxx of the carrier Cosco

> 海运提单的背书

海运提单的背书有多种多样，只要收货人一栏不是记名收货人，海运提单一般可以经背书转让。

1. 海运提单背书的类型

(1) 当收货人一栏填写凭指示(to order)时，由托运人(shipper)背书。

(2) 当收货人一栏填写记名指示(to XXX's order 或 to order of XXX)，由记名的一方背书。

(3) 当收货人一栏填写凭托运人指示时(to shipper's order 或 to order of shipper)，由托运人背书。

(4) 当收货人一栏填写凭申请人或其他商号公司指示时，由申请人或其他商号公司背书。

(5) 当收货人一栏填写凭某银行指示时，由该银行背书。

2. 背书方式

(1) 空白背书——书写背书人的名称及地址。

(2) 记名背书——既书写背书人的名称及地址，又书写被背书人(海运提单转让对象)的名称及地址。

(3) 记名指示背书——既书写背书人的名称及地址，又要书写"to order of"+被背书人(海运提单转让对象)的名称及地址。

> 信用证中有关提单条款列举如下：

● Full set clean on board Ocean Bill of Lading issued to order, blank endorsed marked freight payable at destination notify as ABC company and showing Invoice Value, Unit Price, Trade Terms, Contract No. and L/C No. unacceptable. 整套清洁已装船提单，空白抬头，并注明 ABC 公司作为通知人，运费到付。不能将发票、单价、价格术语、合同号码和信用证号打在提单上。

● Full set of clean on board B/L issued to our order, marked notifying applicant and freight prepaid and showing full name and address of the relative shipping agent in Egypt. 全套清洁已装船提单，做成以开证行指示为抬头，注明通知开证人和"运费预付"，并显示相关在埃及船代的全称和详细地址。

● Full set of clean on board marine Bills of Lading, made out to order of ABC Company, marked freight prepaid notify applicant. 整套已装船海运提单，做成以 ABC 公司指示的抬头，注明运费预付，通知开证人。

● Full set of not less than two clean on board marine Bills of Lading marked freight prepaid and made out to order and endorsed to our order showing Blue Bird Trading Company as notifying party. Short form Bills of Lading are not acceptable. Bill of Lading to state shipment has been effected in containers and container numbers. 全套不少于两份的已装船海运提

单，注明运费预付，空白抬头，背书给开证行，并以蓝鸟贸易公司作为通知人。简式提单不接受，提单注明集装箱装运及集装箱号码。

Task 5 Certificate of Origin 原产地证明书

The Certificate of Origin was issued by the CCPIT in Ningbo.

1. Exporter: NINGBO SAKAI PET CO., LTD. 118 ZHONGSHAN ROAD, NINGBO, CHINA			Certificate No. 085643215 **CERTIFICATE OF ORIGIN** **OF** **THE PEOPLE'S REPUBLIC OF CHINA**		
2. Consignee: TO ORDER					
3. Means of transport and route FROM NINGBO TO MIAMI BY SEA			5. For certifying authority use only		
4. Country/region of destination U.S.A.					
6. Marks & Nos. ABF ST08020 MIAMI C/NO.: 1-UP	7. Number and kind of packages; Description of goods SAY (100) ONE HUNDRED CARTONS ONLY OF FLOCKING SWEATERS L/C NO: BOC070325 ************************	8. H.S. Code 6200.1300	9. Quantity 2,400PCS	10. Numbers and Date of Invoice 08NSP168 JULY 15TH, 2008	
11. Declaration by the exporter The undersigned hereby declares that the above details and statements are correct, that all the goods were produced in China and that they comply with the Rules of Origin of the People's Republic of China. 宁波井通宠物用品有限公司 NINGBO SAKAI PET CO., LTD. NINGBO, CHINA JULY 26TH, 2008 王立 Place and date, signature and stamp of authorized signatory			12. Certification It is hereby certified that the declaration by the exporter is correct. CCPIT NINGBO, CHINA JULY 26TH, 2008 李华 Place and date, signature and stamp of authorized signatory		

Directions 操作指南

1. 原产地证书的作用

原产地证明书(Certificate of Origin)是出口商应进口商要求而提供的、由公证机构或政府或出口商出具的证明货物原产地或制造地的一种证明文件。主要作用有：

(1) 确定税率待遇的依据；

(2) 进行贸易统计的依据；

(3) 实施进口数量限制、反倾销、反补贴等外贸措施的依据；

(4) 控制从特定国家进口货物，确定是否准予放行的依据；

(5) 证明商品内在品质或结汇的依据。

2. 原产地证书的类型

根据签发者不同，原产地证书一般可分为以下三类：

商会出具的产地证书，例如：中国国际贸易促进委员会(CCPIT)出具的一般原产地证书，简称贸促会产地证书(CCPIT CERTIFICATE OF ORIGIN)；

商检机构出具的原产地证书，例如：中华人民共和国检验检疫局(CIQ)出具的普惠制产地证格式 A(GSP FORM A)；一般原产地证书(CERTIFICATE OF ORIGIN)。

制造商或出口商出具的产地证书。

3. 原产地证书的申请

根据我国的规定，企业最迟于货物报关出运前三天向签证机构申请办理原产地证书，并严格按照签证机构的要求，真实、完整、正确地填写以下材料：

(1) 《中华人民共和国出口货物原产地证书/加工装配证明书申请书》；

(2) 《中华人民共和国出口货物原产地证明书》一式四份；

(3) 出口货物商业发票；

(4) 签证机构认为必要的其他证明文件。

4. 一般原产地证书的缮制

(1) 产地证书的编号(CERTIFICATE NO.)

此栏不得留空，否则证书无效。

(2) 出口方(EXPORTER)

填写出口公司的详细地址、名称和国家(地区)名。

(3) 收货方(CONSIGNEE)

填写最终收货人名称、地址和国家(地区)名。通常是外贸合同中的买方或信用证上规定的提单通知人。如信用证规定所有单证收货人一栏留空，在这种情况下，此栏不得留空，应加注"TO WHOM IT MAY CONCERN"或"TO ORDER"。

(4) 运输方式和路线(MEANS OF TRANSPORT AND ROUTE)

填写装运港和目的港、运输方式。若经转运，还应注明转运地。例如：通过海运，由上海港经香港转运至伦敦港，应填为：FROM SHANGHAI TO LONDON BY VESSEL VIA HONG KONG。

(5) 目的地国家(地区)(COUNTRY/REGION OF DESTINATION)

　　填写目的地国家(地区)。一般应与最终收货人或最终目的港(地)国别相一致,不能填写中间商国家名称。

(6) 签证机构用栏(FOR CERTIFYING AUTHORITY USE ONLY)

　　由签证机构在签发后发证、补发证书或加注其他声明时使用。证书申领单位应将此栏留空。一般情况下,该栏不填。

(7) 运输标志(MARKS AND NUMBERS)

　　填写唛头。应按信用证、合同及发票上所列唛头填写完整图案、文字标记及包装号码,不可简单填写"按照发票"(AS PER INVOICE NUMBER)或者"按照提单"(AS PEER B/L NUMBER)。货物如无唛头,应填写"无唛头"(NO MARK)字样。此栏不得留空,如唛头多,本栏填写不够,可填写在第7、8、9栏内的空白处,如还是不够,可用附页填写。

(8) 商品描述、包装数量及种类(NUMBER AND KIND OF PACKAGES; DESCRIPTION OF GOODS)

　　填写商品描述及包装数量。商品名称要填写具体名称,不得用概括性表述,例如:服装、食品(GARMENT, FOOD)等。包装数量及种类要按具体单位填写,应与信用证及其他单据严格一致。包装数量应在阿拉伯数字后加注英文表述。如货物为散装,在商品名称后加注"散装"(IN BULK)字样。有时信用证要求在所有单据上加注合同号码、信用证号等,可加注在此栏内。本栏的末行要打上表示结束的符号(**************),以防添加内容。

(9) 商品编码(H.S. CODE)

　　此栏要求填写 H.S. 编码,应与报关单一致。若同一证书包含有几种商品,则应将相应的税目号全部填写。此栏不得留空。

(10) 数量(QUANTITY)

　　此栏要求填写出口货物的数量及商品的计量单位。如果只有毛重时,则需填"G.W."。

(11) 发票号码及日期(NUMBER AND DATE OF INVOICE)

　　填写商业发票号码及日期。此栏不得留空,为避免对月份、日期的误解,月份一律用英文表述,如2008年3月15日,则为:MARCH 15TH, 2008。

(12) 出口方声明(DECLARATION BY THE EXPORTER)

　　填写出口人的名称、申报地点及日期,由已在签证机构注册的人员签名并加盖有中英文的印章。

(13) 由签证机构签字、盖章(CERTIFICATION)

　　填写签证地点、日期。 签证机构签证人经审核后在此栏(正本)签名,并盖签证印章。

5. 普惠制原产地证书的填制

　　原产地证明书格式(FORM A)是出口商的声明和官方机构的证明合二为一的联合证明。联合国贸发会议优惠问题特别委员会对原产地证明书格式 A 的印刷格式,填制方法都有严格、明确的规定,对所需纸张的质量、重量、大小尺寸,使用文件作了规定,并要求正本加印绿色检索图案,防止涂改或伪造。因此,填制必须十分细心,本证书一律不得涂改,证书不得加盖校正章。本证书一般使用英文填制,也可使用法文。特殊情况下,第二栏可以使用给惠国的文种。唛头标记不受文种限制,可据实填写。

(1) 证书号码(REFERENCE NUMBER)

此栏不得留空，否则，证书无效。

(2) 出口商名称、地址和国家(GOODS CONSIGNED FROM)

此栏填写出口商的详细地址。一般情况下与信用证中的受益人一致。

(3) 收货人名称、地址和国家(GOODS CONSIGNED TO)

根据信用证要求填写给惠国的最终收货人名称(即信用证上规定的提单通知人或特别声明的收货人)。如果信用证未明确最终收货人，可以填写商业发票的抬头人。但不可填写中间商的名称。如果商品直接运往欧盟、挪威等给惠地区和给惠国，而且进口商要求将此栏留空时，则可以不填。

(4) 所知航运方式和航线(MEANS OF TRANSPORT AND ROUTE)

此栏一般填写装货、到货地点(如始运港、目的港)及运输方式(如海运、陆运、空运)等内容，对转运商品应加注转运港，如 FROM SHANGHAI TO LOS ANGELES VIA SINGAPORE BY SEA。

(5) 供官方使用(FOR OFFICIAL USE)

此栏在正常情况下留空。下列特殊情况，签证当局在此栏加注：

货物已出口，签证日期迟于出货日期，签发"后发"证书时，此栏盖上"ISSUED RETROSPECTIVELY"红色印章。

证书遗失、被盗或损毁，签发"复本"证书时盖上"DUPLICATE"红色印章，并在此栏注明原证书的编号和签证日期，并声明原证书作废，其文字是：THIS CERTIFICATE IS IN REPLACEMENT OF CERTIFICATE OF ORIGIN NO…DATED…WHICH IS CANCELLED.

(6) 商品顺序号(ITEM NUMBER)

如同一批出口货物有不同品种，则按不同品种、发票号等分列"1"，"2"，"3"，…单项商品，此栏填"1"。

(7) 唛头及包装号(MARKS AND NUMBERS OF PACKAGES)：

如果没有唛头，应填写"NO MARK"(N/M)。如果唛头过多，此栏不够填写，可填写在第 7、8、9、10 栏之截止线以下(附页的纸张要与原证书一般大小)，在右上角打上证书号，并由申请单位和签证当局授权签字人分别在附页末页的右下角和左下角手签、盖印。附页手签的笔迹、地点、日期均与证书第 11、12 栏相一致。

(8) 包装件数、包装种类及商品的名称(NUMBER AND KIND OF PACKAGES, DESCRIPTION OF GOODS)

该栏目填写时应注意：

包装件数必须用英文和阿拉伯数字同时表示。

商品名称必须具体填写，不能笼统填写"MACHINE"(机器)、"GARMENT"(服装)。

商品的商标、牌名(BRAND)及货号(ART NO.)一般可以不填。商品名称等项列完后，应在下一行加上表示结束的符号，以防止加填伪造内容。

国外信用证有时要求填写合同、信用证号码等，可加填在此栏空白处。

(9) 原产地标准(ORIGIN CRITERION)

此栏是国外海关审核的核心项目。如果本商品完全是出口国自产的，不含任何进口成分，出口到所有给惠国，填写"P"。对含有进口成分的商品，因情况复杂，国外要求严格，极易弄错而造成退证查询，具体填写可参考证书背面的标准。

(10) 毛重和其他数量(GROSS WEIGHT OR OTHER QUANTITY)

此栏应填写商品的正常计量单位。如"只"、"件"、"双"、"台"、"打"等。以重量计算的则填毛重，只有净重的，填净重亦可，但要标上 N.W. (NET WEIGHT)。

(11) 发票的日期和号码(NUMBER AND DATE OF INVOICE)

此栏不得留空。月份一律用英文表示。此栏的日期必须按照正式商业发票填制。

(12) 签证当局的证明(CERTIFICATION)

签证单位要填写商检局签证地点、日期。商检局签证人经审核后在此栏(正本)签名，加盖签证印章。本栏日期不得早于发票日期(第 10 栏)和申报日期(第 12 栏)，但应早于货物出运日期。

(13) 出口商声明(DECLARATION BY THE EXPORTER)

在生产国横线上填写"中国"(CHINA)。进口国横线上填最终进口国，进口国必须与第3 栏的国别一致，如转运内陆目的地，应与内陆目的地的国别一致。凡货物运往欧盟范围内，进口国不明确时，进口国可填 EU。

申请单位应授权专人在此栏手签，标上申报地点、日期，并加盖申报单位中英文印章，手签人手迹必须在商检局注册备案。

此栏日期不得早于发票日期(第 10 栏)(最早是同日)。盖章时应避免覆盖进口国名称和手签人姓名。

6. 信用证中有关原产地证书条款举例

- Certificate of origin G.S.P. FORM A original and one copy, evidencing China as origin of goods. FORM A 原产地证明书一正一副，证明货物的原产地为中国。

- Certificate of China origin issued by a relevant authority. 中国原产地证书，由相关的当局出具。

- Certificate of origin should state that the goods do not contain any component of an Israel origin whatever the proportion of such component, the exporter or supplier has no direct or indirect connection whatsoever with Israel. 产地证明书，须声明货物中不含任何以色列的原料和加工成分，出口商或供应商不曾与以色列有任何直接或间接联系。

- Certificate of origin in two copies indicating that goods are of Chinese origin issued by Chamber of Commerce. 由商会出具的产地证明书两份，证明货物原产地为中国。

- Certificate of origin issued by the Chamber of Commerce certifying that goods are of Chinese origin in one original and one copy the original legalized by the A.R.E. representation in China. 商会出具原产地证明书一正一副，正本须由阿联酋驻中国代表签证。

1. Goods Consigned from (Exporter's name, address, country)			Reference No. **GENERALIZED SYSTEM OF PREFERENCES CERITFICATE OF ORIGIN (Combined declaration and certificate)** # FORM A Issued in **THE PEOPLE'S REPUBLIC OF CHINA**		
2. Goods Consigned to (Consignee's name, address, country)					
3. Means of Transport and Route			4. For Official Use		
5. Item NO.	6. Marks & Nos. of Packages	7. No. of Kind of Packages; Description of Goods	8. Origin Criterion	9. Gross Weight & other Quantity	10. No. and Date of Invoice
11. Certification It is hereby certified, on the basis of control carried out, that the declaration by the exporter is correct.			12. DECLARATION BY THE EXPORTER The undersigned hereby declares that the above details and statements are correct; that all goods were produced in **CHINA** and that they comply with the origin requirements specified for those goods in the Generalized System of preferences for goods exported to _____		
Place and date, signature and stamp of Certifying authority.			Place and date, signature and stamp of authorized signatory.		

Task 6   Other Documents 其他单据

In this L/C, the seller was required to provide the fax of shipping advice, shipping company's certificate and beneficiary's certificate.

宁波井通宠物用品有限公司

NINGBO SAKAI PET CO., LTD.

118 ZHONGSHAN ROAD, NINGBO, CHINA

Shipping Advice

TO: ABF INTERNATIONAL CO., LTD.   July 30th, 2008

RE: INVOICE NO: 08NSP168 L/C NO: B0C070325

We are glad to inform you that the abovementioned goods have been shipped. The details are as follows:

Value of Goods:	USD7,122.00
Quantity:	2,400pcs
Vessel Name and Voy. No.:	WUYING V.198
Port of Discharge:	Ningbo
Container Identification No.:	COSCO123456/98765
Sailing Date:	July 30th, 2008
E.T.A.:	Aug. 28th, 2008

宁波井通宠物用品有限公司

NINGBO SAKAI PET CO., LTD.

王立

CERTIFICATE

TO: ABF INTERNATIONAL CO., LTD.   Ningbo

July 30th, 2008

RE: INVOICE NO: 08NSP168 L/C NO: B0C070325

This is to certify that all the goods indicated on the shipping documents (commercial invoice and packing list) have been really loaded on the container.

COSCO

XXX (signature)

BENEFICIARY'S CERTIFICATE

TO: ABF INTERNATIONAL CO., LTD.   July 30th, 2008

RE: INVOICE NO: 08NSP168 L/C NO: B0C070325

This is to certify that all shipping details have been supplied to the applicant by fax.

宁波井通宠物用品有限公司

NINGBO SAKAI PET CO., LTD.

王立

Directions 操作指南

1. 装船通知(SHIPPING ADVICE)

装船通知是出口商在货物装船后发给进口方的电报通知。其目的是让进口商了解货物已经装船发运，可准备付款接货了。在 FOB、CFR 等条件下成交的合同，需进口方自行办理货物保险的凭证，装船通知书应在装船后立即发出，以便进口商办理投保手续。装船通知也可使买方了解货物装运情况、准备接货或筹措资金。买方为了避免因疏忽未及时通知，所以在信用证中明确规定，卖方必须按时发出装船通知，并规定通知的内容，而且在议付时必须提供该装船通知的副本，与其他单据一起向银行议付，因而装船通知也是提交银行结汇的单据之一。装船通知书并无统一格式，但其内容一定要符合信用证的规定。

➢ 信用证中有关装船通知条款举例

● A certificate from the beneficiary stating that they have advised the applicant by the date of shipment, number of packages, name of commodity, total net and gross weight, name of vessel and number of voyage within 2 days after shipment effected. 受益人证明书，证明他们已经在开航前二天用电传通知开证人有关装运日期、箱数、货物名称，总毛重、净重、船名和航班号。

● Original fax from beneficiary to our applicant evidencing B/L number, name of ship, shipment date, quantity and value of goods. 正本受益人发给开证人传真，证明提单号码、船名、开航日期、数量和货物价值。

● Insurance effected in Iran by Iran insurance company, the name of insurance company and the policy number XXX DD—have to be mentioned on B/L shipment advice to be made to said insurance company via TLX No. XXX indicating policy number and details of shipment, a copy of which is to be accompanied by the original documents. 保险由伊朗保险公司承保，装船通知必须有上述保险公司名称及保单号码、装运细节，一张副本必须和其他正本单据附在一起。

- Beneficiary's certificate certifying that shipment advice and abovementioned documents have been faxed to applicant for insurance purpose before shipment, fax copy with transmission report is required. 受益人证明书，证实装运通知连同上述单据在装船前已传真给开证申请人，同时须提交一份传真副本及传真件。

- Beneficiary must cable advise the applicant for the particulars before shipment effected and a copy of such advice should be presented for negotiation. 受益人必须在装运前电报通知开证申请人装运细节，一份这样的电报通知副本须提示议付。

Example:

SHIPPING ADVICE

No.:

Date:

From:

To:

WE ARE GLAD TO INFORM YOU THE CONTAINER OF S/C NO.: XXX HAS BEEN LOADED. THE DETAILS ARE AS FOLLOWS:

SHIPPING LINE:

BILL OF LADING NO.:

BILL OF LADING DATE:

NAME OF VESSEL:

CONTAINER NO.:

SEAL NO.:

GROSS WEIGHT AND NET WEIGHT:

NUMBER OF PACKAGES:

ETA:

HOPE EVERYTHING IS CLEAR.

BEST REGARDS.

XXX COMPANY

(SIGNATURE)

2. 受益人证明书(BENEFICIARY'S STATEMENT/CERTIFICATE)

受益人证明书是一种由受益人自己出具的证明，以便证明自己履行了信用证规定的条款，如证明所交货物的品质，证明运输包装处理，证明按要求寄单、发电等。

➤ 受益人证明的基本要求

(1) 单据名称。这种单据的名称因所证明事项不同而略异，可能是寄单证明、寄样证明(船样、样卡和码样等)、取样证明、证明货物产地、品质、唛头、包装和标签情况、电抄形式的装运通知、证明产品生产过程、证明商品业已检验、环保人权方面的证明等。

(2) 证明上通常会显示发票号、合同号或信用证号以表明与其他单据的关系。

(3) 证明的内容应严格与合同或信用证规定相符。

(4) 因属于证明性质，按有关规定证明人(受益人)必须签字。

➤ 信用证中有关受益人证明书条款举例

● Beneficiary's declaration certifying that the original of export licence has been sent to the applicant by express courier before shipment effected. 受益人证明，正本出口许可证已在装船前快件邮寄给开证人。

● Copy of letter from beneficiary to our applicant evidencing a non-negotiable Bill of Lading together with copy of other documents were sent directly to them after one days from shipment date. 一张受益人发给开证人的证明信，证明一份非议付提单和其他单据一起已经在装船后的第二天直接寄给开证人了。

● A statement from the beneficiary evidencing that: packing effected in 25kgs/ctn box. 一份受益人声明书，证明货物用 25 千克重的箱体包装。

● A certificate from beneficiary stating that the following documents have been sent to the applicant by speed post after shipment effected: (1) 1/3 original Bill of Lading; (2) Certificate of quality issued by CCIB/CCIC in duplicate. 一份受益人证明，证明以下单据已经在装船后，快件邮寄给开证人了：(1) 1/3 的正本提单；(2) 一式两份由 CCIB/CCIC 出具的质量证明书。

Example:

ABC TRADING COMPANY
BENEFICIARY'S CERTIFICATE

TO WHOM IT MAY CONCERN: DATE: MAY 15TH, 2009

RE: L/C NO.: 12345   INV. NO.: ZJHZ008

WE HEREBY CERTIFY THAT THE FOLLOWING DOCUMENTS HAVE BEEN SENT TO XXX BY UPS.

(1) TWO COPIES OF B/C;

(2) TWO COPIES OF INVOICE;

(3) ONE COPY OF PACKING LIST.

SIGNATURE

3. 船公司证明信(SHIPPING COMPANY'S CERTIFICATE)

船公司证明信是船公司出具的单据，是进口商为了满足当局或为了解货物运输情况等要求出口商提供的单据。常见的船公司证明信有：

(1) 船龄证明信(CERTIFICATE OF VESSEL'S AGE)，这是一种船公司出具的说明载货船舶船龄的证明文件。一般船龄要求在 15 年之内，如在 15 年以上则为超龄船只。一般进口商会将此规定在信用证或合同内，如信用证或合同有此条款，出口商须请船公司出具船龄证明信。

(2) 船级证明信(CERTIFICATE OF CLASSIFICATION)，这是一种船公司出具的证明载货船舶符合一定船级标准的文书。

(3) 黑名单证明信(BLACK LIST CERTIFICATE)，是某些阿拉伯国家将一些与以色列有业务往来的船舶及公司列出的名单，若那些公司及船舶被列入黑名单，阿拉伯国家将不允许他们与本国发生运输业务关系。在阿拉伯国家开出的信用证或合同中常常有此条款规定。因此船公司出具的证明将要满足信用证条款的要求。

(4) 船籍证明信(CERTIFICATE OF SHIP'S NATIONALITY)，此证明信为船公司说明装载货物船舶的国籍证明文件。信用证中如规定有这样的条款，船公司必须出具该证明信，以确定船舶的国籍。

(5) 船长收据(CAPTAIN'S RECEIPT)，船长收据是船长收到随船带交给收货人的单证时的收单证明。进口方为防止单据迟于货物到达或其他原因，常要求出口商将某些单据或一套副本或正本单据在装船时交给载货船舶的船长，随船带交给收货人。

Example:

ITINERARY CERTIFICATE

TO WHOM IT MAY CONCERN: SHANGHAI

   RE: S.S. DONGFENG V.028

THIS IS TO CERTIFY THAT S.S.DONGFENG V.028 FLYING THE PEOPLE'S REPUBLIC OF CHINA FLAG WILL NOT CALL AT ANY XXX PORTS DURING THIS PRESENT VOYAGE, AND SHE IS NOT BLACK LISTED BY THE ARAB COUNTRIES.

               SIGNATURE (船公司/代理签字)

Practice 操作练习

Case No. 1

1. 操作信息

The company named Virson Ltd. has signed the contract with Zhejiang Foreign Trade Imp. & Exp. Corporation to import rugs. Virson Limited has opened the L/C as follows. The seller has delivered the commodity and will make out all the required documents.

FROM: THE HONG KONG AND SHANGHAI BANKING CORP., LONDON

TO: BANK OF CHINA, HANGZHOU BRANCH

SEQUENCE OF TOTAL   27: 1/1

FORM OF DOC. CREDIT 40A: IRREVOCABLE

DOC. CREDIT NUMBER   20: DC LDI58921

DATE OF ISSUE	31C:	070820
EXPIRY	31D:	DATE 071020 PLACE IN COUNTRY OF BENEFICIARY
APPLICANT	50:	VIRSONS LIMITED
		28 COSGROVE WAY
		LONDON
BENEFICIARY	59:	ZHEJIANG FOREIGN TRADE IMP. & EXP. CORPORATION
		09 TIANMUSHAN ROAD, HANGZHOU, CHINA
AMOUNT	32B:	CURRENCY USD54,280.00
AVAILABLE WITH/BY	41D:	ANY BANK
		BY NEGOTIATION
DRAFT AT	42C:	AT SIGHT
DRAWEE	42D:	THE HONG KONG AND SHANGHAI BANKING CORP., LONDON
PARTIAL SHIPMENT:	43P:	ALLOWED
TRANSSHIPMENT	43T:	NOT ALLOWED
LOADING IN CHARGE	44A:	CHINA
FOR TRANSPORT TO	44B:	LONDON
LATEST DATE OF SHIP.	44C:	071005
DESCRIPT: OF GOODS	45A:	DEVORE RUGS AS PER VIRSONS ORDER NO. RAP-599/2008
		CIF LONDON PORT

DOCUMENTS REQUIRED 46A: +ORIGINAL COMMERCIAL INVOICE PLUS THREE COPIES.

+FULL SET OF ORIGINAL CLEAN ON BOARD MARINE BILL OF LADING MADE OUT TO SHIPPER'S ORDER AND BLANK ENDORSED, MARKED FREIGHT PREPAID AND NOTIFY APPLICANT QUOTING FULL NAME AND ADDRESS.

+ORIGINAL PACKING LIST PLUS THREE COPIES INDICATING DETAILED PACKING OF EACH CARTON.

+MARINE INSURANCE POLICY FOR 110PCT OF INVOICE VALUE, BLANK ENDORSED, COVERING ALL RISKS AND WAR RISK, CLAIMS PAYABLE AT DESTINATION.

+ORIGINAL CERTIFICATE OF ORIGIN PLUS ONE COPY ISSUED BY CHAMBER OF COMMERCE.

+ORIGINAL GSP FORM A CERTIFICATE OF ORIGIN IN OFFICIAL FORM ISSUED BY A TRADE AUTHORITY OF GOVERNMENT BODY PLUS ONE COPY.

+CERTIFICATE FROM BENEFICIARY EVIDENCING THAT COPIES OF INVOICE, BILL OF LADING AND PACKING LIST HAVE BEEN FAXED TO APPLICANT ON FAX NO. 01589 45708 WITHIN 3 DAYS OF BILL OF LADING DATE.

ADDITIONAL COND.   47A: +THE NUMBER OF THE L/C MUST BE QUOTED ON ALL DOCUMENTS.

+UNLESS OTHERWISE EXPRESSLY STATE, ALL DOCUMENTS MUST BE IN ENGLISH.

+EXCEPT SO FAR AS OTHERWISE EXPRESSLY STATE, THIS DOCU-MENTARY CREDIT IS SUBJECT TO UNIFORM CUSTOMS AND PRACTICE FOR DOCUMENTARY CREDIT ICC PUBLICATION NO. 500.

+ALL BANKING CHARGES IN CONNECTION WITH THIS DOCUMENTARY CREDIT EXCEPT ISSUING BANK'S OPENING COMMISSION AND TRANS-MISSION COSTS ARE FOR ACCOUNT OF THE BENEFICIARY.

PRESENTAITON PERIOD   48: WITHIN 15 DAYS AFTER THE DATE OF SHIPMENT BUT WITHIN THE VALIDITY OF THE CREDIT.

CONFIRMATION   49: WITHOUT

INSTRUCTION   78: ON RECEIPT OF DOCUMENTS CONFIRMING TO THE TERMS OF THIS DOCUMENTARY CREDIT, WE UNDERTAKE TO REIMBURSE YOU IN THE CURRENCY OF THE CREDIT IN ACCORDANCE WITH YOUR INSTRUCTIONS, WHICH SHOULD INCLUDE YOUR UID NUMBER AND THE ABA CODE OF THE RECEIV-ING BANK.

SEND. TO REC. INFO.   72: DOCUMENTS TO BE DESPATCHED BY COURIER SEVICE IN ONE LOT TO HSBC BANK PLC, TRADE SERVICES LD1TEAM, LEVEL 26, 8 CANADA SQUARE, LONDON E145HQ

有关资料：

发票号码：07ZJFT9832

提单号码：SD1397602183

合同号码：077-218

集装箱号码：TGHU9812780

船名航次：SHANGHAI V.56

海运费：USD2,800.00

FORM A 号码：ZJ/HZ/07/04567

发票日期：2008 年 9 月 20 日

提单日期：2008 年 10 月 4 日

合同日期：2008 年 7 月 18 日

集装箱封号：2897228 1×40′ LCL, CY/CY

保险单号码：07-HZ-07256

保险费：USD165.00

2. 操作要求

请根据上述提供的信用证及其所给的资料缮制整套议付单据。

Case No. 2

1. 操作信息

(1) 信用证

THE HONG KONG AND SHANGHAI BANKING CORPORATION INCORPORATED IN HONG KONG WITH LIMITED LIABILITY

SHANGHAI OFFICE: 185 YUAN MING YUAN ROAD, P.R. CHINA, SHANGHAI 20002

OUR REF. EXP DC 007475

SHANDONG HOPE NATIVE PRODUCE I/E CORP.,

62, GUANGXI ROAD, QINGDAO.

DATE MAY 23TH, 2009

DEAR SIRS,

WE ADVISE HAVING RECEIVED THE FOLLOWING TELETRANSMISSION DATED MAY 22ND, 2009 FROM:

THE HONG KONG AND SHANGHAI BANKING CORP. LTD., DOWNING STREET, PENANG

ISSUE OF AN IRREVOCABLE DOCUMENTARY CREDIT

DC NUMBER: PGH000348DC

DATE OF ISSUE: MAY 21ST, 2009

EXPIRY DATE AND PLACE: JULY 21ST, 2009-CHINA

APPLICANT:

SOO HUP SENG TRADING CO. SDN BHD.,

165 1ST FLOOR, VICTORIA STREET,

10300 PENANG MALAYSIA

BENEFICIARY:

SHANDONG HOPE NATIVE PRODUCE I/E CORP.,

62, GUANGXI ROAD, QINGDAO, CHINA

CCY/AMOUNT: USD46,150.00

AVAILABLE BY NEGOTIATION

DRAFTS: AT SIGHT FOR FULL INVOICE VALUE OF GOODS DRAWN ON OURSELVES.

PARTIAL SHIPMENTS: FORBIDDEN

TRANSSHIPMENT: PERMITTED

SHIPMENT FROM ANY PORT IN CHINA TO PENANG LATEST JULY 6TH 2009 GOODS:

5M/TS SHANDONG BLACK DATES HIGH QUALITY AT USD9,230 PER M/T

CIF PENANG AS PER THE BUYER'S ORDER NO.SOO-6378

DOCUMENTS:

+INVOICE IN TRIPLICATE

+FULL SET ORIGINAL CLEAN ON BOARD BILL OF LADING MADE OUT TO SHIPPER'S ORDER AND ENDORSED IN BLANK AND MARKED "FREIGHT PREPAID" AND NOTIFY APPLICANT AND ISSUING BANK.

+MARINE INSURANCE POLICY OR CERTIFICATE FOR FULL CIF VALUE PLUS 10 PERCENT COVERING OCEAN MARINE CLAUSES ALL RISKS AND WAR RISKS CLAUSES OF THE PICC.

SPECIAL CONDITIONS:

SHIPPING MARKS:SHS/OEBABG/1-UP

BENEFICIARY TO AIRMAIL DIRECT TO OPENER ONE SET OF NON-NEGOTIABLE DOCUMENTS IMMEDIATELY AFTER SHIPMENT AND A CERTIFICATE OF COMPLIANCE TO THIS EFFECT IS REQUIRED.

PLUS/MINUS 0.5 PERCENT ON BOTH QUANTITY AND AMOUNT ACCEPTABLE.

A USD30.00 (OR EQUIVALENT) FEE SHOULD BE DEDUCTED FROM THE REIMBURSEMENT CLAIM FOR EACH PRESENTATION OF DISCREPANT DOCUMENTS UNDER THIS DOCUMENTARY CREDIT NOTWITHSTANDING ANY INSTRUCTIONS TO THE CONTRARY, THIS CHARGE SHALL BE FOR THE ACCOUNT OF THE BENEFICIARY.

BNAK TO BANK INFO:

WE HEREBY ENGAGE WITH DRAWERS AND/OR BONA FIDE HOLDERS THAT DRAFTS DRAWN AND NEGOTIATED ON PRESENTATION, SO LONG AS THERE HAS BEEN STRICT COMPLIANCE WITH ALL TERMS AND CONDITIONS OF THIS CREDIT, SAVE TO THE EXTENT THAT THE SAME HAVE BEEN AMENDED IN WRITING AND SIGNED ON OUR BEHALF.

CHARGES:

ALL BANKING CHARGES OUTSIDE MALAYSIA INCLUDING ADVISING, NEGO- TIATING COMMISSION AND REIMBURSING BANK'S FEES ARE FOR APPLICANT'S ACCOUNT.

PERIOD OF PRESENTATION: DOCUMENTS TO BE PRESENTED WITHIN 16 DAYS AFTER THE ISSUANCE OF THE SHIPPING DOCUMENTS BUT WITHIN THE VALIDITY OF THE CREDIT.

CONFIRMATION: WITHOUT

THIS CREDIT IS SUBJECT TO UCP600 AND IS AN OPERATIVE CREDIT INSTRUMENT AND NO MAIL CONFIRMATION TO FOLLOW.

COL HKD45,150.00

(2) 制单参考资料

Commodity: Shandong Black Dates

Quantity: 5 m/ts

Packed in cardboard cartons of 25 kgs each and then shipped in one container of 200 cartons

Container No: EISU2628205

G.W: 5,240KGS   N.W: 48,40KGS

Measurements: 13.427CBM

Shipping Marks: SHS/PENANG/1-up

Shipped per Victoria V. 29 on July 5th, 2009 B/L No.:19

Invoice No.: SHNP018

B/L No.: 009312

2. 操作要求

请根据上述提供的信用证及其所给的资料缮制整套议付单据。

BILL OF EXCHANGE

Drawn under _____

L/C No.   Dated

Payable with interest at   %

No._____

Exchange for_____ _____China   Dated _____

At_____sight of this FIRST of Exchange (Second of Exchange being unpaid) pay to the

order of _____

The sum of _____

Value received _____

_____

To_____

COMMERCIAL INVOICE

Invoice No.: _____

Date: _____

Issuer: _____

S/C No.: _____

_____

L/C No.: _____

To: _____

_____

Shipped per _____ From _____ To _____

_____

Shipping Mark	Description of Goods	Quantity	Unit Price	Amount

Issuer:	装箱单 **PACKING LIST**				
To:	No.:				
	Date:				
	L/C No.:				
	S/C No.:				
Transport Details: From:　　　　To:　　　　By:					
Marks & Nos.	No. & Kind of Pkgs.	Description of Goods	Gross Weight	Net Weight	Measurement

Shipper

Consignee

Notify Party

B/L NO.

BILL OF LADING

Pre-carriage by	Place of Receipt
Ocean Vessel Voy. No.	Port of Loading

Port of Discharge	Place of Delivery	Final Destination (of the Goods)

Marks & Nos. Container. Seal No.	Kind of Packages Description of Goods	Gross Weight	Measurement

TOTAL NO. OF CONTAINERS
OR PACKAGES (IN WORDS)

FREIGHT & CHARGES	Revenue' Tons	Rate	Per	Prepaid
Ex. Rate:	Prepaid at	Payable at	Place and Date of Issue	
	Total Prepaid	No. of Original B(s)/L	Signed for the Carrier	

中国人民保险公司杭州市分公司

The People's Insurance Company of China Hangzhou Branch

Head Office Beijing   Established in 1949

货物运输保险单 Cargo Transportation Insurance Policy

发票号(INVOICE NO.):   保单号次:

合同号(CONTRACT NO.):   POLICY NO.:

信用证号 (L/C NO.):

被保险人:

Insured: _____

MARKS & NOS.	QUANTITY	DESCRIPTION OF GOODS	AMOUNT INSURED

总保险金额：TOTAL AMOUNT INSURED: _____

保费: 启运日期: 装载运输工具

PREMIUM _____ DATE OF COMMENCEMENT _____ PER CONVEYANCES:_____

自   经   至

FROM_____ VIA _____ TO _____

承保险别:

CONDITIONS:

所保货物，如发生保险单项下可能引起索赔的损失或损坏，应立即通知本公司下述代理人查勘。如有索赔，应向本公司提交保单正本(本保单共有 _1_ 份正本)及有关文件。

IN THE EVENT OF LOSS OR DAMAGE WHICH MAY RESULT IN A CLAIM UNDER THIS POLICY, IMMEDIATE NOTICE MUST BE GIVEN TO THE COMPANY'S AGENT AS MENTIONED HEREUNDER CLAIMS, IF ANYONE OF THE ORIGINAL POLICY WHICH HAS BEEN ISSUED IN __ONE__ ORIGINAL(S) TOGETHER WITH THE RELEVANT DOCUMENTS SHALL BE SURRENDERED TO THE COMPANY.

中国人民保险公司杭州市分公司

The People's Insurance Company of China, Hangzhou Branch

_____

赔款偿付地点

CLAIM PAYABLE AT _____

出单日期 ISSUING DATE _____

1. Exporter	Certificate No.
2. Consignee	**CERTIFICATE OF ORIGIN** **OF** **THE PEOPLE'S REPUBLIC OF CHINA**
3. Means of Transport and Route	5. For Certifying Authority Usc Only
4. Country / Region of Destination	

6. Marks and Nos.	7 No. and Kind of Packages; Description of Goods	8. H.S. Code	9. Quantity	10. No. and Date of Invoices

11. Declaration by the Exporter The undersigned hereby declares that the above details and statements are correct, that all the goods were produced in China and that they comply with the Rules of Origin of the People's Republic of China. ——————————— Place and date, signature and stamp of authorized signatory.	12. Certification It is hereby certified that the declaration by the exporter is correct. ——————————— Place and date, signature and stamp of certifying authority.

1. Goods Consigned from (Exporter's business name, address, country)	Reference No.
	GENERALIZED SYSTEM OF PREFERENCES **CERTIFICATE OF ORIGIN** (Combined declaration and certificate)
2. Goods Consigned to (Consignee's name, address, country)	**FORM A** Issued in **THE PEOPLE'S REPUBLIC OF CHINA**

3. Means of Transport and Route (as far as known)	4. For Official Use

5. Item No.	6 Marks and Nos. of Packages	7. No. and Kind of Packages; Description of Goods	8. Origin Criterion (see Notes overleaf)	9. Gross Weight or Other Quantity	10. No. and Date of Invoices

11. Certification It is hereby certified, on the basis of control carried out, that the declaration by the exporter is correct.	12 Declaration by the exporter The undersigned hereby declares that the above details and statements are correct, that all the goods were produced in **CHINA** and that they comply with the origin requirements specified for those goods in the Generalized System of Preferences for goods exported to _____ _____
Place and date, signature and stamp of certifying authority.	Place and date, signature and stamp of authorized signatory.

PRACTICE 10

Cancellation after Verification of Export and Tax Rebate
出口核销与退税

Example & Analysis 操作实例及解析

Task 1　Cancellation after Verification of Export 出口收汇核销

◆ Case Lead-in

The 2,400pcs of Flocking Sweaters under S/C No. ST08020 supplied by Ningbo Sakai Pet Co., Ltd. have been honored by the buyer. After payment, what the seller should do next is to fill out the verification sheet to get it written off.

◆ 案例导入

ST08020 合同项下的 2400 件宠物用植绒毛衣，已经买方确认。办理定制单结汇以后，出口企业还需填写出口核销单，办理核销退税手续。

➤ **Procedure of cancellation after verification 出口核销流程**
出口核销程序概而述之可分为以下四个阶段：

1. **领单**

出口单位在开展出口业务之前，须向外管局领取出口收汇核销单。出口企业到外管局领取核销单之前，先在网上或其他途径申请核销单领用的份数。外管局确认后发放核销单，核销单领用后仅用于领单企业报关出口，不得借用、冒用、转让或买卖。

2. **报关**

出口企业凭核销单、报关单向海关报关。海关在核销单正本和报关单上盖"验讫"章，并退还出口单位。

3. **交单**

金融机构收妥货款后向出口企业出具注记核销号编号等信息供核销专用的结汇水单/收账通知。对于预计收款日期超过报关日期90天以上(含90天)的远期收汇，企业应当在报关后进行网上交单，凭远期出口合同、报关单、核销单向外汇局备案，并在核销单的"收汇方式"栏注明远期收汇天数。凡未向外汇局备案的，一律视作即期出口收汇。

4. **收汇核销**

出口单位按规定时限向外管部门交回核销单正本结汇水单/收账通知等附件办理核销。即期出口项下，企业应当在出口报关之日起100天内凭核销单、报关单、出口收汇核销专用联到外汇局办理出口收汇核销手续；远期出口项下，企业应当在合同规定收汇日起10天内持上述材料到外汇局办理出口收汇核销手续。

出口收汇核销单 存根

(浙)编号：435849673

出口单位：宁波井通宠物用品有限公司
单位代码：74596223-7
出口币种汇总：USD7122.00
收汇方式：L/C
预计收款日期：SEPT. 2 ND, 2008
报关日期 JULY 28TH, 2008
备注
此单报关有效期截止到

出口收汇核销单

(浙)编号：435849673

出口单位盖章 / 海关盖章

出口单位：宁波井通宠物用品有限公司				
单位代码：74596223-7				
银行签注栏	类别	币种金额	日期	盖章
海关签注栏				
外汇局签注栏		年　月　日 (盖章)		

出口收汇核销单

(浙)编号：435849673

出口单位盖章 / 海关盖章

出口单位：宁波井通宠物用品有限公司		
单位代码：74596223-7		
货物名称	数量	币种总价
报关单编号：		
外汇局签注栏	年　月　日 (盖章)	

Directions 操作指南

> **Basic knowledge of cancellation after verification of export** 核销基本概念和原则

The State Administration of Foreign Exchange (SAFE) is the institution to draft foreign exchange administration rules, supervising and monitoring foreign exchange transactions in international market. Every deal of foreign trade is controlled by verification sheet issued by the SAFE.

我国是外汇管制国家，核销是我国外汇管理项目之一。根据国务院、国家外汇管理局、国家税务局的有关规定，我国出口企业在办理货物装运出口以及制单结汇以后，应及时办理出口收汇和核销退税、手续。出口核销，是以出口货物的价值为标准，核对是否有相应的外汇收回国内的事后管理措施。出口核销制度，是国家加强出口收汇管理，确保国家外汇收入，防止外汇流失的一项重要措施。

1. 出口收汇核销的对象

出口收汇核销的对象是指经对外贸易经济合作部及其授权单位批准有经营出口业务的公司、有对外贸易经营权的企业和外商投资企业，简称为出口单位。

2. 出口收汇核销的原则

(1) 属地管理。由出口单位向其注册所在地的外管部门申领核销单，一般说来，在何地申领的核销单，就由何地办理核销。

(2) 专单专用。谁申领的核销单就由谁用，不得相互借用，核销单的交回核销或作废遗失、注销手续也由原领用该核销单的出口单位向其所在地的外管部门办理。

(3) 领用衔接。核销单的发放，一般按多用多发、不用不发的原则，也就是根据出口单位的业务量来决定核销单的领用量。一般续发核销单与已用核销单以及已核销情况和预计出口用单的增减量相呼应。

(4) 单单对应。原则一份核销单对应一份报关单；报关单、核销单、发票、汇票副本上的有关栏目的内容应相一致，如有变动，应附有关更改单或凭证。

> **Verifying and writing-off instrument** 出口收汇核销单

出口收汇核销单分为存根、正联、退税联三部分，各部分填写方法是：

1. 存根

(1) 编号。应与出口报关单的编号一致。

(2) 出口单位。填写领取核销单的单位的名称。

(3) 单位代码。填写领取核销单的单位在外汇管理局备案的号码。

(4) 出口币种总价。此栏填写出口成交货物总价及使用币种。一般情况下，须与报关单一致。溢短装出口时，可以不一致，但须提供该笔出口的货运提单副本(提单上有实际出口的数量和重量，根据发票或报关单上的单价与提单上的重量或数量相乘，即可得出实际出口的总金额)。

(5) 收汇方式。填写信用证、托收、汇付。

(6) 预计收款日期。依付款期限、地点不同按规定填写：

即期信用证和即期托收项下的货款，从寄单之日起，近洋地区(香港和澳门)20 天内，远洋地区(香港和澳门以外的地区)30 天内结汇或收账。例如：2008 年 6 月 1 日寄单，预计收款日期即应填写 2008 年 6 月 21 日。

　　远期信用证和远期托收项下货款，从汇票规定的付款日起，港澳地区 30 天内，远洋地区 40 天内结汇或收账。如港澳地区，预计收款日期为寄单日期加上邮程日期加上汇票规定的远期天数加上 30 天。例如：寄单日期为 2008 年 6 月 1 日，汇票为远期 180 天，则预计收款日期应为 2008 年 6 月 1 日+10 天+180 天+30 天，则为 2009 年 1 月 8 日。

(7) 报关日期。同出口报关单右上角的出单日期。

(8) 备注。填写出口单位就该核销单项下需说明的事项。例如：北京甲进出口公司代广西乙进出口公司出口，收汇后，原币划转广西进出口公司，则该事项连同该受托公司的联系地址和电话应批注在备注栏内并加盖批注单位的公章。

(9) 有效期。自领单日起四个月。此栏由外汇管理局填。

2．正联

(1) 出口单位。同存根。

(2) 单位代码。同存根。

(3) 银行签审。(类别、币种金额、日期、公章)填写收汇方式、币种总价、收结汇日期银行盖章。

(4) 海关签注栏。海关验放该核销单项下的出口货物后，在该栏目内加盖"放行"或"验讫"章，并填写放行日期。如遇退关，海关需在该栏加盖有关更正章。

(5) 外汇管理局签注栏。由外汇管理部门将核销单、报关单、发票等配对审核无误后，在该栏内签注意见，并由核销人员签字，加盖"已核销"章。

3．退税联

(1) 编号。同存根。

(2) 出口单位。同存根。

(3) 单位代码。同存根。

(4) 货物名称。同报关单。

(5) 出口数量。同报关单。

(6) 币种总价。同存根。

(7) 报关单编号。按报关单左上角号码填写。

(8) 外汇局签注栏。同正联。

Task 2　Tax Rebate 出口退税

➢ **Basic knowledge of tax rebate and conditions** 退税基本概念和条件

　　出口产品退税，简称出口退税，是指税务机关将其出口前在生产和流通环节中已征收的中间税款返还给出口企业，从而使出口商品以不含税价格进入国际市场，参与国际竞争的一种政策制度。

　　一般来说，出口产品只有在同时具备下述 3 个条件的情况下才予以退税：

(1) 必须是属于产品税、增值税和特别消费税范围的产品。

(2) 必须报关离境。所谓出口，即是输出关口。这是区分产品是否属于应退税出口产品的主要标准之一，以加盖海关验讫章的出口报关单和出口销售发票为准。

(3) 必须在财务上做出口销售。

　　但是国家对退税的产品也做了特殊规定，特准某些产品视同出口产品予以退税。

> **Procedures of tax rebate of export 出口退税流程**

1. 出口退税登记的一般程序

(1) 有关证件的送验及登记表的领取

企业在取得有关部门批准其经营出口产品业务的文件和工商行政管理部门核发的工商登记证明后，应于 30 日内办理出口企业退税登记。

(2) 退税登记的申报和受理

企业领到"出口企业退税登记表"后，即按登记表及有关要求填写，加盖企业公章和有关人员印章后，连同出口产品经营权批准文件、工商登记证明等证明资料一起报送税务机关，税务机关经审核无误后，即受理登记。

(3) 填发出口退税登记证

税务机关接到企业的正式申请，经审核无误并按规定的程序批准后，核发给企业"出口退税登记证"。

(4) 出口退税登记的变更或注销

当企业经营状况发生变化或某些退税政策发生变动时，应根据实际需要变更或注销退税登记。

2. 出口退税附送材料

● 外贸企业申报出口退税所需单证

(1) 两票三单

1) 出口货物报关单(出口退税专用联)；2) 出口商业发票；3) 购进货物的增值税发票(税款抵扣联)或普通发票；4) 出口收汇核销单(出口退税专用)。远期收汇货物不需提供出口收汇核销单，但需提供远期收汇证明；5) 税收(出口货物专用)缴款书(第二联)或出口货物完税分割单(第二联)。

委托出口的货物除提供上述资料外，还需提供代理出口协议、代理出口货物证明。

(2) 出口货物退(免)税申报表

1) 出口退税进货凭证申报表(一式两份)，退消费税的，还应提供消费税进货凭证申报表(一式两份)；2) 出口货物退税申报明细表(一式四份)；3) 出口退税汇总申报表(一式四份)，并经商务主管部门稽核盖章。

(3) 出口货物核销明细账

出口货物明细账记载内容与申报资料、申报表、申报软盘内容一致。

(4) 退税申报软盘(一张)，软盘中申报数据的顺序、内容要与申报资料、申报表一致。

● 生产企业申报出口退税所需单证

(1) 两单一票退税单证

1) 出口货物报关单(出口退税专用联)；2) 出口收汇核销单(出口退税专用联)；3) 出口商业发票。

外商投资企业须提供国家统一印制的出口商业发票。委托出口的货物还须提供代理出口协议和《代理出口货物证明》，进料加工复出口货物须提供《生产企业进料加工贸易申请表》；实行"免、抵、退"税的生产企业，季度纳税额为正数，须提供征税机关审核盖章的税收缴款书(复印件)。

(2) 出口货物退税申报表

　　1) 出口货物退税申报表(一式四份)。2) 出口退税汇总申报表(一式四份)。3) 出口货物销售明细账。

Practice 操作练习

Case No. 1

1. 操作信息

Zhejiang Xinlong Arts & Crafts Co., Ltd. signed the contract of exporting porcelain wares to Indigo Trading Co., Ltd. in Holland.

Description of goods: porcelain wares

Total amount: USD45,290.00

Terms of payment: L/C

Quantity: 6,000 sets

浙江新龙工艺品有限公司与荷兰 Indigo Trading Co., Ltd. 成交一批瓷器制品，合同总价为 USD45,290.00，信用证方式结汇，2008 年 9 月 10 日装运。货物名称：瓷器制品(porcelain wares)，成交数量：6,000 sets。货物已备妥，准备报关。

出口收汇核销单
存根

(浙)编号：435849675

出口单位：
单位代码：
出口币种汇总：
收汇方式：
预计收款日期：
报关日期
备注
此单报关有效期截止到

出口收汇核销单

(浙)编号：435849675

出口单位盖章

出口单位：				
单位代码：				
银行签注栏	类别	币种金额	日期	盖章
海关签注栏				
外汇局签注栏				
		年　　月　　日 (盖章)		

出口收汇核销单

(浙)编号：435849675

出口单位盖章　海关盖章

出口单位：		
单位代码：		
货物名称	数量	币种总价
报关单编号：		
外汇局签注栏		
年　　月　　日 (盖章)		

2. 操作要求

根据上述资料填写出口核销单。

Case No. 2

1. 操作信息

浙江正阳贸易有限公司与澳大利亚 Overseas Trading Co., Ltd. 成交一批茶叶，合同总价为 USD49,380.00,信用证方式结汇，2008 年 10 月 8 日装运。货物名称：红茶。成交数量：2,000KGS。

2. 操作要求

根据上述资料填写出口核销单。

出口收汇核销单 存根	出口收汇核销单	出口收汇核销单

出口收汇核销单 存根

(浙)编号：435849675

出口单位：
单位代码：
出口币种汇总：
收汇方式：
预计收款日期：
报关日期
备注
此单报关有效期截止到

出口单位盖章

出口收汇核销单

(浙)编号：435849675

出口单位：				
单位代码：				
银行签注栏	类别	币种金额	日期	盖章
海关签注栏				
外汇局签注栏				
年　　月　　日 (盖章)				

出口收汇核销单

(浙)编号：435849675

出口单位：			
单位代码：			
	货物名称	数量	币种总价
报关单编号：			
外汇局签注栏			
年　　月　　日 (盖章)			

出口单位盖章

海关盖章

Import Procedure

进口贸易流程

*P*RACTICE *1*

Preparation for Import
进口准备

Task 1　Investigation and Study 调查研究

Example & Analysis 操作实例及解析

◆ Case Lead-in

Hangzhou Zhongda Trading Co., Ltd. is a considerable size of IMP. & EXP. company, mainly engaged in mineral business. In the beginning of the year 2008, Mr. Wang Gang, the salesman of the company, got the information that the commodity of chrome ore was in short supply and decided to import 1,200MT of lumpy chrome ore. He knew the main countries of origin for chrome ore are Turkey, Pakistan, Zimbabwe, South Africa, etc.

Wang Gang got on the Internet to look for the potential suppliers. According to the information from the Internet, he chose two of them.

Detailed information for supplier (1):

AVRASYALI MINING LTD. STI. is one of the group companies of Eurasian Holding. It is a manufacturer in supply business of chrome, as ores lump and concentrated in different grades.

Add: Bagdat CAD. 78 / 7 Kiziltoprak, Istanbul, Turkey

Contact person: Mr. Ozgur Cakir

Tel: 90-216-4180810

Fax: 90-216-4182452

Email: ocakir@avrasyalimining.com

Website: http://www.avrasyalimining.com

Detailed information for supplier (2):

DELTA EXPORTS PTE LTD., a trading company, was founded in March, 1993. With a founding mission of the Business Link, Delta has continuously maintained this philosophy by being the linking pin and a steady liaison among its business partners. It is a chrome ore owner in Turkey.

Add.: 221 Henderson Road #08-15 Henderson Building, Singapore Zip: 159557

Contact person: Mr. Vasudevan Vairavan

Tel No.: 65-6276 6646

Fax No.: 65-6276 7045

Email: vvairavan@deltaonnet.com

Website: http://www.deltaonnet.com

Meanwhile, from Mr. Zhang in the same industry Wang Gang knew a Taiwan Company, TOP CHAMPION DEVELOPMENTS CO., LTD., which is a chrome ore owner in Turkey and can supply chrome ore. It is a comprehensive trading company with certain scope and good business reputation. The company where Mr. Zhang works has maintained business relationships with this company for years.

Detailed information for supplier (3):

TOP CHAMPION DEVELOPMENTS CO., LTD.

Add: No. 259, Dahan St., Kang Lo Village, Hsin Cheng Hsiang, Hualien, Taiwan, China

Contact person: Mr. Peter Liu

Tel No.: 886-3-8260781

Fax No.: 886-3-8266331

Email: peterliu@topchampion.com

Website: http://www.topchampion.com

Wang Gang planned to choose the above three companies as his potential suppliers for further negotiation.

◆ 案例导入

杭州中大贸易有限公司 (Hangzhou Zhongda Trading Co., Ltd., Add: No. 216 Yan'an Rd., Hangzhou, China, Tel: 86-571-65726860, Fax: 86-571-85726688)是杭州市一家颇具规模的进出口贸易公司，主要经营矿产。该公司业务员王刚(Email: Tom9898@hotmail.com)在 2008 年初得知最近国内市场铬矿(chrome ore)紧缺，欲进口 1200 公吨块状铬矿。他了解到国际市场上铬矿的主要出产国家有土耳其、巴基斯坦、津巴布韦、南非等。

王刚上网去寻找潜在的供货商。根据网上各公司的资料，他选定了其中的两家供货商(土耳其的 AVRASYALI MINING LTD STI. 和新加坡的 DELTA EXPORTS PTE LTD.）。

供货商 AVRASYALI MINING LTD. STI. 是能提供不同级别的块状铬矿和精铬矿的生产商。该公司的主要市场在东亚地区。

供货商 DELTA EXPORTS PTE LTD. 是一家贸易公司，成立于 1993 年。该公司在土耳其拥有铬矿。

期间，王刚又从一个同行张先生中得知一家台湾公司 TOP CHAMPION DEVELOPMENTS CO., LTD. 在土耳其拥有铬矿，可提供铬矿。该公司是一家有一定规模、信誉良好的综合性贸易公司。张先生所在公司与该公司已有多年的贸易往来。

王刚决定将上述三家公司作为潜在的供货商，准备与他们进一步洽谈磋商。

Directions 操作指南

Prior to an import business, we shall make some international and domestic market investigations in relation to goods and their suppliers, especially the situation of the goods supply, the trend of the commodities prices and the suppliers' credit of the main countries of origin.

在进口交易之前，必须对国内外市场进行调查研究，包括有关商品的产、供、销和客户情况，尤其要搞清主要生产国家和生产厂家的供应情况、商品的价格趋势及供应商的资信情况。

> **The trend of commodities prices 商品价格趋势**

不同商品的价格走势不同，了解价格的途径也不同。

工业品。价格大多较稳定，但受原料价格的涨落而变化。可向外商直接询价了解。

机械设备。价格波动较小，但不同的生产厂商、规格牌号价格往往相差很大，可从专业杂志上查阅了解、分析比较，也可邀请几家外商来我国进行技术交流，直接洽谈比较技术和价格。

农产品。价格受主要生产国播种面积和气候变化的影响较大。一般可从报纸杂志中了解，还应根据农作物的生长情况对远期交易的价格趋势进行预测。

原材料。市场变化快，投机性强，国际市场价格经常变化，同时受该商品的上游产品价格的影响，国际政治局势的变化、突发事件的影响（如主要生产厂家的工人罢工、厂区安全事故的影响），造成生产能力锐减等。因此，进口商要关心国际政治局势的变化，随时了解国内外大事，掌握供求关系，做到知己知彼。

> **Suppliers credit investigation 供应商的资信调查**

在进口业务中，供应商的主要责任是提供品质、数量、包装符合买卖合同规定的货物，并按合同规定的时间、地点和方式交付货物。由于我国大多数进口业务都是以信用证方式付款，信用证的特点决定了供应商的资信在进口业务中尤为重要。因此，对供应商的资本情况、经营作风、能力和范围、商业信誉及商号的性质、结构等调查是极为重要的。

对供应商资信的调查，有多种多样，如可通过银行、与其有业务往来的采购商、同行了解。该供应商以往的履约资信等，必要时可通过我驻外商务机构、商会、行业协会及咨询机构等进行。

Task 2　Calculation of Importation Cost 进口成本核算

Example & Analysis 操作实例及解析

Composition of the importation cost = contract price + importation charges

Information for chrome ore：

Contractual price (FOB Mersin, Turkey)	USD437.85
Import duty	0%
VAT rate	17%
Ocean freight (from Mersin, Turkey to Shanghai, China)	US$1,800/20' FCL
	US$3,200/40' FCL
Marine cargo insurance: (ALL RISKS)	0.8% (for 110% of CIF value)
Customs declaration charges	￥250 per sale
Customs censoring charges	￥200 per sale
Lump sum	￥300 /20' FCL
	￥500 /40' FCL
Local charge: inland transport charge	￥1,700 /20' FCL
(from Shanghai to Hangzhou)	￥2,000 /40' FCL
Verification charges	￥10 per sale
Banking charges: L/C opening fee	￥0.12% of contract price
L/C amendment fee and other additional charges	￥100 per sale
Fixed charges	1.5% of contract price
Exchange rate：	1USD=7RMB

进口预算表(Budget)

Item 项目	Estimated Amount 预算金额
Purchase Cost 进口合同价格	￥3,064.95/MT
Ocean Freight 海洋运费	￥484.61/MT
Insurance Premium 保险费	￥31.5/MT
Banking Charges 银行费用	￥4,513.53/sale
Import Duty 进口关税	0
VAT 增值税	￥608.78/MT
Customs Declaration Charges 报关费	￥250/sale
Customs Censoring Charges 报检费	￥200/sale
Iump Sum 码头包干费	￥11,100/sale
Inland Freight 内陆运费	￥62,900/sale

Item 项目	Estimated Amount 预算金额
Warehouse Fee 仓储费	-------
Interest 利息	包含在定额费里
Verification Charge 核销费	￥10/sale
Fixed Charges 定额费	￥55,169.10/sale

Analysis:

进口商品成本=进口合同价格+进口费用

进口合同价格 FOB= USD437.85/MT×7=￥3064.95/MT

进口费用=海洋运费+保险费+银行费用+进口关税+增值税+报关费+报检费+码头包干费
　　　　+内陆运费(上海港至杭州指定仓库)+仓储费+利息+其他费用(核销费+定额费)

其中:

- 海洋运费=USD1800/26MT=USD69.23/MT×7=￥484.61/MT
- CFR= FOB+海洋运费=USD437.85+USD69.23=507.08/MT×7=￥3549.56/MT

  CIF=CFR/[1－保险费率×(1+投保加成率)]=507.08/(1－0.8%x110%)

  　　=USD511.58×7=￥3581.06/MT

  保险费=保险金额×保险费率=CIF×(1+投保加成率)×保险费率

  　　　　=USD511.58×110%×0.8%

  　　　　=USD4.50×7=￥31.5/MT
- 银行费用=￥0.12%×USD437.85/MT×7×1200MT+￥100per sale

  　　　　　=￥4513.53/1200=￥3.76/MT
- 进口关税=0
- 增值税=进口货物完税价格×进口货物增值税税率

  　　　　=USD511.58×7×17%=￥608.78/MT
- 报关费=￥250 per sale/1200=￥0.21/MT
- 报检费=￥200 per sale/1200=￥0.17/MT
- 码头包干费=￥300×37FCL=￥11100/1200=￥9.25/MT
- 内陆运费(上海港至杭州指定仓库)=￥1700×37FCL=￥62900/1200=￥52.42/MT
- 其他费用(核销费、定额费)=￥10/1200MT +1.5%×￥3064.95=￥45.98/MT

计算结果: 进口商品成本=￥4301.63/ MT

Directions 操作指南

1. 进口成本的构成

进口商品成本=进口合同价格+进口费用

进口费用包括很多内容,每一笔业务由于成交条件不同,进口商承担的费用也不同。如以 FOB 条件成交,进口费用有如下内容:

(1) 国外运输费用

(2) 运输途中货物的保险费用

(3) 包括卸货费、驳船费、码头建设费、码头仓租费等的卸货费用

(4) 进口关税、增值税、工商统一税及地方附加税等

(5) 进口商品的检验费和其他公证费用

(6) 银行费用，如开证费及其他手续费

(7) 报关提货费

(8) 国内运输费、仓储费

(9) 从开证付款到收回货款之间所发生的利息支出

(10) 其他费用(如定额费，指进口公司管理费等)

● 海洋运费的计算

计算步骤：

首先要根据报价数量计算产品体积与重量，比照集装箱规格，如果报价数量正好够装整箱(20 英尺集装箱或 40 英尺集装箱)，则直接取单位包箱费率为基本运费；如果不够装整箱，则用产品总体积(或总重量，或取两者较高者)×拼箱运费率来算出海运费。

(1) 班轮运费的计算

计算公式：$F = F_b \times (1 + \sum S) \times Q$

F 为班轮运费总额，F_b 为基本运费率，$\sum S$ 为附加费率之和，Q 为总货运量。

(2) 集装箱运费的计算

以集装箱为运费的单位，20'集装箱的有效容积为 25CBM，限重 17.5TNE，40'集装箱的有效容积为 55CBM，限重 24.5TNE。

常见的包箱费率有三种：

FAK 包箱费率(Freight for all kinds)，对每个集装箱部分货物种类统一收取运费；

FCS 包箱费率(Freight for class)，按不同货物的等级制定的包箱费率；

FCB 包箱费率(Freight for class & basis)，按不同货物的等级或货物类别以及计算标准制定的费率。

● 保险费的计算

保险费=保险金额×保险费率

保险金额=CIF(或 CIP)×(1+投保加成率)

CIF=CFR / [1－保险费率×(1+投保加成率)]

● 银行手续费

银行手续费是银行向客户提供汇兑、结算等相关服务时所收取的费用。

计算方式一般为：按每笔交易收取，或按报价或成交价格的一定百分比收取。

● 进口关税的计算

进口货物应纳关税=进口货物完税价格×进口货物关税税率

进口货物完税价格是以 CIF 价格为基础的。因此，进口业务中，无论采用 FOB 条件还是 CFR 条件，在交纳进口关税和增值税时，都要折算成 CIF 价格，以作为进口总成本核算的基础。

● 进口增值税的计算

　　进口货物应纳增值税=(进口货物完税价格+进口关税)×进口货物增值税税率

2. 进口商品盈亏率的计算

　　进口商品盈亏率是指该商品的进口盈亏额与进口总成本的比率。

　　进口商品盈亏率=(国内销售价格-进口总成本) / 进口总成本

　　在进口费用不变的情况下,进口总成本的大小取决于成交价格的高低及汇率的变动等。

Practice 操作练习

Case No. 1

1. 操作信息

　　宁波新宇进出口公司(Ningbo Xinyu Imp. & Exp. Co., ADD: 306 Jianguo Road, Ningbo, China, TEL: 0574-88223260, FAX: 0574-88223348, Email: Jennyli@hotmail.com)是一家颇具规模的进出口贸易公司,主要经营原材料的进口。最近得知国内紧缺电解铜(electrolytic copper),欲进口500吨。

2. 操作要求

(1) 请你以业务员李萍的身份,进行进口交易前的调查研究。

(2) 请你以业务员李萍的身份,根据以下资料核算进口成本。

　　假设货物最终将从荷兰鹿特丹出运至宁波。其中,核算资料如下:

　　进口价格: USD7,780/MT FOB Rotterdam, Holland

　　进口关税：2%

　　增值税：17%

　　海运费：从荷兰鹿特丹港至中国宁波港,一个20英尺集装箱的包箱费率为1900美元,一个40英尺集装箱的包箱费率为3400美元,散货基本运费为每运费吨116美元,计算标准为W/M。

　　保险：CIF基础上加成10%投保中国人民保险公司海运货物保险条款中的一切险,费率为0.8%。

　　商检费：￥200/sale

　　报关费：￥200/sale

　　银行费用：0.15%

　　码头包干费：￥300/20' FCL，￥500/40' FCL

　　国内运输费：￥400/20' FCL，￥700/40' FCL

　　其他费用：1.5%

　　汇率：7元人民币兑换1美元。

Case No. 2

1. 操作信息

杭州凯凯贸易有限公司(Hangzhou K.K. Trading Co., Ltd., ADD: 186 Xixi Road, Hangzhou, China, TEL: 0571-87157288, FAX: 0571-87156338, Email: Tomwang2006@yahoo.com.cn)是一家民营企业，主要经营原材料的进口。最近得知国内紧缺白卡纸(Duplex Board with Grey Back)，欲进口 200 公吨。

2. 操作要求

(1) 请你以业务员王浩的身份，进行进口交易前的调查研究。

(2) 请你以业务员王浩的身份，根据以下资料核算进口成本。

假设货物最终将从韩国釜山用集装箱运至上海。其中：核算资料如下：

进口价格：USD340/MT CFR PUSAN, KOREA (R.O.)

进口关税：8%

增值税：17%

保险：CIF 基础上加成 10%投保中国人民保险公司海运货物保险条款中的一切险，费率为 0.8%。

商检费：￥200 sale

报关费：￥200 sale

银行费用：0.15%

码头包干费：￥300/20' FCL，￥500/40' FCL

国内运输费：￥1,700/20' FCL，￥2,000/40' FCL

其他费用：1.5%

汇率：7 元人民币兑换 1 美元。

PRACTICE 2

Negotiation for Import Business
进口交易磋商

learning Objectives 学习目标

◇ To grasp the procedure of the Negotiation for Import Business 掌握进口交易磋商的流程

◇ To be able to write letters for inquiry, offer, counter-offer and acceptance 询盘、发盘、还盘、接受电函的撰写

◇ To be able to sign a purchase contract with the exporter 与出口商签订购买合同

Task 1　Negotiation for Import Business 进口交易磋商

一、Inquiry 询盘

Example & Analysis 操作实例及解析

◆ Case Lead-in

Mr. Wang Gang, the salesman of Hangzhou Zhongda Trading Co., Ltd. (Add: No.216 Yan'an Rd., Hangzhou, China, Tel: 86-571-65726860, Fax: 86-571-85726688, Email: Tom9898@hotmail.com), decided to negotiate with the three companies, AVRASYALI MINING LTD. STI., DELTA EXPORTS PTE LTD., and TOP CHAMPION DEVELOPMENTS CO., LTD., as the potential suppliers and finally succeed in making a deal with one of them by signing a purchase contract.

◆ 案例导入

杭州中大贸易有限公司(Hangzhou Zhongda Trading Co., Ltd.)业务员王刚决定将寻找到的三家公司：(1) AVRASYALI MINING LTD. STI.; (2) DELTA EXPORTS PTE LTD.; (3) TOP

CHAMPION DEVELOPMENTS CO., LTD. 作为潜在的供货商，准备与他们进一步洽谈磋商，并且从中选定一家公司，与之达成交易，签订贸易合同。

The following is one of the three inquiries Wang Gang sent:

Jan. 22nd, 2008
From: Wang Gang of Hangzhou Zhongda Trading Co., Ltd.
To: TOP CHAMPION DEVELOPMENTS CO., LTD.
Attn: Mr. Peter Liu
Subject: Inquiry for lumpy chrome ore

Dear Mr. Liu,

　　Your name was referred to me by my friend Mr. Zhangwei of ABC Co. that you are exporters of lumpy chrome ore in Taiwan. It will be our pleasure to establish business relationship with you. We, Hangzhou Zhongda Trading Co., Ltd., are an import and export trading company in Hangzhou China, mainly engaged in mineral business. Recently we are buying Lumpy chrome ores which the terms and conditions are as follows:

　　Lumpy chrome ores, on FOB basis, above 45% Chrome Grade, Quantity: 1,000MT, Packing in bulk in container, Prompt shipment, Payment: L/C at sight.

　　Would you please let us have your favourable quotations of the above mentioned goods? Should you have any questions, please feel free to contact me.

　　Your early reply will be highly appreciated.

　　Looking forward to doing business with you in the coming future.

Thanks & best regards.

Yours faithfully,
Wang Gang

Directions 操作指南

1. 进口业务中，询盘常常是由进口人向供应商发出的。

2. 询盘的对象事先应有所选择。一般可根据以往的业务资料或从其他方面查询来选择适当的对象进行询盘，既不宜只局限于个别客户而无法进行比较，也不宜在同一地区多头询盘而影响市场价格。对数量较大的采购任务，应适当安排采购进度，防止在一个时期内大量集中订购，遭到对方抬价。

3. 询盘中要注意策略。不要过早透露需采购的数量、可接受的价格等，以免在磋商中处于不利地位。对技术含量较高的机械设备，可直接向生产厂商询盘，以减少中间环节。

4. 询盘时一般不直接用"询盘"的术语，而通常用下列一类词句：

- 对……有兴趣请发盘(Interested in…, please offer)
- 请告……(Please advise…)
- 请电传告……(Please advise by telex…)
- 请报价……(Please quote…)

➢ **Useful sentences 典型例句**

- Your name was referred / recommended to me by the New York Chamber of Commerce. Would you let me know the details of your Star Brand Eye Glasses?

- Would you please send us information / a catalogue / a brochure / a price list / prices?

- We are very much interested in your Electronic Calculators and should like you to send us a copy of the newest catalogue together with the prices.

- We would like to have samples of various sizes of your shirts together with the best prices.

- Please advise by telex your best price for three copy machines.

- Would you please let us know the minimum export quantities per color and per design?

- If you quote reasonable prices, we shall place large orders with you in future.

- I look forward to hearing from you / I hope to hear from you soon.

二、Offer 发盘

Example & Analysis 操作实例及解析

◆ **Case Lead-in**

After receiving Mr. Wang's inquiry for 1,000MT lumpy chrome ore, the three companies sent firm offers to Hangzhou Zhongda Trading Co., Ltd.

◆ **案例导入**

三家公司收到杭州中大贸易有限公司王刚关于 1000 公吨块状铬矿的询盘后，随即发来了实盘。

The following is one of the three offers Wang Gang received:

Jan. 24th, 2008

From: Peter Liu of TOP CHAMPION DEVELOPMENTS CO., LTD.

To: Hangzhou Zhongda Trading Co., Ltd.

Attn: Mr. Wang Gang

Subject: Our offer for lumpy chrome ore

Dear Mr. Wang,

It is gratifying to learn from your email of Jan. 22nd, 2008 that you are interested in an offer from us for 1,000MT lumpy chrome ore.

We take pleasure in making you, subject to your acceptance reaching us not later than Jan. 31st, 2008, the following offer:

Turkish Lumpy Chrome Ore

Specifications:		
	Cr_2O_3	46% Min
	Cr/Fe	2.6% Min
	Al_2O_3	12% Max
	MgO	24% Max
	SiO_2	12% Max
	P	0.007% Max
	S	0.01% Max
	Size: 10—300 mm	65% Min
	Below 10 mm	35% Max

Price: USD442/MT FOB MERSIN, TURKEY

Quantity: 1,000MT

Packing: In bulk in container.

Shipment: From Mersin, Turkey to Shanghai, China not later than March 31st, 2008.

Payment: By irrevocable L/C at sight to reach the sellers 30 days before the time of shipment

As the prices will inevitably be raised soon because of the low stock and increasing demand, your early order is absolutely essential.

Thanks & best regards.

Yours faithfully,

Peter Liu

Directions 操作指南

1. 进口业务中，进口人往往先发询盘，请对方发盘，但也有不进行询盘而直接向外方发盘。有时，进口人还可向外方提出发盘的邀请。

2. 发盘一般采用下列术语和语句：

- 发盘(offer)
- 发实盘(offer firm, firm offer)
- 报价(quote)
- 可供应(can supply)
- 订购(book, booking)
- 订货(order, ordering)
- 递盘(bid, bidding)
- 递实盘(bid firm, firm bid)

> **Useful sentences 典型例句**

● It is gratifying to learn that…

● Subject to your acceptance reaching us not later than …

● We are pleased to know that you are interested in our products.

● In reply to your inquiry, we take pleasure in making you an offer as follows, provided your reply reaches us within 5 days from today.

● As you requested, we are pleased to make you an offer, subject to our final confirmation, as follows:

● By irrevocable Letter of Credit in our favor payable by draft at sight to reach the Sellers one month before shipment and remain valid for negotiation in…till the 15th day after shipment.

三、Counter-offer 比价和还盘

Example & Analysis 操作实例及解析

◆ Case Lead-in

After receiving the quotations from the three companies, Wang Gang made a counter-offer by increasing the quantity from 1,000MT to 1,200MT.

◆ 案例导入

王刚收到三家公司分别的报价后，进行还盘，并把订购数量增加到 1200 吨。

The following is one of the three counter-offers Wang Gang sent:

Jan. 28th, 2008
From: Wang Gang of Hangzhou Zhongda Trading Co., Ltd.
To: TOP CHAMPION DEVELOPMENTS CO., LTD.
Attn: Mr. Peter Liu
Subject: Counter-offer for lumpy chrome ore

Dear Mr. Liu,

We thank you for your letter of Jan. 24th, 2008 offering us 1,000MT of the subject goods at USD442/MT FOB MERSIN, TURKEY.

In reply, we regret to say that your quotation is too high for us. Information indicates that the same goods of other origin have been sold at the level of USD438/MT on FOB basis. In view of our sincerity, we would like to increase our quantity from 1,000MT to 1,200MT. Should you be prepared to reduce your price by 1%, we might come to terms.

We hope you will consider our counter-offer most favorably.

Should you have any questions, please feel free to contact me.

Your early reply will be highly appreciated.

Thanks & best regards.

Yours faithfully,

Wang Gang

Directions 操作指南

1. 比价的方式通常有：

● 不同外商的同期报价比较；

● 历史价格比较；

● 对各种不同交易条件的发盘进行综合分析比较。

2. 一笔交易有时不经过还盘即可达成，有时要经过还盘，其至往返多次的还盘才能达成。

3. 还盘不仅可以对商品价格，也可以对交易的其他条件提出意见。在还盘时，对对方已经同意的条件一般不必重复列出。

4. 进行还盘时，可用"还盘"术语，但一般仅将不同条件的内容通知对方，即意味着还盘。

➢ **Useful sentences 典型例句**

● In reply, we very much regret to state that our end-users here find your price too high and out of line with the prevailing market level.

● Should you be prepared to reduce your limit by, say 10%, we might come to terms.

● We would like…and welcome the opportunity to do business with you.

● However, such practice will mean no profit to us.

四、Acceptance 接受

Example & Analysis 操作实例及解析

◆ Case Lead-in

After receiving the new inquiry for 1,200MT lumpy chrome ore from TOP CHAMPION DEVELOPMENTS CO., LTD., Wang Gang compared all the terms and conditions of the three companies' offers in respect of their capital situation, style of management, ability and scope of business, business reputation, etc., and decided to accept the new quotation from TOP CHAMPION DEVELOPMENT CO., LTD.

◆ 案例导入

王刚收到 TOP CHAMPION DEVELOPMENT CO., LTD. 的重新报价后，对这三家公司报价的各个条款进行了综合比较，又考虑到它们的资本情况、经营作风、能力和范围、商业信誉等因素，决定接受 TOP CHAMPION DEVELOPMENT CO., LTD. 的新报价。

The following is the new offer Wang Gang received:

Jan. 30th, 2008

From: Peter Liu of TOP CHAMPION DEVELOPMENT CO., LTD.

To: Hangzhou Zhongda Trading Co., Ltd.

Attn: Mr. Wang Gang

Subject: Our new offer for lumpy chrome ore

Dear Mr. Wang,

Thank you for your mail dated Jan. 28th, 2008.

After the second thought, to express our sincerity, we take pleasure in making you, subject to your acceptance reaching us not later than Feb. 2nd, 2008, our rock-bottom price of USD437.85/MT FOB MERSIN, TURKEY, on order of 1,200MT.

Other terms and conditions unchanged.

Should you have any questions, please feel free to contact me.

Looking forward to your reply soon.

Thanks & best regards.

Yours faithfully,

Peter Liu

The following is the acceptance Wang Gang sent:

Feb. 2nd, 2008

From: Wang Gang of Hangzhou Zhongda Trading Co., Ltd.

To: TOP CHAMPION DEVELOPMENT CO., LTD.

Attn: Mr. Peter Liu

Subject: Our acceptance for 1,200MT lumpy chrome ore

Dear Mr. Liu,

Thank you for your letter of Jan. 30th, 2008

We would like to confirm your new order as follows:

Turkish Lumpy Chrome Ore

Specifications:	Cr_2O_3	46% Min
	Cr/Fe	2.6% Min
	Al_2O_3	12% Max

MgO	24% Max
SiO$_2$	12% Max
P	0.007% Max
S	0.01% Max
Size: 10-300 mm	65% Min
Below10 mm	35% Max

Price: USD437.85/MT FOB MERSIN, TURKEY

Quantity: 1,200MT

Packing: In bulk in container.

Shipment: From Mersin, Turkey to Shanghai, China not later than March 1st, 2008

Payment: By irrevocable L/C at sight to reach the sellers 30 days before the time of shipment

  We are glad that through our mutual effort we finally have reached the agreement.

  Should you have any questions, please feel free to contact me.

Thanks & best regards.

Yours faithfully,

Wang Gang

Directions 操作指南

1. 发盘一经接受，交易即告达成，合同即告订立；双方就应分别履行各自所承担的合同义务。

2. 表示接受，一般用"接受"(accept)、"同意"(agree)和"确认"(confirm)等术语。

Task 2　Signing the Contract 进口合同的签订

Example & Analysis 操作实例及解析

◆ Case Lead-in

  After friendly negotiation, on Feb. 10th, 2008, Hangzhou Zhongda Trading Co., Ltd. finally signed a Purchase Contract (see below) with TOP CHAMPION DEVELOPMENTS CO., LTD. according to the stipulations in the letter of Feb. 2nd, 2008.

◆ 案例导入

  经过友好协商，杭州中大贸易有限公司终于按照 2008 年 2 月 2 日的电邮内容规定，在 2008 年 2 月 10 日与台湾 TOP CHAMPION DEVELOPMENT CO., LTD. 签订了购买合同。

购买合同
PURCHASE CONTRACT

正本
ORIGINAL

The Buyers:

　HANGZHOU ZHONGDA TRADING CO., LTD.

Add: No. 216 Yan'an Rd., Hangzhou, China

Tel: 86-571-65726860　　Fax: 86-571-85726688

The Sellers:

　TOP CHAMPION DEVELOPMENT CO., LTD.

Add: No. 259, Dahan St., Kang Lo Village, Hsin Cheng Hsiang,

　　Hualien, Taiwan, China

Tel: 886-3-8260781　　Fax: 886-3-8266331

编号
Contract No.:　ZD080210TW

日期
Date:　　FEB. 10TH, 2008

地点
Place:　　Hangzhou, China

下列签字双方同意按以下条款达成交易

The undersigned Buyers and Sellers have agreed to close the transaction according to the following terms and conditions.

唛头 Shipping Mark	品名及规格 Description of Goods		数　量 Quantity	单　价 Unit Price	金　额 Amount
N/M	Turkish Lumpy Chrome Ore Specifications: Cr_2O_3 Cr/Fe Al_2O_3 MgO SiO_2 P S Size: 10—300 mm 　Below 10 mm	46% Min 2.6% Min 12% Max 24% Max 12% Max 0.007% Max 0.01% Max 65% Min 35% Max	1,200MT +/-10%	USD437.85/MT FOB MERSIN, TURKEY	USD525,420.00
总值 TOTAL VALUE: SAY U.S. DOLLARS FIVE HUNDRED AND TWENTY-FIVE THOUSAND FOUR HUNDRED AND TWENTY ONLY.					

包装 PACKING: In bulk in container

装运港 PORT OF LOADING: Mersin, Turkey

目的港 PORT OF DESTINATION: Shanghai, China

装运期限 SHIPMENT: March 31st, 2008

保险 INSURANCE: To be covered by the buyers

付款方式 PAYMENT: By irrevocable L/C at sight to reach the sellers 30 days before the time of shipment

THE BUYERS

HANGZHOU ZHONGDA TRADING CO., LTD.

王刚(盖章)

THE SELLERS

TOP CHAMPION DEVELOPMENT CO., LTD.

刘锡莲(盖章)

Directions 操作指南

1. 进口合同磋商达成协议后，通常由一方缮制正本合同一式两份，经签署后寄送对方，要求对方签署后寄回一份存查，并作为履行和处理争议的依据。对于对方寄回或签退的要认真审查，如有与达成的协议不一致的，应视具体情况处理，或接受或要求更改。合同条款对买卖双方的权利和义务必须明确具体地列明，并符合法律规范。

2. 合同的样式有多种。进口合同的内容一般都有三个部分：

(1) 约首

　　主要包括合同名称、订约日期和地点、当事人名称、地址以及前文。

(2) 基本条款

　　包括商品的名称、质量、包装、数量条款、价格条款、装运条款、付款条款、保险条款以及格式条款或称一般交易条款。

● 进口合同中，商品质量条款是非常重要的条款。商品名称要作明确的规定，进口许可证和其他单证中的商品名称要与进口合同严格一致。为预防或避免卖方交货品质不符要求或以次充好，合同中的商品规格、标准、牌号、型号、等级等应订得具体明确。

● 数量条款中，应明确规定计算数量的时间和地点。一般商品尤其是初级产品还可规定溢短装幅度。

● 装运条款中，如以 FOB 计价的，除了在合同中规定装运港外，还应规定合理的装运时间和装运通知。

● 进口合同中，采用的付款方式有汇付、托收、信用证等。对小额合同，可采用交货后汇款或托收方式，多数合同采用信用证付款方式。

● 格式条款是适用于所有合同的共性条款，如商检、罚金、索赔、不可抗力、仲裁等一些通用的条款。

(3) 约尾

　　包括合同的有效期、合同使用的文字及其效力、买卖双方的签字等。

3. 以下是空白合同样式(格式条款略)。

购买合同
PURCHASE CONTRACT

正本
ORIGINAL

The Buyers:

Add:

Tel:　　　　　　　　Fax:

The Sellers:

Add:

Tel:　　　　　　　　Fax:

编号
Contract No.:_____
日期
Date:　_____
地点
Place:　_____

下列签字双方同意按以下条款达成交易

The undersigned Buyers and Sellers have agreed to close the transaction according to the following terms and conditions.

唛头 Shipping Mark	品名及规格 Description of Goods	数　量 Quantity	单　价 Unit Price	金　额 Amount
总值 TOTAL VALUE:				

包装
PACKING:

装运港
PORT OF LOADING:

目的港
PORT OF DESTINATION:

装运期限
SHIPMENT:

保险
INSURANCE:

付款方式
PAYMENT:

THE BUYERS　　　　　　　　　　　THE SELLERS

　　(盖章)　　　　　　　　　　　　　　(盖章)

Practice 操作练习

Case No. 1

1. 操作信息

杭州伟星进出口公司(Hangzhou Winstar Imp. & Exp. Corp., ADD: 56 Jianfang Road, Hangzhou, China, TEL: 0571-85573210, Email: Charlesli@Winstar.com)是杭州市一家民营企业，最近欲进口一批电子手掌玩具(electron palm bauble)。公司业务员李力(Charles Li)上网查得一家香港出口商(YOU DA TRADE CO., LTD., ADD: 101 QUEENS ROAD, CENTRAL, HONG KONG, TEL: 852-23923210, Email: Lilygao@Youda.com)，于是及时与对方取得联系并进行贸易磋商：

(1) 7月6日伟星公司向 YOU DA 公司询价：2000套电子手掌玩具。要求对方报价。

(2) 7月7日伟星公司收到对方公司的报盘：电子手掌玩具，货号：H3203A，2000套，每50套装一个出口纸箱，每套35美元 CIF 上海，不可撤销即期信用证，2008年9月30前从香港装运至上海。

(3) 7月10日伟星公司回复 YOU DA 公司，提出报价高于目前国际市场价格，我方无法接受。要求价格降10%。

(4) 7月12日 YOU DA 公司回复伟星公司，重新报价：考虑到贵方诚意，我方同意将报价改为我方最优惠的价格：每套32美元 CFR 上海。其他条款不变。

(5) 7月13日伟星公司发接受函，双方达成交易，进入签订合同阶段。

(6) 7月16日伟星公司与 YOU DA 公司签订了编号为 WS080716HK 的合同。签约地为杭州。

2. 操作要求

(1) 请你以双方业务员李力(Charles Li)和 Lily Gao 的身份，根据上述资料用英语拟写询盘函、报盘函、还盘函和接受函。

(2) 请你以业务员李力(Charles Li)的身份，根据上述资料拟订一份进口合同。

购买合同   正本
PURCHASE CONTRACT   ## ORIGINAL

The Buyers:

编号
Contract No.:_____

Add:

日期
Tel: Fax: Date: _____

The Sellers:

地点
Place: _____

Add:

Tel: Fax:

下列签字双方同意按以下条款达成交易

The undersigned Buyers and Sellers have agreed to close the transaction according to the following terms and conditions.

唛头 Shipping Mark	品名及规格 Description of Goods	数　量 Quantity	单　价 Unit Price	金　额 Amount
总值 TOTAL VALUE:				

包装
PACKING:

装运港
PORT OF LOADING:

目的港
PORT OF DESTINATION:

装运期限
SHIPMENT:

保险
INSURANCE:

付款方式
PAYMENT:

THE BUYERS   THE SELLERS

    (盖章)   (盖章)

Case No. 2

1. 操作信息

杭州利星贸易有限公司(Hangzhou Lixing Trading Co., Ltd., ADD: No. 152 Wensan Road, Hangzhou, China, TEL: 0571-88187288, FAX: 0571-88187338, Email: Tinawang1999@yahoo.com.cn)是杭州市一家颇具规模的进出口贸易公司，主要经营原材料的进口。最近得知国内紧缺天然橡胶，欲进口 500 公吨天然橡胶。业务员王燕(Tina Wang)上网查得马来西亚出口商(KSK GLOBALINK MARKETING, ADD: 2, Jalan Iks Simpang Ampat, Taman Iks, S.P.S., Penang, Malaysia, TEL: 60-4-5889811, Fax: 60-4-5882811, Email: Vivianpoh@KSK.com)，于是及时与对方取得联系并进行贸易磋商：

(1) 4 月 12 日利星公司向 KSK 公司询价：马来西亚 20 号标胶(SMR20)，要求对方报价。

(2) 4 月 13 日利星公司收到对方公司的报盘：马来西亚天然橡胶(20 号标胶)，货号：SMR20CB，16 pallets/20 foot container 每包 35 千克，一个托盘装 30 包，一个 20 英尺集装箱装 16 个托盘，每吨 2,075 美元 CIF 上海，不可撤销即期信用证，2008 年 7 月 31 前从马来西亚槟城(Penang)装运至上海。

(3) 4 月 15 日利星公司回复 KSK 公司，提出报价高于目前国际市场价格，我方无法接受。要求价格降至每吨 1,998 美元，我方可订 500 公吨，同时要求改贸易术语为 FOB Penang。

(4) 4 月 18 日 KSK 公司回复伟星公司，重新报价：考虑到贵方诚意，我方同意将报价改为我方最优惠的价格：每吨 2,002 美元 FOB Penang。其他条款不变。

(5) 4 月 20 日利星公司发接受函，双方达成交易，进入签订合同阶段。

(6) 4 月 24 日利星公司与 KSK 公司签订了编号为 LS080424MA 的合同。签约地为杭州。

附产品规格：

Parameter	SMR20+CB
SMR20 20	99 % min
Dirt (max), %wt	0.16
Ash (max), %wt	1.00
Nitrogen (max), %wt	0.60
Volatile Matter (max), %wt	0.80
Po (min)	30.0
PRI (min)	40.0

2. 操作要求

(1) 请你以双方业务员王燕(Tina Wang)和 Ms. Vivian Poh 的身份，根据上述资料用英语拟写询盘函、报盘函、还盘函和接受函。

(2) 请你以业务员王燕的身份，根据上述资料拟订一份进口合同。

购买合同
PURCHASE CONTRACT

正本
ORIGINAL

The Buyers:

Add:

Tel:　　　　　　　　　Fax:

The Sellers:

Add:

Tel:　　　　　　　　　Fax:

编号
Contract No.:_____

日期
Date:　　_____

地点
Place:　　_____

下列签字双方同意按以下条款达成交易

The undersigned Buyers and Sellers have agreed to close the transaction according to the following terms and conditions.

唛头 Shipping Mark	品名及规格 Description of Goods	数　量 Quantity	单　价 Unit Price	金　额 Amount

总值
TOTAL VALUE:

包装
PACKING:

装运港
PORT OF LOADING:

目的港
PORT OF DESTINATION:

装运期限
SHIPMENT:

保险
INSURANCE:

付款方式
PAYMENT:

THE BUYERS　　　　　　　　　　　　　THE SELLERS

　　(盖章)　　　　　　　　　　　　　　　(盖章)

PRACTICE 3

Applying for Import License
申请进口许可证

learning Objectives 学习目标

◇ To know how to apply for the import license 了解如何申请进口许可证
◇ To be able to fill out the application of import license 掌握进口许可证申请表的填制

Example & Analysis 操作实例及解析

◆ Case Lead-in

Hangzhou Zhongda Trading Co., Ltd. has signed a Purchase Contract to import Turkish lumpy chrome ore with TOP CHAMPION DEVELOPMENT CO., LTD. on Feb. 10th, 2008. According to the rules, they should apply for the import license.

◆ 案例导入

杭州中大贸易有限公司于 2008 年 2 月 10 日与台湾 TOP CHAMPION DEVELOPMENT CO., LTD. 签订了购买块状铬矿合同，根据规定，他们将申请进口许可证。

以下是进口许可证申请表的填写。

中华人民共和国进口许可证申请表

1. 进口商： 杭州中大贸易有限公司 576809-200987-1	代码	3. 进口许可证号：0856456215		
2. 收货人： 杭州中大贸易有限公司		4. 进口许可证有效截止日期： 2009 年 4 月 10 日		
5. 贸易方式：一般贸易		8. 出口国(地区)：土耳其		
6. 外汇来源：银行购汇		9. 原产地国(地区)：土耳其		
7. 报关口岸：上海		10. 商品用途：生产用		
11. 商品名称： 块状铬矿		商品编码：2610.0000		

12. 规格、型号	13. 单位	14. 数 量	15. 单价(币别)	16. 总值(币别)	17. 总值折美元
Size:10—300mm 65% Min Below10mm 35% Max	DMT	1,200	USD437.85	USD525,420.00	USD525,420.00
18. 总 计：		1,200		USD525,420.00	USD525,420.00

19. 领证人姓名： 王刚 联系电话： 0571-65726860 申请日期： 2008.2.20 下次联系日期：	20. 签证机构审批(初审)： 终审：

中华人民共和国商务部监制　　　　　　　　　　　　　第一联(正本)签证机构存档

Directions 操作指南

An import license is a document issued by a national government authorizing the importation of certain goods into its territory. Import licenses are considered to be non-tariff barriers to trade when used as a way to discriminate against another country's goods in order to protect a domestic industry from foreign competition.

➢ 申领进口许可证应提交的一般文件和材料

● 各类进出口企业在申领进口许可证时,应向发证机关提供的一般文件和材料包括:

(1) 进口许可证申请表。申请表(正本)需填写清楚并加盖申领单位公章。所写内容必须规范。

(2) 申领单位的公函或申领人的工作证,代办人员应出示委托单位的委托函。

(3) 非外贸单位(指没有外贸经营权的机关,团体和企事业单位)申领进口许可证,需提供其主管部门(司、局级以上)证明。

(4) 第一次办理进口许可证的申领单位,应提供外经贸部或经其授权的地方外经贸主管部门批准企业进出口经营权的文件(正本复印件)。

(5) 外商投资企业第一次申领进口许可证,应提供政府主管部门批准该企业的批准证书和营业执照(复印件),由发证机关存档备案。

● 一般贸易项下进口,还应分别提交以下材料:

(1) 配额管理进口商品:机电产品,应提交国家机电产品进口办公室(以下简称国家机电办) 签发的《进口配额证明》;一般商品,应提交国家计委授权的配额管理部门签发的《一般商品进口配额证明》。

(2) 非配额管理进口商品:粮食、植物油、农药、酒和彩色感光材料,应提交国家计委授权的进口登记部门签发的《特定商品进口登记证明》;碳酸饮料,应提交国家经贸委签发的《进口证明》;军民通用化学品,应提交化工部的批件;易制毒化学品,应提交外经贸部的批件。

● 外商投资企业申领进口许可证,还应分别提交以下文件和材料:

(1) 外商投资企业作为投资、自用而进口实行配额管理的一般商品,应提交各地外经贸主管部门批准的进口设备、物料清单;如进口实行许可证管理的特定登记商品,应提交各地外经贸主管部门批准的进口设备、物料清单。

(2) 外商投资企业为生产内销产品而进口实行配额管理的一般商品,应提交各地外经贸主管部门签发的《外商投资企业进口配额证明》;为生产内销产品而进口特定登记商品,应提交各地外经贸主管部门签发的《外商投资企业特定商品进口登记证明》。

(3) 外商投资企业作为投资、自用和生产内销产品进口成品油,应提交国家计委授权的进口配额管理部门签发的《一般商品进口配额证明》。

(4) 外商投资企业为生产内销产品而进口实行配额管理的机电产品,应提交国家机电办签发的《进口配额证明》。

➢ 进口许可证申请表的填制

1. 进口商(IMPORTER)

指进口合同签订单位。进口商代码为《中华人民共和国进出口企业资格证书》、《对外贸易经营者备案登记表》或《外商投资企业批准证书》中的 13 位企业代码。

接受赠送、无偿捐赠、援助进口的货物，该项为"赠送"，编码为"0000000000001"。

2. 收货人(CONSIGNEE)

指实际进口用货单位。

3. 进口许可证号(IMPORT LICENSE NO.)

结构为：XX-XX-XXXXXX

(1) - (2) - (3)

(1) 为年份；(2) 为发证机构代码；(3) 为顺序号，由发证系统自动生成。

4. 进口许可证有效截止日期(EXPIRY DATE)

按《货物进口许可证管理办法》确定的许可证有效期，由发证系统自动生成。

5. 贸易方式(TERMS OF TRADE)

指该项进口货物的贸易性质。包括：一般贸易、进料加工、来料加工、外资企业进口、边境贸易、赠送等，只能填报一种。

6. 外汇来源(TERMS OF FOREIGN EXCHANGE)

常见的有：银行购汇、现金、外资等，只能填报一种。

7. 报关口岸(PLACE OF CLEARANCE)

指进口口岸，只能填报一个。进口许可证实行"一证一关"制。对指定口岸的进口商品，按国家有关规定执行。

8. 出口国(地区)(COUNTRY/REGION OF EXPORTATION)

指签约国(地区)名称，只能填报一个。不能使用区域名，如欧盟等。如从中国保税区进口，出口国(地区)应填报"中国"。

9. 原产地国(地区)(COUNTRY/REGION OF ORIGIN)

指商品进行实质性加工的国家(地区)。

10. 商品用途(USE OF GOODS)

包括自用、生产用、内销、维修、样品、加工后返回、加工复出口、加工贸易内销，只能填报一种并应与批准文件一致。

11. 商品名称、商品编码(DESCRIPTION OF GOODS, CODE OF GOODS)

商品编码按商务部公布的年度《进口许可证管理货物目录》中的 10 位商品编码填报，商品名称由系统自动生成。只能填报一个商品编码并应与进口批准文件一致。

12. 规格、型号(SPECIFICATION)

只能填报同一商品编码下的 4 种不同规格型号，超过 4 种规格型号的，另行申请许可证。

13. 单位(UNIT)

指计量单位。按商务部公布的年度《进口许可证管理货物目录》中的计量单位执行，由发证系统自动生成。如合同使用的计量单位与规定的计量单位不一致，应换算成规定的计量单位。无法换算的，可在备注栏注明。

14. 数量(QUANTITY)

指申请进口的商品数量，最大位数为 9 位阿拉伯数字，最小保留小数点后 1 位。如数量过大，可分证办理；如数量过小，可在备注栏内注明。计量单位为"批"的，此栏均为"1"。

中华人民共和国进口许可证
IMPORT LICENCE OF THE PEOPLE'S REPUBLIC OF CHINA

No.

1. 进口商: Importer 杭州中大贸易有限公司	3. 进口许可证号: Import License No. ZJ082345
2. 收货人: Consignee 杭州中大贸易有限公司	4. 进口许可证有效截止日期: Import License Expiry Date April 10th, 2009
5. 贸易方式: Terms of Trade 一般贸易	8. 出口国(地区): Country/Region of Exportation 土耳其
6. 外汇来源: Terms of Foreign Exchange 银行购汇	9. 原产国(地区): Country/Region of Origin 土耳其
7. 报关口岸: Place of Clearance 上海	10. 商品用途: Use of Goods 生产用
11. 商品名称: Description of Goods 块状铬矿	商品编码: Code of Goods 2610.0000

12. 规格型号 Specification	13. 单位 Unit	14. 数量 Quantity	15. 单价 Unit Price	16. 总值 Amount	17. 总值折美元 Amount in USD
Size:10—300mm 65% Min Below10mm 35% Max	MT	1,200	USD437.85	USD525,420.00	USD525,420.00
18. 总 计 Total		1,200	USD437.85	USD525,420.00	USD525,420.00

19. 备 注 Supplementary Details	20. 发证机关签章: Issuing Authority's Stamp & Signature 21. 发证日期: License Date

对外贸易经济合作部监制

15. 单价(币别)(UNIT PRICE)

指与第十三项"单位"所使用的计量单位相应的单价和货币种类。计量单位为 1 批的，此栏为总金额。

16、17、18.总值、总值折美元、总计(AMOUNT; AMOUNT IN USD; TOTAL)

由发证系统自动计算。

19. 备注(SUPPLEMENTARY DETAILS)

用于注明其他需要说明的情况。如不是一批一证报关的进口许可证，在此栏注明"非一批一证"。

20. 发证机关签章

发证机构在发放进口许可证前在此栏加盖《中华人民共和国进口许可证专用章》。

申请通过后，公司将获得进口许可证，以下是进口许可证的样本。

➤ **进口许可证更改、展期、遗失的处理**

各类进出口企业领取进口许可证后，因故需要对进口许可证更改、延期时，应按以下规定办理：

申领单位因故需要更改进口许可证，应在有效期内进行。申领单位应填写进口许可证更改申请表，按表中要求填写清楚，连同原许可证第一、二联交原发证机关；

更改进口商、收货单位、商品名称、规格和数量等内容，须重新申领进口许可证；

进口许可证有效期需要延期，申领单位一般应在有效期内提出申请并提供进口合同。如确实签订了进口合同，发证机关可视情况给予延期，最长延期半年，延期后不得再展期；如在有效期内未签订合同，不得再申请展期。

申领单位如丢失许可证，应及时向发证机关和该证的报关口岸海关挂失。由发证机关审查确属丢失后按规定办理。

➤ **申领单位的法律责任**

申领单位不得伪造、变造、买卖进口许可证，对违反者，将按《中华人民共和国对外贸易法》和海关法规追究刑事责任。

Practice 操作练习

Case No. 1

1. **操作信息**

浙江新民化工厂是一家从事化学品生产的企业，最近公司业务员陈新华(0575-87609822)打算从日本进口一批高锰酸钾，具体资料如下：

商品名称：高锰酸钾　　　　　　　　　　数量：10 吨

单价：USD1,600/T　　　　　　　　　　总价：USD16,000.00

出口国：日本　　　　　　　　　　　　商品编码：2841.6100

贸易方式：一般贸易　　　　　　　　　外汇来源：银行购汇

2. 操作要求

　　请根据所提供的资料填写进口许可证申请书一份。

中华人民共和国进口许可证申请表

1. 进口商：　代码				3. 进口许可证号：	
2. 收货人：				4. 进口许可证有效截止日期： 　　　　　　年　　　月　　　日	
5. 贸易方式：				8. 出口国(地区)：	
6. 外汇来源：				9. 原产地国(地区)：	
7. 报关口岸：				10. 商品用途：	
11. 商品名称：　　　　　　　　　　　商品编码：					
12. 规格、型号	13. 单位	14. 数量	15. 单价(币别)	16. 总值(币别)	17. 总值折美元
18.总　　计：					
19.领证人姓名： 联系电话： 申请日期： 下次联系日期：	20. 签证机构审批(初审)： 终审：				

中华人民共和国商务部监制　　　　　　　　　　　　第一联(正本)签证机构存档

中华人民共和国进口许可证
IMPORT LICENCE OF THE PEOPLE'S REPUBLIC OF CHINA

No.

1. 进口商: Importer	3. 进口许可证号: Import License No.
2. 收货人: Consignee	4. 进口许可证有效截止日期: Import License Expiry Date
5. 贸易方式: Terms of trade	8. 出口国(地区): Country/Region of Exportation
6. 外汇来源: Terms of Foreign Exchange	9. 原产国(地区): Country/Region of Origin
7. 报关口岸: Place of Clearance	10. 商品用途: Use of Goods

11. 商品名称:　　　　　　　　　　商品编码:
Description of Goods　　　　　　　Code of Goods

12. 规格型号 Specification	13. 单位 Unit	14. 数量 Quantity	15. 单价 Unit Price	16. 总值 Amount	17. 总值折美元 Amount in USD
18. 总 计 Total					

19. 备 注 Supplementary Details	20. 发证机关签章: Issuing Authority's Stamp & Signature
	21. 发证日期: License Date

对外贸易经济合作部监制

PRACTICE 4

L/C Business
信用证业务

Learning Objectives 学习目标

✧ To be able to fill in the L/C application 填写信用证开证申请书
✧ To be able to make L/C amendment 填写信用证修改申请书

Task 1   Opening the L/C 开立信用证

Example & Analysis 操作实例及解析

◆ Case Lead-in

According to the stipulations of the Purchase Contract (C/T No.: ZD080210TW) signed in Feb. 10th, 2008 between Hangzhou Zhongda Trading Co., Ltd. and TOP CHAMPION DEVELOP-MENTS CO., LTD. (see below), Mr. Wang Gang of Hangzhou Zhongda Trading Co., Ltd. filled in the L/C application and submitted it with the purchase order, etc., to Bank of China, Zhejiang Br. for opening the L/C.

◆ 案例导入

杭州中大贸易有限公司(Hangzhou Zhongda Trading Co., Ltd.)王刚根据 2008 年 2 月 10 日与台湾公司 TOP CHAMPION DEVELOPMENT CO., LTD. 签订的如下合同的规定,填写了信用证开证申请书,将该开证申请书随附合同等有关材料一起提交给中国银行浙江省分行,申请开立信用证。

购买合同
PURCHASE CONTRACT

正本
ORIGINAL

The Buyers:

HANGZHOU ZHONGDA TRADING CO., LTD.

Add: No. 216 Yan'an Rd., Hangzhou, China

Tel: 86-571-65726860　　　　Fax: 86-571-85726688

The Sellers:

TOP CHAMPION DEVELOPMENT CO., LTD.

Add: No. 259, Dahan St., Kang Lo Village, Hsin Cheng Hsiang, Hualien, Taiwan, China

Tel: 886-3-8260781　　　　Fax: 886-3-8266331

编号

Contract No.:　__ZD080210TW__

日期

Date:　__FEB. 10TH, 2008__

地点

Place:　__Hangzhou, China__

下列签字双方同意按以下条款达成交易

The undersigned Buyers and Sellers have agreed to close the transaction according to the following terms and conditions.

唛头 Shipping Mark	品名及规格 Description of Goods	数　量 Quantity	单　价 Unit Price	金　额 Amount
N/M	Turkish Lumpy Chrome Ore Specifications: Cr_2O_3　　46% Min Cr/Fe　　2.6% Min Al_2O_3　　12% Max MgO　　24% Max SiO_2　　12% Max P　　0.007% Max S　　0.01% Max Size: 10—300 mm　65% Min 　　　Below 10 mm　35% Max	1,200DMT +/-10%	USD437.85/DMT FOB MERSIN, TURKEY	USD525,420.00
总值 TOTAL VALUE: SAY U.S. DOLLARS FIVE HUNDRED AND TWENTY-FIVE THOUSAND FOUR HUNDRED AND TWENTY ONLY.				

包装

PACKING: In bulk in container

装运港

PORT OF LOADING: Mersin, Turkey

目的港

PORT OF DESTINATION: Shanghai, China

装运期限

SHIPMENT: March 31st, 2008

保险

INSURANCE: To be covered by the buyers

付款方式

PAYMENT: By irrevocable L/C at sight to reach the sellers 30 days before the time of shipment

THE BUYERS

HANGZHOU ZHONGDA TRADING CO., LTD.

王刚(盖章)

THE SELLERS

TOP CHAMPION DEVELOPMENTS CO., LTD.

刘锡莲(盖章)

已填妥的开证申请书：

APPLICATION FOR ISSUING LETTER OF CREDIT

To: BANK OF CHINA   Date: Feb. 18th, 2008

Please issue on our behalf and for our account the following IRREVOCABLE LETTER OF CREDIT

By (X) TELEX/(   ) AIRMAIL: L/C No.   (left for bank to fill)

Beneficiary: (full name &detailed address)	Advising Bank: (left for bank to fill)
TOP CHAMPION DEVELOPMENT CO., LTD.	The Hong Kong and Shanghai Banking Corporation,
No. 259, Dahan St., Kang Lo Village, Hsin Cheng	Hualien Br.
Hsiang, Hualien, Taiwan, China	
Tel: 886-3-8260781 Fax: 886-3-8266331	
Applicant: (full name & detailed address)	Date of Expiry: April 21st, 2008
HANGZHOU ZHONGDA TRADING CO., LTD.	Place of Expiry: Hualien, Taiwan, China
No. 216 Yan'an Rd., Hangzhou, China	
Tel: 86-571-65726860 Fax: 86-571-85726688	

Amount: (both in figure and words)

USD525,420.00

SAY U.S. DOLLARS FIVE HUNDRED AND TWENTY-FIVE THOUSAND FOUR HUNDRED AND TWENTY ONLY.

Dear Sirs,

We hereby issue our IRREVOCABLE LETTER OF CREDIT in your favour for account of the above applicant available by your draft(s) drawn [X] at sight / [   ] _____ on [X] us / [   ] advising bank / [   ] applicant for __100__ % of invoice value marked as drawn under this L/C accompanied by following documents marked with X;

A1 [X] Signed commercial invoice in __3__ copies indicating Contract No. ZD080210TW

A2 [X] Full set 3/3 clean on board ocean Bills of Lading _____ [X] made out to order and endorsed in blank / [X] notifying [X] China National Foreign Trade Transportation Corp. at destination / [X] applicant / [   ] China National Foreign Trade Transportation Corp. at destination and applicant marked freight [X] to collect / [   ] prepaid [   ] indicating freight amount.

A3 [   ] Airway Bill _____ consigned to [   ] China National Foreign Trade Transportation Corp. at destination / [   ] applicant / [   ] us marked air freight [   ] to collect / [   ] prepaid [   ] indicating freight amount.

A4 [   ] Memorandum, issued by China Travel Service (H.K.) Ltd., Hong Kong _____

A5 [   ] Forwarding Agent's cargo receipt _____

A6 [   ] Insurance policy or certificate in _____ copies endorsed in blank covering [   ] All Risks / [   ] Air Transportation All Risks / [   ] Overland Transportation All Risks, War Risks including _____ per _____ clause for _____% of invoice value.

A7 [X] Packing list/weight memo in __3__ copies indicating quantity / gross and net weight of each package.

A8 [X] Quality certificate in __3__ copies issued by [   ] below mentioned manufacturer / [X] public recognized surveyor / [   ] _____

A9 [X] Copy of your telex advising applicant within __48__ hours after Shipment indicating Contract No., L/C No., goods name, quantity invoice value, vessel's name/air flight No., packages, loading port and shipment date.

AA [　　] Copy of applicant's / ZHONGZU's or it's agent's shipping instruction indicating vessel name, Contract No., approximate shipment date.

AB [X] Your letter certifying that one extra copy of each document called for herein has been [X] disposed of according to relative contract stipulations / [X] Sent to the applicant by express mail with 10 days after shipment.

AC [X] Other documents if any:

Certificate of Origin in 2 copies issued by Chamber of Commerce.

Certificate of Quantity in 3 copies issued by public recognized surveyor.

B. Evidencing shipment of:

Turkish Lumpy Chrome Ore

Specifications:

Cr_2O_3	46% Min
Cr/Fe	2.6% Min
Al_2O_3	12% Max
MgO	24% Max
SiO_2	12% Max
P	0.007% Max
S	0.01% Max
Size: 10—300 mm	65% Min
Below 10 mm	35% Max

Quantity: 1200DMT+/-10%

Unit price: USD437.85/DMT FOB MERSIN, TURKEY

Total amount: USD525,420.00

Packing: In bulk in container　　　　　　　　　Price term: CIF/CFR/FOB ____FOB____

Manufacturer:　　　　　　　　　　　　　　　Shipping Mark: N/M

C. Special instructions: (if any marked with X)

C1 [　　] Your signed receipt instead of draft is acceptable.

C2 [　　] The remaining _____% of invoice value _____

C3 [X] Both quantity and amount ____10____% more or less are allowed.

C4 [X] All banking charges [X] outside China / [　　] in Hong Kong are for the beneficiaries' account.

C5 [　　] Prepaid freight drawn in excess of L/C amount is acceptable against presentation of original charges voucher issued by Shipping Co. / Air Line/or it's agent.

D. Documents should be presented within ____21____ days from the date of shipment, but in any event within the validity of this L/C.

E. Shipment from Mersin, Turkey to _Shanghai, China_ not later than _March 31st, 2008_ transshipment is [X] allowed / [　　] not allowed; partial shipments are [　　] allowed / [X] not allowed; on deck shipment is [　　] allowed / [X] not allowed; third party transport documents are [　　] allowed / [X] not allowed.

*May leave in blank.

Sealed & Signed by: _杭州中大贸易有限公司　王刚_

Account No._XXXXXXXXX_　　　　　　with _BANK OF CHINA, ZHEJIANG BR._

Telephone No.: 0571-65726860　　　　　　　　　(name of bank)

Directions 操作指南

1. 信用证开证申请书的缮制方法

● 根据合同的规定，用 "X" 选择开证方式。

● 填写出口商的全称和详细地址。

● 填写信用证的有效日期和地点。

● 按照合同总金额用大小写表示。

● 填写信用证的种类和汇票金额。

● 根据合同的规定或进口商的要求，用 "X" 选择单据的类别及要求。

● 填写合同号码。

● 根据合同的规定，填写货物名称、规格、数量、单价、总价、包装方式、唛头以及生产厂商。

● 根据合同的规定，填写贸易术语。

● 根据合同的规定或进口商的要求，用 "X" 选择相关内容。

● 根据合同对分批装运的规定，用 "X" 选择允许或不允许。

● 根据合同对转运的规定，用 "X" 选择允许或不允许。

● 根据合同的规定，填写运输路线和装运日期。

● 填写进口商的开户银行账号。

● 填写开户银行名称。

● 填写开证申请人及经办人名称。

● 填写开证申请人的电话号码。

2. 开证申请书样式

APPLICATION FOR ISSUING LETTER OF CREDIT

To: Date: _____

Please issue on our behalf and for our account the following IRREVOCABLE LETTER OF CREDIT.

By ( ) TELEX/( ) AIRMAIL: L/C No.   (left for bank to fill)

Beneficiary: (full name & detailed address)	Advising Bank: (left for bank to fill)
Applicant: (full name & detailed address)	Date of Expiry:

Amount:(both in figure and words)

Dear Sirs,

We hereby issue our IRREVOCABLE LETTER OF CREDIT in your favour for account of the above applicant available by your draft(s) drawn [　　] at sight / [　　] _____ on [　　] us / [　　] advising bank / [　　] applicant for _____% of invoice value marked as drawn under this L/C accompanied by following documents marked with X;

A1 [　　] Signed commercial invoice in _____ copies indicating Contract No._____

A2 [　　] Full set 3/3 clean on board ocean Bills of Lading _____ [　　] made out to order and endorsed in blank / [　　] notifying [　　] China National Foreign Trade Transportation Corp. at destination / [　　] applicant / [　　] China National Foreign Trade Transportation Corp. at destination and applicant marked freight [　　] to collect / [　　] prepaid [　　] indicating freight amount.

A3 [　　] Airway Bill _____ consigned to [　　] China National Foreign Trade Transportation Corp. at destination / [　　] applicant / [　　] us marked air freight [　　] to collect / [　　] prepaid [　　] indicating freight amount.

A4 [　　] Memorandum, issued by China Travel Service (H.K.) Ltd., Hong Kong _____

A5 [　　] Forwarding Agent's cargo receipt _____

A6 [　　] Insurance policy or certificate in _____ copies endorsed in blank covering [　　] All Risks / [　　] Air Transportation All Risks / [　　] Overland Transportation All Risks, War Risks including _____ per _____ clause for _____% of invoice value.

A7 [　　] Packing list/weight memo in _____ copies indicating quantity / gross and net weight of each package.

A8 [　　] Quality certificate in _____ copies issued by [　　] below mentioned manufacturer / [　　] public recognized surveyor / [　　] _____

A9 [　　] Copy of your telex advising applicant within _____ hours after Shipment indicating Contract No., L/C No., goods name, quantity invoice value, vessel's name/air flight No., packages, loading port and shipment date.

AA [　　] Copy of applicant's / ZHONGZU's or it's agent's shipping instruction indicating vessel name, Contract No., approximate shipment date.

AB [　　] Your letter certifying that one extra copy of each document called for herein has been [　　] disposed of according to relative contract stipulations / [　　] _____

AC [　　] Other documents if any:

Certificate of Origin in 3 copies issued by Chamber of Commerce.

Certificate of Quantity in 3 copies issued by public recognized surveyor.

B. Evidencing shipment of:

Packing:　　　　　　　　　　　　　　　　　　　Price term: CIF/CFR/FOB _____

Manufacturer:　　　　　　　　　　　　　　　　　Shipping Mark:

C. Special instructions: (if any marked with X)

    C1 [   ] Your signed receipt instead of draft is acceptable.

    C2 [   ] The remaining _____% of invoice value _____

    C3 [   ] Both quantity and amount _____% more or less are allowed.

    C4 [   ] All banking charges [   ] outside China / [   ] in Hong Kong are for beneficiaries' account.

    C5 [   ] Prepaid freight drawn in excess of L/C amount is acceptable against presentation of original charges voucher issued by Shipping Co. / Air Line/or it's agent.

D. Documents should be presented within _____ days from the date of shipment, but in any event within the validity of this L/C.

E. Shipment from _____ to _____ not later than _____ transshipment is [   ] allowed / [   ] not allowed; partial shipments are [   ] allowed / [   ] not allowed; on deck shipment is [   ] allowed / [   ] not allowed; third party transport documents are [   ] allowed / [   ] not allowed.

*May leave in blank.

Sealed & Signed by: _____

Account No._____   with _____

Telephone No.:   (name of bank)

Task 2　Amendment of the L/C 修改信用证

Example & Analysis 操作实例及解析

◆ Case Lead-in

After receiving the relevant L/C (L/C No. 0011LC123756), the beneficiary, TOP CHAMPION DEVELOPMENT CO., LTD., examined the L/C with the contract. As the goods would not be available at the time stipulated in the contract and L/C, the beneficiary asked for postponing the time of shipment and L/C validity for 15 days respectively and the amendment of the L/C accordingly. The applicant agreed to the request of the exporter and submitted the Application for Amendment to the opening bank.

◆ 案例导入

信用证受益人台湾 TOP CHAMPION DEVELOPMENT CO., LTD. 收到由中国银行浙江省分行开来的号码为 0011LC123756 的信用证后，根据买卖合同审核了该信用证。由无法按时交货，受益人与买方协商，提出将信用证交货期和有效期分别推迟 15 天，同时要求买方修改信用证。开证申请人同意了出口方的请求，向开证行提交了信用证修改申请书(如下)，要求开证行修改信用证。

已填妥的信用证修改申请书：

中国银行
BANK OF CHINA
信用证修改申请书
APPLICATION FOR AMENDMENT

Date of Amendment: Feb. 28th, 2008   No. of Amendment: 1

Amendment to Our Documentary Credit No. 0011LC123756

To: Bank of China, Zhejiang Br.

Applicant HANGZHOU ZHONGDA TRADING CO., LTD. No. 216 Yan'an Rd., Hangzhou, China Tel: 86-571-65726860 Fax: 86-571-85726688	Advising Bank The Hong Kong and Shanghai Banking Corporation, Hualien Br.
Beneficiary (before this amendment) TOP CHAMPION DEVELOPMENTS CO., LTD. No. 259, Dahan St., Kang Lo Village, Hsin Cheng Hsiang, Hualien, Taiwan, China Tel: 886-3-8260781 Fax: 886-3-8266331	Amount USD525,420.00

The above mentioned credit is amended as follows:

☒ Shipment date extended to ___April 15th, 2008_____

☒ Expiry date extended to _____May 6th, 2008_____

☐ Amount increased/decreased by _____ to _____

☐ Other terms:

☒ Banking charges:

   The amendment charges are for the beneficiary's account.

All other terms and conditions remain unchanged.

Authorized Signature(s)

HANGZHOU ZHONGDA TRADING CO., LTD.

Wang Gang   王刚

This Amendment is Subject to Uniform Customs and Practice for Documentary Credits (2007 Revision) International Chamber of Commerce Publication No. 600.

Directions 操作指南

1. 信用证修改申请书的缮制方法

● 填写信用证修改的日期以及信用证修改申请书的编号；

● 填写要修改的信用证的号码；

- 填写开证行的名称；
- 填写开证申请人名称；
- 填写通知行的名称；
- 填写信用证受益人名称；
- 填写该信用证的原金额；
- 填写信用证要修改的内容，用"X"表示，如修改申请书上未列出的项目，可在 other terms 中列明；
- 注明该信用证修改的费用由哪方承担；
- 填写信用证修改方(开证申请人)名称。

2. 信用证修改申请书样式

中国银行
BANK OF CHINA
信用证修改申请书
APPLICATION FOR AMENDMENT

Date of Amendment: No. of Amendment:

Amendment to Our Documentary Credit No.

To:

Applicant	Advising Bank
Beneficiary (before this amendment)	Amount

The above mentioned credit is amended as follows:

☐ Shipment date extended to _____

☐ Expiry date extended to _____

☐ Amount increased/decreased by _____ to _____

☐ Other terms:

☐ Banking charges:

All other terms and conditions remain unchanged.

Authorized Signature(s)

This Amendment is Subject to Uniform Customs and Practice for Documentary Credits (2007 Revision) International Chamber of Commerce Publication No. 600.

Practice 操作练习

1. 操作信息

　　江苏好跃贸易公司(JIANGSU HAO YUE TRADING CO.)是南京市一家主要经营轻工产品的进出口贸易公司。公司业务员陈平欲进口一批钓鱼穿的靴子(FISHING BOOTS)。陈平在互联网上获悉美国 JAMES BROWN AND SONS 是一家专门生产户外用品的公司，于是与对方取得联系。双方经过友好磋商，签订了如下合同。陈平根据合同规定，以电开的方式按时开出了信用证。美国方面收到号码为 M3271NS00121 的信用证后，在生产过程中发现其中一款 ART. NO. JB702 产品由于原料问题，只能提供 200 箱，要比合同规定的少 20 箱。于是要求买方据此修改信用证。

　　其中：开证行：Bank of China, Suzhou Br.
　　　　　通知行：Bank of China, Miami Br.
　　　　　需提交的单据：发票一式五份
　　　　　　　　　　　　装箱单一式三份
　　　　　　　　　　　　海运提单一式三份
　　　　　　　　　　　　产地证一式两份
　　　　　　　　　　　　质量证书一式三份(由独立的公证行出具)
　　　　　　　　　　　　数量证书一式三份(由独立的公证行出具)
　　　　　　　　　　　　装运通知
　　　　　　　　　　　　受益人证明(全套副本单据已寄给申请人)

购买合同
PURCHASE CONTRACT　　　正本
ORIGINAL

The Buyers: JIANGSU HAO YUE TRADING CO., LTD.
Add: 12 HONGQI ROAD, NANGJING, CHINA
Tel: 025-23494668　　　　Fax: 025-23494400
The Sellers: JAMES BROWN AND SONS
Add: 2116 NW21 STREET, MIAMI FL. 33142, U.S.A.
Tel:　　　　　　　Fax:

编号
Contract No.:　04JB558
日期
Date:　JAN. 5th, 2009
地点
Place:　NANGJING, CHINA

下列签字双方同意按以下条款达成交易

The undersigned Buyers and Sellers have agreed to close the transaction according to the following terms and conditions.

唛头 **Shipping Mark**	品名及规格 **Description of Goods**	数 量 **Quantity** (PAIRS)	单 价 **Unit Price**	金 额 **Amount**
JBAS 04JB558 SHANGHAI CHINA NO. 1-520	FISHING BOOTS ART. NO. JB702 ART. NO. JB703 AS PER S/C NO. 4JB558 ******************** TOTAL:	 2,640 3,600 ********* 6,240	CFR SHANGHAI CHINA USD15.00/PAIR USD12.00/PAIR ************** 	 USD39,600.00 USD43,200.00 ************* USD82,800.00

总值
TOTAL VALUE: SAY U.S.DOLLARS EIGHTY-TWO THOUSAND EIGHT HUNDRED ONLY.

包装

PACKING: 12 PAIRS PER CARTON

装运港

PORT OF LOADING: MIAMI, U.S.A.

目的港

PORT OF DESTINATION: SHANGHAI, CHINA

装运期限

SHIPMENT: NOT LATER THAN APRIL 15TH, 2009

保险

INSURANCE: TO BE COVERED BY THE BUYERS

付款方式

PAYMENT: BY IRREVOCABLE L/C AT SIGHT. THE RELEVANT L/C MUST REACH THE SELLERS 30
　　　　　DAYS BEFORE THE TIME OF SHIPMENT.

THE BUYERS　　　　　　　　　　　　　　THE SELLERS

JIANGSU HAO YUE TRADING CO.　　　　　　JAMES BROWN AND SONS

陈平(盖章)　　　　　　　　　　　　　　JAMES BROWN (盖章)

2. 操作要求

(1) 请你以业务员陈平的身份，根据上述购买合同填写开证申请书；

(2) 请你以业务员陈平的身份，根据上述要求填写信用证修改申请书。

开证申请书：

APPLICATION FOR ISSUING LETTER OF CREDIT

To: BANK OF CHINA   Date:_____

Please issue on our behalf and for our account the following IRREVOCABLE LETTER OF CREDIT

By (   ) TELEX/(   ) AIRMAIL: L/C No.   (left for bank to fill)

Beneficiary: (full name & detailed address)	Advising Bank: (left for bank to fill)
Applicant: (full name & detailed address)	Date of Expiry:

Amount:(both in figure and words)

Dear Sirs,

We hereby issue our IRREVOCABLE LETTER OF CREDIT in your favour for account of the above applicant available by your draft(s) drawn [   ] at sight / [   ] _____ on [   ] us / [   ] advising bank / [   ] applicant for _____% of invoice value marked as drawn under this L/C accompanied by following documents marked with X;

A1 [   ] Signed commercial invoice in _____ copies indicating Contract No._____

A2 [   ] Full set 3/3 clean on board ocean Bills of Lading _____ [   ] made out to order and endorsed in blank / [   ] notifying [   ] China National Foreign Trade Transportation Corp. at destination / [   ] applicant / [   ] China National Foreign Trade Transportation Corp. at destination and applicant marked freight [   ] to collect / [   ] prepaid [   ] indicating freight amount.

A3 [   ] Airway Bill _____ consigned to [   ] China National Foreign Trade Transportation Corp. at destination / [   ] applicant / [   ] us marked air freight [   ] to collect / [   ] prepaid [   ] indicating freight amount.

A4 [   ] Memorandum, issued by China Travel Service (H.K.) Ltd, Hong Kong _____

A5 [   ] Forwarding Agent's cargo receipt _____

A6 [   ] Insurance policy or certificate in _____ copies endorsed in blank covering [   ] All Risks / [   ] Air Transportation All Risks / [   ] Overland Transportation All Risks, War Risks including _____ per _____ clause for _____% of invoice value.

A7 [   ] Packing list/weight memo in _____ copies indicating quantity / gross and net weight of each package.

A8 [   ] Quality certificate in _____ copies issued by [   ] below mentioned manufacturer / [   ] public recognized surveyor / [   ] _____

A9 [   ] Copy of your telex advising applicant within _____ hours after Shipment indicating Contract No., L/C No., goods name, quantity invoice value, vessel's name/air flight No., packages, loading port and shipment date.

AA [   ] Copy of applicant's / ZHONGZU's or it's agent's shipping instruction indicating vessel name, Contract No., approximate shipment date.

AB [   ] Your letter certifying that one extra copy of each document called for herein has been [   ] disposed of according to relative contract stipulations / [   ] _____

AC [   ] Other documents if any:

Certificate of Origin in 3 copies issued by Chamber of Commerce.

Certificate of Quantity in 3 copies issued by public recognized surveyor.

B. Evidencing shipment of:

Packing: In bulk in container.   Price term: CIF/CFR/FOB _____

Manufacturer: Shipping Mark:

C. Special instructions: (if any marked with X)

C1 [   ] Your signed receipt instead of draft is acceptable.

C2 [   ] The remaining _____% of invoice value _____

C3 [   ] Both quantity and amount _____% more or less are allowed.

C4 [   ] All banking charges [   ] outside China / [   ] in Hong Kong are for beneficiaries' account.

C5 [   ] Prepaid freight drawn in excess of L/C amount is acceptable against presentation of original charges voucher issued by Shipping Co. / Air Line/or it's agent.

D. Documents should be presented within _____ days from the date of shipment, but in any event within the validity of this L/C.

E. Shipment from _____ to _____ not later than _____ transshipment is [   ] allowed / [   ] not allowed; partial shipments are [   ] allowed / [   ] not allowed; on deck shipment is [   ] allowed / [   ] not allowed; third party transport documents are [   ] allowed / [   ] not allowed.

*May leave in blank.

Sealed & Signed by:_____

Account No._____   with _____

Telephone No.:   (name of bank)

信用证修改申请书：

中国银行
BANK OF CHINA
信用证修改申请书
APPLICATION FOR AMENDMENT

Date of Amendment: No. of Amendment:

Amendment to Our Documentary Credit No.

To:

Applicant	Advising Bank
Beneficiary (before this amendment)	Amount

The above mentioned credit is amended as follows:

☐ Shipment date extended to _____

☐ Expiry date extended to _____

☐ Amount increased/decreased by _____ to _____

☐ Other terms:

☐ Banking charges:

All other terms and conditions remain unchanged.

Authorized Signature(s)

This Amendment is Subject to Uniform Customs and Practice for Documentary Credits (2007 Revision) International Chamber of Commerce Publication No. 600.

Case No. 2

1. **操作信息**

　　杭州捷达贸易有限公司(HANGZHOU JIEDA TRADING CO. LTD.)是杭州市一家民营企业，主要经营建材产品。公司业务员张丽欲进口一批抛光大理石饰面砖(POLISHED MARBLE TILES)。张丽通过友人介绍，与英国一家专门做建材的公司 ALEXANDER FRASER AND SON LTD. 取得联系。双方经过友好磋商，签订了如下合同。张丽根据合同规定，以电开的方式按时开出了信用证。英国方面收到号码为 SH8774AH00451 的信用证后，发现需提交的单据中，一份正本海运提单需寄给开证申请人。对此，卖方不同意，坚持全套正本提单交银行。同时要求买方修改信用证。

其中：开证行：Bank of China, Zhejiang Br.

通知行：Bank of China, London Br.

需提交的单据：发票一式六份

装箱单一式六份

海运提单一式二份(另一份直接寄给开证申请人)

产地证一式两份

质量证书一式三份(由独立的公证行出具)

重量证书一式三份(由独立的公证行出具)

装运通知

受益人证明(全套副本单据已寄给申请人)

购买合同
PURCHASE CONTRACT

正本
ORIGINAL

The Buyers: HANGZHOU JIEDA TRADING CO., LTD.

Add: 201 FENGQI ROAD, HANGZHOU, CHINA

Tel: 86-571-85235716   Fax: 86-571-85235800

The Sellers: ALEXANDER FRASER AND SON LTD.

Add: FRANKLAND MOORE HOUSE, 185/187 HIGH ROAD,

CHADWELL HEATH, ROMFORD, ESSEX. RM6 2NR.

Tel: 0044-1-35786482   Fax: 0044-1-35786600

编号

Contract No.:　PET/CAN/5

日期

Date:　　JAN. 16TH, 2009

地点

Place: HANGZHOU, CHINA

下列签字双方同意按以下条款达成交易

The undersigned Buyers and Sellers have agreed to close the transaction according to the following terms and conditions.

唛头 Shipping Mark	品名及规格 Description of Goods	数量 Quantity (SQM)	单价 Unit Price	金额 Amount
PETRICO PET/CAN/5 TORONTO, CANADA 1-16 **********	POLISHED MARBLE TILES, 30.5×30.5×1CM. +/- 0.5 MM AS PER APPLICANT C/T NO. PET/CAN/5 ART NO.425 ART NO.424 ************************	 312.56 312.56 ********** 625.12SQM	FOB TORONTO, CANADA USD24.00 USD24.00 **********	 USD7,501.44 USD7,501.44 ************* USD15,002.88
总值 TOTAL VALUE: SAY U.S. DOLLARS FIFTEEN THOUSAND AND TWO AND CENTS EIGHTY-EIGHT. ONLY				

包装

PACKING: IN WOODEN CRATES WITH PLASTIC FOAM BOX, CONTAINERIZED

装运港

PORT OF LOADING: TORONTO, CANADA

目的港

PORT OF DESTINATION: SHANGHAI, CHINA

装运期限

SHIPMENT: NOT LATER THAN APRIL 15TH, 2009

保险

INSURANCE: TO BE COVERED BY THE BUYERS

付款方式

PAYMENT: BY IRREVOCABLE L/C AT SIGHT. THE RELEVANT L/C MUST REACH THE SELLERS 30
DAYS BEFORE THE TIME OF SHIPMENT.

THE BUYERS   THE SELLERS

HAGNZHOU JIEDA TRADING CO. LTD.   ALEXANDER FRASER AND SON LTD.

张丽(盖章)   JAMES BROWN (盖章)

2. 操作要求

(1) 请你以业务员张丽的身份，根据上述购买合同填写开证申请书；

(2) 请你以业务员张丽的身份，根据上述要求填写信用证修改申请书。

开证申请书：

APPLICATION FOR ISSUING LETTER OF CREDIT

To: BANK OF CHINA   Date: _____

Please issue on our behalf and for our account the following IRREVOCABLE LETTER OF CREDIT

By ( ) TELEX/( ) AIRMAIL: L/C No.   (left for bank to fill)

Beneficiary: (full name & detailed address)	Advising Bank: (left for bank to fill)
Applicant: (full name &detailed address)	Date of Expiry:
Amount:(both in figure and words)	

Dear Sirs,

We hereby issue our IRREVOCABLE LETTER OF CREDIT in your favour for account of the above applicant available by your draft(s) drawn [   ] at sight / [   ] _____ on [   ] us / [   ] advising bank / [   ] applicant for _____% of invoice value marked as drawn under this L/C accompanied by following documents marked with X;

A1 [   ] Signed commercial invoice in _____ copies indicating Contract No._____

A2 [   ] Full set 3/3 clean on board ocean Bills of Lading _____ [   ] made out to order and endorsed in blank / [   ] notifying [   ] China National Foreign Trade Transportation Corp. at destination / [   ] applicant / [   ] China National Foreign Trade Transportation Corp. at destination and applicant marked freight [   ] to collect / [   ] prepaid [   ] indicating freight amount.

A3 [   ] Airway Bill _____ consigned to [   ] China National Foreign Trade Transportation Corp. at destination / [   ] applicant / [   ] us marked air freight [   ] to collect / [   ] prepaid [   ] indicating freight amount.

A4 [   ] Memorandum, issued by China Travel Service (H.K.) Ltd., Hong Kong _____

A5 [   ] Forwarding Agent's cargo receipt _____

A6 [   ] Insurance policy or certificate in _____ copies endorsed in blank covering [   ] All Risks / [   ] Air Transportation All Risks / [   ] Overland Transportation All Risks, War Risks including _____ per _____ clause for _____% of invoice value.

A7 [   ] Packing list/weight memo in _____ copies indicating quantity / gross and net weight of each package.

A8 [   ] Quality certificate in _____ copies issued by [   ] below mentioned manufacturer / [   ] public recognized surveyor / [   ] _____

A9 [   ] Copy of your telex advising applicant within _____ hours after Shipment indicating Contract No., L/C No., goods name, quantity invoice value, vessel's name/air flight No., packages, loading port and shipment date.

AA [   ] Copy of applicant's / ZHONGZU's or it's agent's shipping instruction indicating vessel name, Contract No., approximate shipment date.

AB [   ] Your letter certifying that one extra copy of each document called for herein has been [   ] disposed of according to relative contract stipulations / [   ] _____

AC [   ] Other documents if any:

Certificate of Origin in 3 copies issued by Chamber of Commerce.

Certificate of Quantity in 3 copies issued by public recognized surveyor.

B. Evidencing shipment of:

Packing: In bulk in container.   Price term: CIF/CFR/FOB _____

Manufacturer: Shipping Mark:

C. Special instructions: (if any marked with X)

C1 [   ] Your signed receipt instead of draft is acceptable.

C2 [   ] The remaining _____% of invoice value _____

C3 [   ] Both quantity and amount _____% more or less are allowed.

C4 [   ] All banking charges [   ] outside China / [   ] in Hong Kong are for beneficiaries' account.

C5 [   ] Prepaid freight drawn in excess of L/C amount is acceptable against presentation of original charges voucher issued by Shipping Co. / Air Line/or it's agent.

D. Documents should be presented within _____ days from the date of shipment, but in any event within the validity of this L/C.

E. Shipment from _____ to _____ not later than _____ transshipment is [　　]

　　allowed / [　　] not allowed; partial shipments are [　　] allowed / [　　] not allowed; on deck shipment is

　　[　　] allowed / [　　] not allowed; third party transport documents are [　　] allowed / [　　] not allowed.

　　*May leave in blank.

Sealed & Signed by:_____

Account No.:_____　　　　　　　　with _____

Telephone No.:　　　　　　　　　　　　　　　　　　　(name of bank)

信用证修改申请书：

中国银行

BANK OF CHINA

信用证修改申请书

APPLICATION FOR AMENDMENT

Date of Amendment:　　　　　　　　　　　　　　No. of Amendment:

Amendment to Our Documentary Credit No.

To:

Applicant	Advising Bank
Beneficiary (before this amendment)	Amount

The above mentioned credit is amended as follows:

☐ Shipment date extended to _____

☐ Expiry date extended to _____

☐ Amount increased/decreased by _____ to _____

☐ Other terms:

☐ Banking charges:

All other terms and conditions remain unchanged.

Authorized Signature(s)

This Amendment is Subject to Uniform Customs and Practice for Documentary Credits (2007 Revision)
International Chamber of Commerce Publication No. 600.

PRACTICE 5

Import Shipment
进口运输

Example & Analysis 操作实例及解析

◆ Case Lead-in

Hangzhou Zhongda Trading Co., Ltd. was requested by TOP CHAMPION DEVELOPMENT CO., LTD. to make L/C amendment accordingly, and then sent Notification of Amendment to the seller through Hong Kong and Shanghai Banking Corporation Hualien Branch. As contract is concluded under FOB terms, the buyer should fulfill commitment of charting or booking space and covering insurance.

◆ 案例导入

杭州中大贸易有限公司(Hangzhou Zhongda Trading Co. Ltd.)按照出口方台湾 TOP CHAMPION DEVELOPMENT CO., LTD. 提出的要求,对信用证作了修改,并通过汇丰银行花莲分行向卖方寄送了改证通知书。由于这是一笔以 FOB 贸易术语成交的进口合同,由买方负责做好派船接货、投保等一系列工作,因此业务员王刚开始着手办理租船订舱手续。

Directions 操作指南

➢ **Procedure for booking shipping space for ocean freight 海运租船订舱流程**

按 FOB 交货条件成交的进口合同，由我方负责租船或订舱。大宗货物需要整船装运的，可租适当船舶承运；小批量的杂货，大多向班轮公司订舱。不论租船或订舱，均需办理租船或订舱手续。

按照合同规定，卖方在交货前一定时间内，将预期货物备妥待装运日期时通知我方，我方在接到上述通知后及时办理租船或订舱手续。

除个别情况外，一般均委托代理来办理。在我国，一般是委托中国对外贸易运输总公司及其分公司来办理。具体程序为：在收到国外出口商发来的备货装运通知后，委托人按合同规定填写《进口租船订舱联系单》(Cargo Note)，连同合同副本提交给外运公司，委托其办理进口运输事宜。

外运公司接到进口公司的订舱单后，根据订舱单的要求进行配船，安排货物的装运。进口企业接到船方的配船通知后，应立即将船名及船期等事项通知卖方，以便卖方准备装货。

对 CIF 和 CFR 条件下的进口合同，系由卖方负责租船、订舱，安排装运，但我方也应及时与卖方联系，掌握卖方的备货和装运情况。

国外供货商往往由于原材料或劳动力成本上涨，出口许可证未及时获得，国际市场该商品价格上扬或无法按期安排生产等各种原因，不能或不愿按期交货。为此，进口企业必须督促对方按期或提前装运。对于成交数量大或重要的、急需的物资，在交货期前的一定时间即应发出函电催装，必要时还可以委托我驻外商务机构就地了解，督促对方及时履行交货义务。

➢ **进口租船订舱联系单的内容**

一般包括货名、重量、尺码、合同号、包装种类、装卸港口、交货期、交货条款、发货人名称地址、发货人电挂或电传号码等项目。

进口租船订舱联系单

第 号　　　　　　　　　　　　　　　　　年　　月　　日

货名			
重量		尺码	
合同号		包装	
装卸港		交货期	
交货条款			
发货人名称地址			
发货人电挂/电传			
订妥船名		预抵港期	
备注		委托单位	

➢ 填写联系单时应注意以下几点

(1) 货名、重量、尺码、包装要用中、英文两种文字填写。对重量一项，应填毛重。对长大件货物，要列明其长、宽、高的尺寸。对集重货物，要列明最大件的重量和件数。

(2) "交货条款"一栏要与贸易合同条款相一致，对合同中的装运条件另有规定者，要在联系单上详细列明，以便划分责任、风险和费用。

(3) 贵重物品要列明其售价。

(4) 危险货物要注明危险品性质和国际危规的页码 IMDGC (International Maritime Dangerous Goods Code Page)及联合国编号(UN No.)。国际危规把危险品分为爆炸品、气体、易燃液体、易燃固体、氧化剂和有机氧化物、有毒和有感染性的物质、放射性物品、腐蚀性物品和其他危险物品等九大类。在填联系单时还需注明其类别。填写货物品名时，必须用其学名(技术名称)，不要使用其俗名。对易燃液体还必须注明其闪点(Flash Point)。

(5) 联系单的内容必须与贸易合同完全一致，还须附贸易合同副本。

Practice 操作练习

1. 操作信息

(1) LETTER OF CREDIT

CREDIT NO:	LCD7904921
DATE OF ISSUE:	JULY 5TH, 2008
EXPIRY:	AUG. 20TH, 2008
APPLICANT:	NINGBO YONGSHEN GARMENT TRADING CO., LTD.
BENEFICIARY:	GOLDWING INTERNATIONAL COMPANY LTD.
AMOUNT:	USD 14,100.00
PARTIAL SHIPMENT:	ALLOWED
TRANSSHIPMENT:	ALLOWED
SHIPMENT PERIOD:	NOT LATER THAN JULY 20TH, 2008
SHIPMENT FROM:	HAMBURG, GERMANY
FOR TRANSPORT TO:	NINGBO, CHINA
COVERING:	100% CASHMERE SWEATER CFR NINGBO PORTSHIPPING MARKS:
	NBYS
	NBYS9090
	NINGBO
	C/NO. 1—300
DOCUMENTS REQUIRED:	FULL SET OF ORIGINAL CLEAN ON BOARD OCEAN BILLS OF LADING MADE OUT TO THE SHIPPERS' ORDER AND BLANK ENDORSED, MARKED FREIGHT PREPAID AND NOTIFY APPLICANT QUOTING FULL NAME AND ADDRESS.

ADDITIONAL CONDITIONS: ...

(2) SHIPPMENT ADVICE

DEAR SIRS,

WE ARE PLEASED TO ADVICE YOU OF THE SHIPPING DETAILS AS FOLLOWS:

L/C NO. LCD7904921

NAME & VOYAGE OF VESSEL: "NIPPON MARU" V630

DATE OF SHIPMENT: JULY 20TH, 2008

PORT OF LOADING: HAMBURG

PORT OF DESTINATION: NINGBO

QUANTITY: 300PCS

PACKING: 20PCS IN A CARTON

2.　操作要求

请以进口商业务员的身份，填制进口租船订舱联系单，向船公司订舱。

进口租船订舱联系单

第　　　号　　　　　　　　　　　　　　　　　　　年　　　月　　　日

货名			
重量		尺码	
合同号		包装	
装卸港		交货期	
交货条款			
发货人名称地址			
发货人电挂/电传			
订妥船名		预抵港期	
备注		委托单位	

*P*RACTICE 6

Inspection of Import Commodities
进口报检

Learning Objectives 学习目标

◇ To understand the procedures of inspection 了解进口商品报检程序
◇ To master how to make out application for inspection 掌握如何填写进口商品报验单

Example & Analysis 操作实例及解析

◆ Case Lead-in

Hangzhou Zhongda Trading Co., Ltd. was informed that the commodity has got to the port of Shanghai. One of the important things they should do next is to arrange the inspection of imported commodity.

◆ 案例导入

杭州中大贸易有限公司得到通知货物已经到达上海港，在海关进口报关的同时，他们还必须做好进口货物的报检工作。

Directions 操作指南

➢ 入境货物报检的一般规定

入境货物报检的一般规定为：法定检验检疫入境货物的货主或其代理人首先向卸货口岸或到达站的出入境检验检疫机构报检；检验检疫机构受理报检，转施检部门签署意见，对来自疫区、可能传播检疫传染病、可能夹带有害物质的入境货物的交通工具或运输包装实施必要的检疫、消毒、卫生除害处理后，签发入境货物通关单(入境废物、活动物等除外)供报检人输海关的通关手续；货物通关后，入境货物的货主或其代理人须在规定的时间和地点联系指定的检验检疫机构对货物实施检验检疫，经检验检疫合格的入境货物，签发入境货物检验检疫证明，经检验检疫不合格的入境货物，签发检验检疫处理通知书，需要索赔的入境货物，签发检验检疫证书。

> 入境货物检验检疫报检方式

入境货物检验检疫报检方式可分为 3 类：进境一般报检、进境流向报检、异地施检报检。

1. 进境一般报检

进境一般报检指法定检验检疫入境货物的货主或其代理人，持有关单证向卸货口岸检验检疫机构申请取得入境货物通关单，并对货物进行检验检疫的报检。对进境一般报检业务而言，签发入境货物通关单和对货物的检验检疫都由口岸检验检疫机构完成，货主或其代理人在输完通关手续后，应主动与检验检疫机构联系落实施检工作。

2. 进境流向报检

进境流向报检亦称口岸清关转异地进行检验检疫的报检，是指法定检验检疫入境货物的收货人或其代理人持有关单证在卸货口岸向口岸检验检疫机构报检，获取入境货物通关单并通关后由进境口岸检验检疫机构进行必要的检疫处理，货物调往目的地后再由目的地检验检疫机构进行检验检疫监管。申请进境流向报检货物的通关地与目的地属于不同辖区。

3. 异地施检报检

异地施检报检是指已在卸货口岸完成进境流向报检，货物到达目的地后，该批进境货物的货主或其代理人在规定的时间内，向目的地检验检疫机构申请进行检验检疫的报检。进境流向报检只在卸货口岸对装运货物的运输工具和外包装进行了必要的检疫处理，并未对整批货物进行检验检疫，因此，只有当检验检疫机构对货物实施了具体的检验检疫，确认其符合有关检验检疫要求及合同、信用证的规定后，货主才能获得相应的准许进口货物销售使用的合法凭证，完成进境货物的检验检疫工作。异地施检报检时应提供口岸检验检疫机构签发的《入境货物调离通知单》。

> 入境货物报检时间与地点限制

1. 入境货物报检时间限制

入境货物报检的时间限制体现在以下几个方面：

(1) 申请货物品质检验和鉴定的，一般应在索赔有效期到期前 20 天内报检；

(2) 输入动物的应当在进境前 15 天报检；

(3) 输入植物、种子、种苗及其他繁殖材料的，应当在进境前 7 天报检；

(4) 动植物性包装物、铺垫材料进境时应当及时报检；

(5) 运输动植物、动植物产品和其他检疫物过境的，应当在进境时报检；

(6) 入境的集装箱货物、废旧物品在到达口岸时，必须向检验检疫机构报检并接受检疫，经检疫或实施消毒、除鼠、除虫或其他必要的卫生处理合格后，方准入境；

(7) 输入微生物、人体组织、生物制品、血液及其制品或种畜、禽及其精液、胚胎、受精卵的，应当在入境前 30 天报检。

2. 入境货物报检地点限制

入境货物报检的地点限制体现在以下几个方面：

(1) 法律、法规规定必须经检验检疫机构检验的进口商品的收货人或者其代理人，应当向报关地检验检疫机构报检；审批、许可证等有关政府批文中规定了检验检疫地点的，在规定的地点报检；

(2) 大宗、散装进口货物及合同规定凭卸货口岸检验检疫机构的品质、重量检验证书作为计算价格结算货款的货物，应向卸货口岸或到达站检验检疫机构报检；

(3) 进口粮食、原糖、化肥、硫磺、矿砂等散装货物，按照国际贸易惯例，应在卸货口岸报检，并须在目的地口岸承载货物的船舱内或在卸货过程中，按有关规定抽取代表性样品进行检验；

(4) 进口化工原料和化工产品，分拨调运后，不易按原发货批号抽取代表性样品，应在卸货口岸报检；

(5) 在国内转运过程中，容易造成水分挥发、散失或易腐易变质的货物，应在卸货口岸报检；

(6) 在卸货时，发现货物残损或短少时，必须向卸货口岸或到达站检验检疫机构报检；

(7) 需要结合安装调试进行检验的成套设备、机电仪器产品以及在卸货口岸开箱检验难以恢复包装的货物，可以向收、用货人所在地检验检疫机构报检；

(8) 输入动植物、动植物产品和其他检疫物的，应向进境口岸检验检疫机构报检，并由口岸检验检疫机构实施检疫；

(9) 进境后需办理转关手续的检疫物，除活动物和来自动植物疫情流行国家或地区的检疫物须由进境口岸检疫外，其他均应到指定检验检疫机构报检，并实施检疫。

➢ 入境货物报检单填制要求

入境货物报检时，应填写入境货物报检单，并提供外贸合同、发票、提(运)单、装箱单等有关单证。入境货物报检单填制要求如下：

(1) 编号：企业发送电子报检信息后，收到尾号为"E"预报检号，正式编号由检验检疫机构报检受理人员填写，前6位为申报地检验检疫局机关代码，第7位为报检类代码(入境01，出境02)，第8、9位为年代码，第10至15位为流水号。

(2) 报检单位登记号：报检单位在检验检疫机构登记的号码。

(3) 联系人：报检人员姓名。电话：报检人员的联系电话。

(4) 报检日期：检验检疫机构实际受理报检的日期。

(5) 收货人：外贸合同中的收货人。应中英文对照填写并录入其在检验检疫机构的注册代码。

(6) 发货人：外贸合同中的发货人。

(7) 货物名称(中/外文)：进口货物的品名，应与进口合同、发票名称一致，如为废旧货物应注明。

(8) H.S.编码：进口货物的商品编码。以当年海关公布的商品税则编码分类为准，目前为10位。录入次序为应先录入法检货物，然后为非法检货物，有木质包装的应按00类包装编码申报，最后为001类的集装箱(散货除外)。

(9) 原产国(地区)：该进口货物的原产国家或地区，有产地证的，以产地证标注的为准。

(10) 数量/重量：以商品编码分类中标准数量、重量单位为准，并与提单和箱单相符。

(11) 货物总值：入境货物的总值及币种，应与合同、发票或报关单上所列的货物总值一致。

(12) 包装种类及数量：货物实际运输包装的种类及数量(有木质包装的此处的种类填写其他)。

(13) 运输工具名称号码：运输工具的名称和号码。

(14) 合同号：对外贸易合同、订单或形式发票的号码。

(15) 贸易方式：该批货物进口的贸易方式。

(16) 贸易国别(地区)：进口货物的贸易国别，指合同的卖方。

(17) 提单/运单号：货物海运提单号或空运单号，有二程提单的应同时填写。

(18) 到货日期：进口货物到达口岸的日期。

(19) 启运国家(地区)：货物的启运国家或地区，以提单为准。

(20) 许可证/审批号：需办理进境许可证或审批的货物应填写有关许可证号或审批号。

(21) 卸毕日期：货物在口岸的卸毕日期。

(22) 启运口岸：货物的启运口岸，以提单为准。

(23) 入境口岸：货物的入境口岸。

(24) 索赔有效期至：对外贸易合同中约定的索赔期限。

(25) 经停口岸：货物在运输中曾经停靠的外国口岸。

(26) 目的地：货物的境内目的地。

(27) 集装箱规格、数量及号码：货物若以集装箱运输应填写集装箱的规格，数量及号码。

(28) 合同订立的特殊条款以及其他要求：在合同中订立的有关检验检疫的特殊条款及其他要求应填入此栏。

(29) 货物存放地点：货物存放的地点。

(30) 用途：本批货物的用途。

(31) 随附单据：在随附单据的种类前划"√"或补填。

(32) 标记及号码：货物的标记号码，应与合同、发票等有关外贸单据保持一致。若没有标记号码则填"N/M"。

(33) 外商投资财产：由检验检疫机构报检受理人员填写。

(34) 签名：由持有报检员证的报检人员手签。

(35) 检验检疫费：由检验检疫机构计费人员核定费用后填写。

(36) 领取证单：报检人在领取检验检疫机构出具的有关检验检疫证单时填写领证日期及领证人姓名。

报检人要认真填写"入境货物报检单"，内容应按合同、国外发票、提单、运单上的内容填写，报检单应填写完整、无漏项，字迹清楚，不得涂改，且中英文内容一致，并加盖申请单位公章。

中华人民共和国出入境检验检疫
入境货物报验单

报检单位(加盖公章) 杭州中大贸易有限公司　　　　　　*编号__ZJ3927_____
报检单位登记号：33013111　联系人：王刚　电话：0571-65726860　报检日期：2008 年 4 月 20 日

发货人	(中文)台湾冠军发展有限公司				
	(外文)TAIWAN CHAMPION DEVELOPMENT CO., LTD.				
收货人	(中文)杭州中大贸易有限公司				
	(外文)Hangzhou Zhongda Trading Co., Ltd.				
货物名称(中外文)	H.S. 编码	产地	数/重量	货物总值	包装种类及数量
块状铬矿 chrome ore	26100000	土耳其	1,200MT	USD525,420.00	散装
运输工具名称号码	贸易方式 一般贸易			货物存放地点 仓库	
合同号 ZD080210TW	信用证号 0011LC123756			用途　进口生产	
发货日期　Apr. 20th, 2008					
启运地　土耳其					
集装箱规格、数量及号码	1×20′				

合同、信用证订立的检验 检疫条款或特殊要求	标记及号码	随附单据(画√或补填)	
	N/M	☑合同	□包装性能结果单
		☑信用证	☑许可/审批文件
		☑发票	□
		□换证凭单	□
		☑装箱单	□
		□厂检单	□

需要证单名称(画√或补填)		检验检疫费
☑品质证书　　1 正 2 副 □重量证书　　__正__副 □数量证书　　__正__副 □兽医卫生证书　__正__副 □健康证书　　__正__副 □卫生证书　　__正__副 □动物卫生证书　__正__副	□植物检疫证书　　__正__副 □熏蒸/消毒证书　　__正__副 □出境货物换证凭单　__正__副 √出境货物通关单　　1正_2副	总金额 (人民币元) 计费人 收费人
报检人郑重声明： 1. 本人被授权报检。 2. 上列填写内容正确属实，货物无伪造或冒用他人的厂名、标志、认证标志，并承担货物质量责任。 　　　　　　　　　　签名：__王刚_____		领取证单 日期 签名

注：有"*"号栏由出入境检验检疫机构填写

进口货物经检验、检疫合格后，商检机构签发《入境货物通关单》，作为海关核放货物的依据。

中华人民共和国出入境检验检疫
入境货物通关单

编号：**ZJ3927**

1. 发货人 TOP CHAMPION DEVELOPMENTS CO., LTD.	5. 标记及号码
2. 收货人 杭州中大贸易有限公司	N/M

3.合同号/信用证号 ZD080210TW/0011LC123756	4.输出国家或地区 土耳其	
6.运输工具名称及号码	7.到货日期 Apr. 20th, 2008	8.集装箱规格及日期 $1 \times 20'$

9.货物名称及规格	10.H.S.编码	11.申报总值	12.数/重量，包装数量及种类
块状铬矿 chrome ore	26100000	USD525,420.00	1,200MT

13. 证明

上述货物业经检验检疫，请海关予以放行

本通关单有效期至　　2008　年　6　月　25　日

签字：　　　　　　　　　　　日期：2008　年　4　月　25　日

14. 备注

Practice 操作练习

1. 操作信息

浙江恒星贸易有限公司(Zhejiang Hengxing Trading Co., Ltd., ADD: No. 15, Wensan Road, Hangzhou, China, TEL: 0571-88187398, FAX: 0571-88187512)业务员陈军与马来西亚出口商 (ABC Trading Co., Ltd., ADD: 2, Jalan Iks Simpang Ampat, Taman Iks, S.P.S., Penang, Malaysia, TEL: 60-4-5889811, Fax: 60-4-5882811)达成了进口天然橡胶的合同,卖方已经将货物运出并将到达港口。

货物名称:天然橡胶,货号:SMR20CB

数量:20 吨,100 Bags

单价:USD2,000.00/吨 总计:USD40,000.00

合同号:HX08932 L/C NO.: ZJ983020

装运港:Penang

目的港:上海

到货日期:2008.8.20

船名、航次:Xinfeng V. 28

1×20 FCL COSCO9823210

2. 操作要求

请根据所提供的资料填写入境货物报检单和入境货物通关单。

中华人民共和国出入境检验检疫
入境货物报验单

报检单位(加盖公章)　　　　　　　　　　　　　*编号＿＿＿＿＿＿＿＿

报检单位登记号：　　　联系人：　　电话：　　　报检日期：　年　月　日

发货人	(中文)				
	(外文)				
收货人	(中文)				
	(外文)				

货物名称(中外文)	H.S. 编码	产地	数/重量	货物总值	包装种类及数量

运输工具名称号码		贸易方式		货物存放地点	
合同号		信用证号		用途	
发货日期					
启运地					
集装箱规格、数量及号码					

合同、信用证订立的检验检疫条款或特殊要求	标记及号码	随附单据(画√或补填)	
		□合同	□包装性能结果单
		□信用证	□许可/审批文件
		□发票	□
		□换证凭单	□
		□装箱单	□
		□厂检单	□

需要证单名称(画√或补填)		检验检疫费	
□品质证书　　__正__副	□植物检疫证书　　__正__副	总金额	
□重量证书　　__正__副	□熏蒸/消毒证书　　__正__副	(人民币元)	
□数量证书　　__正__副	□出境货物换证凭单　__正__副		
□兽医卫生证书　__正__副	□出境货物通关单　　__正__副	计费人	
□健康证书　　__正__副			
□卫生证书　　__正__副		收费人	
□动物卫生证书　__正__副			

报检人郑重声明：	领取证单
1. 本人被授权报检。	
2. 上列填写内容正确属实，货物无伪造或冒用他人的厂名、标志、认证标志，并承担货物质量责任。	日期
签名：＿＿＿＿＿＿＿	签名

注：有"*"号栏由出入境检验检疫机构填写

中华人民共和国出入境检验检疫
入境货物通关单

编号：

1. 发货人			5. 标记及号码
2. 收货人			
3.合同号/信用证号		4.输出国家或地区	
6.运输工具名称及号码		7.到货日期	8.集装箱规格及日期
9.货物名称及规格	10.H.S.编码	11.申报总值	12.数/重量，包装数量及种类

13. 证明

上述货物业经检验检疫，请海关予以放行

本通关单有效期至　　　年　　月　　　日

签字：　　　　　　　　　　日期：　　年　　月　　　日

14. 备注

PRACTICE 7

Goods Insurance
货物投保

✧ To understand the procedure of effecting insurance for import 熟悉进口货物投保流程

✧ To know the structure and main content of open policy 熟悉进口货物预约保险合同的格式内容

Example & Analysis 操作实例及解析

◆ Case Lead-in

Under FOB trade terms, Hangzhou Zhongda Trading Co., Ltd. as the importer was responsible for booking space and effecting insurance. After receiving the equipment interchange receipt from shipping company, the importer was preparing for covering insurance on goods. Wang Gang filled in the application form for insurance, and submitted to the Insurance Company together with relevant documents.

◆ 案例导入

在 FOB 条件下，进口商杭州中大贸易有限公司(Hangzhou Zhongda Trading Co., Ltd.)订妥舱位收到配舱回单后，向保险公司办理进口投保手续，业务员王刚根据合同的要求填制投保单，并准备好相关的资料一并提交给保险公司。

Directions 操作指南

➢ **The procedure of effecting insurance 国际货物运输保险程序**

按 FOB，CFR，FCA 和 CPT 条件成交的进口货物，由进口企业自行办理保险。为简化投保手续和避免漏保或来不及办理投保等情况，进口企业一般采用预约保险(Open Policy)的做法，即被保险人(投保人)和保险人就保险标的物的范围、险别、责任、费率以及赔款处理等条款与保险公司签订长期性的保险合同。保险公司对属于预约保险合同范围内的商品，一经起运，即自动承担保险责任。但同时要求进口企业在接到外商的装运通知后，立即填制"起运通知书"(或以出口商的"装船通知"代替)，将合同号、起运口岸、船名、起运日期、航线、货物名称、数量、金额等必要内容——列明，送达保险公司，完成投保手续。

在获悉每批货物起运时，应将船名、开船日期及航线、货物品名及数量、保险金额等内容，书面定期通知保险公司。

未与保险公司签订预约保险合同的进口企业，则采用逐笔投保的方式，在接到国外出口方的装船通知或发货通知后，应立即填"装货通知"或投保单交保险公司，"装货通知"注明有关保险标的物的内容，装运情况，保险金额和险别等，保险公司接受投保后签发一份正式保险单。

进口货物运输预约保险合同

合同号 　　　　　　　年/号
甲方：_____
乙方：中国人民保险公司_____分公司
双方就进口货物的运输预约保险议定下列各条以资共同遵守：

1. 保险范围

甲方从国外进口的全部货物，不论运输方式，凡贸易条件规定由买方办理保险的，都属于本合同范围之内。甲方应根据本合同规定，向乙方办理投保手续并支付保险费。

乙方对上述保险范围内的货物，负有自动承保的责任，在发生本合同规定范围内的损失时均按本合同的规定负责赔偿。

2. 保险金额

保险金额以进口货物的到岸价格(CIF)即货价加运费加保险费为准(运费可用实际运费，亦可由双方协定一个平均运费率计算)。

3. 保险险别和费率

各种货物需要投保的险别由甲方选定并在投保单中填明。乙方根据不同的险别规定不同的费率。现暂定如下：

货物种类	运输方式	保险险别	保险费率

4. 保险责任

各种险别的责任范围，按照所属乙方制定的"海洋货物运输保险条款"、"海洋货物运输战争险条款"、"航空运输综合险条款"和其他有关条款的规定为准。

5. 投保手续

甲方一经掌握货物发运情况，即应向乙方寄送起运通知书，办理投保。通知书一式五份，由保险公司签认后退回一份。如果不办理投保，货物发生损失，乙方不予理赔。

6. 保险费

乙方按甲方寄送的起运通知书照前列相应的费率逐笔计收保费，甲方应及时付费。

7. 索赔手续和期限

本合同所保货物发生保险范围以内的损失时，乙方应按制定的"关于海运进口保险货物残损检验和赔款给付办法"迅速处理。甲方应尽力采取防止货物扩大受损的措施，对已遭受损失的货物必须积极抢救，尽量减少货物的损失。向乙方办理索赔的有效期限，以保险货物卸离海轮之日起满一年终止。如有特殊需要可向乙方提出延长索赔期。

8. 合同期限

本合同自　　年　　月　　日开始生效。

甲方(签章)　　　　　　　　　　　　　　　　乙方(签章)

国际运输预约保险起运通知书

被保险人　　　　　　　　　　　　　　　　　　编号：

唛头	包装及数量	保险货物项目	价格条件	货价(原币)

合同号：	发票号：	提单号：
运输方式：	运输工具名称：	运费：

开航日期：　年　　月　　日		运输路线：自　　　　　　　　至	
投保险别	费率	保险金额	保险费

中国人民保险公司	被保险人签章	备　注
年　　月　　日	年　　月　　日	

本通知书填写一式五份送保险公司。保险公司签章后退回被保险人一份。

Practice 操作练习

1. 操作信息

浙江省香化实业有限公司向泰国 JUR TAI ZUN IMP. & EXP. (THAILAND) CO., LTD. 进口 6000 块纯手工香皂，每块 5.00 美元，FOB 宁波、纸箱包装，每箱 200 块。合同规定投保一切险，保险费率 0.6%。香化实业与中国人民保险公司订有预约保险协议，依靠泰国公司装船通知办理进口投保手续。

SHIPPING ADVICE

To   ZHEJIANG XIANGHUA INDUSTRY CO., LTD.

     NO. 12, YANGMING ROAD.

COMMODITY: CHABA LANG MAN-MADE SOAP

QUANTITY: 6,000PCS

INVOICE VALUE: USD30,000.00 FOB NINGBO

CONTRACT NO.:   08MP560

L/C NO.:   T-027651

INVOICE NO.:   NM234

NAME OF VESSEL: DONGFENG VOY. No. 208

     FROM BANGKOK, THAILAND TO NINGBO, CHINA

DATE ON OR ABOUT: MAY 15TH, 2008

SHIPPING MARKS: 08MP560

     NINGBO

     C/NO. 1—30

注意事项：

起运通知书中的保险金额的计算应参照预约合同中的条款计算。

起运通知书签章时间：2008 年 5 月

美元汇率以 7.00 计算。

2. 操作要求

(1) 填制进口货物运输预约保险起运通知书。

(2) 根据上述条件填制保险单。

国际运输预约保险起运通知书

被保险人			编号:	
唛头	包装及数量	保险货物项目	价格条件	货价（原币）

| 合同号: | 发票号: | | 提单号: |
| 运输方式: | 运输工具名称: | | 运费: |

| 开航日期： 年 月 日 | 运输路线：自 至 |

| 投保险别 | | 费率 | | 保险金额 | | 保险费 | |

| 中国人民保险公司 | 被保险人签章 | 备 注 |
| 年 月 日 | 年 月 日 | |

中国人民保险公司宁波市分公司
The People's Insurance Company of China Ningbo Branch

总公司设于北京　　　一九四九年创立

Head Office Beijing　　　Established in 1949

货物运输保险单
CARGO TRANSPORTATION INSURANCE POLICY

保单号次

POLICY NO.

被保险人：

INSURED:

中国人民保险公司(以下简称本公司)根据被保险人的要求，由被保险人向本公司缴付约定的保险费，按照本保险单承保险别和背面所载条款与下列特款承保下述货物运输保险，特立本保险单。

THIS POLICY OF INSURANCE WITNESSES THAT THE PEOPLE'S INSURANCE COMPANY OF CHINA (HEREINAFTER CALLED "THE COMPANY") AT THE REQUEST OF THE INSURED AND IN CONSIDERATION OF THE AGREED PREMIUM PAID TO THE COMPANY BY THE INSURED, UNDERTAKES TO INSURE THE UNDERMENTIONED GOODS IN TRANSPORTATION SUBJECT TO THE CONDITIONS OF THIS POLICY AS PER THE CLAUSES PRINTED OVERLEAF AND OTHER SPECIAL CLAUSES ATTACHED HEREON.

标 记 MARKS & NOS.	包装及数量 QUANTITY	保险货物项目 DESCRIPTION OF GOODS	保险金额 AMOUNT INSURED

总保险金额

TOTAL AMOUNT INSURED: _____

保费   启运日期   装载运输工具：

RATE _____ SLG. ON OR ABT.:_____ PER CONVEYANCE S. S. _____

自   经   至

FROM:_____ VIA:_____ TO:_____

承保险别：

CONDITIONS:

所保货物，如发生保险单项下可能引起索赔的损失或损坏，应立即通知本公司下述代理人查勘。如有索赔，应向本公司提交保单正本(本保险单共有____份正本)及有关文件。如一份正本已用于索赔，其余正本自动失效。

IN THE EVENT OF LOSS OR DAMAGE WHICH MAY RESULT IN A CLAIM UNDER THIS POLICY, IMMEDIATE NOTICE MUST BE GIVEN TO THE COMPANY'S AGENT AS MENTIONED HEREUNDER. CLAIMS, IF ANYONE OF THE ORIGINAL POLICY WHICH HAS BEEN ISSUED IN ORIGINAL(S) TOGETHER WITH THE RELEVANT DOCUMENTS SHALL BE SURRENDERED TO THE COMPANY. IF ONE OF THE ORIGINAL POLICY HAS BEEN ACCOMPLISHED. THE OTHERS TO BE VOID.

中国人民保险公司宁波市分公司

The People's Insurance Company of China Ningbo Branch

赔款偿付地点

CLAIM PAYABLE AT: _____

出单日期   宁波   _____

ISSUING DATE: _____NINGBO   Authorized Signature

*P*RACTICE *8*

Customs Declaration for Entry of Goods
进口报关

◇ To understand the basic procedure of customs declaration for entry 熟悉一般进口货物的报关程序

◇ To be able to fill in the declaration form 填制进口货物报关单

Example & Analysis 操作实例及解析

◆ Case Lead-in

After Hangzhou Zhongda Trading Co., Ltd. finished the work of booking space and effecting insurance, the next thing the importer should do is to apply to the customs for declaration and pay for import duty.

◆ 案例导入

杭州中大贸易有限公司(Hangzhou Zhongda Trading Co., Ltd.)办妥租船订舱、投保等工作后，接下来就着手准备向海关办理货物进口手续以及缴纳进口税。

Directions 操作指南

➢ **The procedure of effecting customs declaration 进口货物报关流程**

1. **申报**

进口商可以自行向海关申报，也可以委托专业报关行代为申报。委托专业报关行申报时要办理报关委托手续，填写代理报关委托书。

如果进口商没有能够在规定时间内向海关申报货物，海关要对其征收滞报金。按照《海关法》的规定，进口货物的收货人应当自载运该货物的运输工具申报进境之日起 14 日内向海关办理进口申报手续，超过 14 日期限未向海关申报的，从第 15 日起按日征收 CIF 价格 5% 的滞报金。如果货物抵港后三个月内没有申报，海关有权变卖货物。

报关时，申报人应填写进口货物报关单，并向海关提交下列单据：进口许可证或其他批准文件，提单或运单，发票，装箱单，减税、免税或免验的证明文件，报验单或检验证书，产地证以及其他海关认为有必要提供的文件。进口货物报关单的填制方法可参见出口部分中出口货物报关单的填制说明。

进口商向海关提交报关单据后，海关接受报关并进行审单。如果单据内容无误，则可以进入进口报关的下一个环节。

2. 查验

进口货物查验是指海关在接受申报并审核报关单证的基础上对进口货物进行实际校对检查。查验的目的是核对实际进口货物与报关单证所报内容是否相符，有无错报、漏报、瞒报、伪报等情况，审查货物的进口是否合法，确定货物的物理性质和化学性质。进口货物除海关总署特准免验外，都应接受海关查验。

查验货物一般在海关监管区域内的码头、机场、车站、邮局或其他监管场所进行。对大宗散货、危险品、鲜活商品等，经收发货人申请，海关也可以在装卸作业现场查验放行。查验要求货物的收货人或其代理人必须到场，并按海关的要求负责办理货物的搬移、拆装箱和重封货物的包装等工作。

3. 纳税

与出口报关相同，进口货物收货人或其代理人持海关的税款缴纳书，应在规定期限内缴纳进口税款。

4. 放行

一般进口货物，报关人如实向海关申报并如数缴清应纳税款和有关费用，海关应在进口货运单据上签盖"放行章"，进口货物凭放行章到海关监管仓库提货进境。放行即解除海关监管，进境货物可以由收货人自由处置。

中华人民共和国海关进口货物报关单

预录入编号： 海关编号：

进口口岸 上海海关	备案号		进口日期 2008.04.07	申报日期 2008.04.08
经营单位 杭州中大贸易有限公司	运输方式 江海运输	运输工具名称 Cosco Mersin/HV300		提运单号 Cosco080331
收货单位 杭州中大贸易有限公司	贸易方式 一般贸易 0110		征免性质 一般征收 101	征税比例
许可证号 0856456215	起运国(地区) 土耳其		装货港 梅尔辛港	境内目的地 杭州
批准文号	成交方式 FOB	运费 USD83,076.00	保费 USD47,52	杂费
合同协议书 ZD080219TW	件数 1	包装种类 散装	毛重(千克) 1,200	净重(千克) 1,200
集装箱号 0	随附单据		用途 外贸自营内销(01)	

标记唛码及备注
N/M

项号	商品编号	商品名称、规格型号	数量及单位	原产国(地区)	单价	总价	币制	征免
01	2610.0000	块状铬矿 Lumpy Chrome Ore	1,200 公吨	土耳其	437.85	525,420.00	USD	

税费征收情况

录入员　　录入单位	兹声明以上申报无讹并承 担法律责任	海关审单批注及放行日期(签章) 审单　　　　审价
报关员　　海声 BP 机号 　　　　　　申报单位(签章) 单位地址 邮编　　　　电话　　　　填制日期		征税　　统计 查验　　放行

Practice 操作练习

1. 操作信息

(1) 上海新斐雅进出口有限公司(经营单位编码：2201212307)于 2008 年 4 月 8 日进口货物一批，次日向上海浦东海关(关区代码 2201)自理报关。商品编码为：90191010 法定计量单位：台。保险费率：0.2%。

(2) 装箱单 PACKING LIST

HOME DECORATION LTD.
VIA FALERINA, 70 CIVITA CASTELLANA
ITALY

PACKING LIST

NO. SH08-10-001   DATE: MARCH 28TH, 2008

         B/L NO: SHC0580

PACKING LIST OF

FOR ACCOUNT AND RISK MESSES SHANGHAI NEW FEIYA IMP. & EXP. CO., LTD.

NO. 106 SHANGHUA RD, SHANGHAI, P.R. CHINA, 200040   **MARKS & NOS.**

SHIPPED BY HOME DECORATION LTD. PER QIAN JIN 220   HDEC

SAILING ON OR ABOUT APR. 3RD, 2008   ITALY

FROM SAVONA ITALY TO PUDONG PORT, SHANGHAI, CHINA   C/NO.1-20

Packing No.	Description of Goods	Quantity	Net Weight	Gross Weight	Measurement
1-20	BM-B180 MASSAGE BATHTUB TOTAL: 20 CASES SAY TOTAL TWENTY (20) CASES ONLY. 40′ CONTAINER CONTAINER NO: ABTU253990	20PCS	78KG	84KG	1800×1300×750MM

(3) 商业发票 COMMERCIAL INVOICE

HOME DECORATION LTD
VIA FALERINA, 70 CIVITA CASTELLANA
ITALY

INVOICE

NO. SH08-10-001   DATE: MARCH 28TH, 2008

INVOICE OF

FOR ACCOUNT AND RISK MESSES SHANGHAI NEW FEIYA IMP. & EXP. CO., LTD.

　　　　　　　　　　　　　NO. 106 SHANGHUA RD, SHANGHAI P.R. CHINA 200040

SHIPPED BY HOME DECORATION LTD PER QIAN JIN 220

SAILING ON OR ABOUT APR. 3RD, 2008 FROM SAVONA ITALY TO PUDONG PORT, SHANGHAI, CHINA

L/C NO. 360LC010115   CONTRACT NO. SHD01-16HH024

Marks & Nos.	Description of Goods	Quantity	Unit Price	Amount
ITALY C/NO. 1—10	BM-B180 MASSAGE BATHTUB COUNTRY OF ORIGIN: ITALY	20PCS	CFR SHANGHAI USD610.00	USD12,200.00
TOTAL AMOUNT (IN WORD): SAY U.S. DOLLARS TWELVE THOUSAND TWO HUNDRED ONLY.				

2. 操作要求：

　　根据所给的信息资料填制进口报关单。

中华人民共和国海关进口货物报关单

预录入编号： 　　　　　　　　　　　　　　海关编号：

进口口岸		备案号		进口日期		申报日期	
经营单位		运输方式	运输工具名称		提运单号		
收货单位		贸易方式		征免性质		征税比例	
许可证号		起运国(地区)		装货港		境内目的地	
批准文号		成交方式	运费		保费		杂费
合同协议书		件数	包装种类		毛重(千克)		净重(千克)
集装箱号		随附单据		用途 外贸自营内销(01)			

标记唛码及备注

项号	商品编号	商品名称、规格型号	数量及单位	原产国(地区)	单价	总价	币制	征免

税费征收情况

录入员　　　录入单位	兹声明以上申报无讹并承担法律责任	海关审单批注及放行日期(签章) 审单　　　　审价
报关员　　海声 BP 机号 　　　　申报单位(签章) 单位地址 邮编　　　电话　　　填制日期		征税　　统计
		查验　　放行

$\boldsymbol{P}$RACTICE 9

Import Verification
进口付汇核销

Example & Analysis 操作实例及解析

◆ Case Lead-in

Hangzhou Zhongda Trading Co., Ltd. paid the seller according to the terms of the L/C and got the relative commodity. The last step in finishing the deal is to get the verification sheet written off.

◆ 案例导入

杭州中大贸易有限公司根据信用证条款付清了货款并收到了相应的货物,交易的最后一步是进行进口付汇的核销。

Directions 操作指南

进口付汇核销就是采用贸易进口付汇核销单(代申报单)的形式,对每一笔通过外汇指定银行向境外付汇的情况进行统计,到货后再逐笔核对注销的一种监管制度。

➢ 进口付汇核销业务流程
(1) 进口单位经商务部或其授权单位批准或备案取得进出口权,并取得中国电子口岸 IC 卡;
(2) 进口单位持有关材料向注册所在地外汇局申请办理列入"对外付汇进口单位名录";

(3) 外汇局审核无误后，为进口单位办理"对外付汇进口单位名录"手续；

(4) 进口单位付汇或开立信用证前，判断是否需到外汇局办理"进口付汇备案表"手续。如需要，持有关材料到外汇局办理进口付汇备案手续，领取进口付汇备案表；如不需要，进口单位持有关材料到外汇指定银行办理开证或购汇手续；

(5) 进口单位在有关货物报关后一个月内到外汇局办理进口核销报审手续(货到付款结算方式的进口付汇除外)。

➤ 进口付汇核销单

根据国家外汇管理局的规定，进口商在对国外客户支付外汇货款时需要填写进口付汇核销单。上部由进口商根据付汇实际情况填写，下部由有关外汇指定银行填写并签章。经过签章的核销单由进口商定期汇总向当地外汇管理局申报核销。

<table>
<tr><td colspan="3" align="center">**进口付汇核销单(代申报单)**</td></tr>
<tr><td colspan="2">印单局代码：</td><td>核销单编号：</td></tr>
<tr><td>单位代码</td><td>单位名称</td><td>所在地外汇局名称</td></tr>
<tr><td>付汇银行名称</td><td>收汇人国别</td><td>交易编码</td></tr>
<tr><td>收款人是否在保税区：是 否</td><td colspan="2">交易附言</td></tr>
<tr><td colspan="3">对外付汇币种   对外付汇金额
其中：购汇金额   现汇金额   其他方式金额
            人民币账号   外汇账号</td></tr>
<tr><td colspan="3">付 汇 性 质
正常付汇
不在名录   90 天以上信用证   90 天以上托收   异地付汇
90 天以上到货   转口贸易   境外工程使用物资   真实性审查
                     备案表编号</td></tr>
<tr><td>预计到货日期 / /</td><td>进口批件号</td><td>合同/发票号</td></tr>
<tr><td colspan="3">结 算 方 式</td></tr>
<tr><td colspan="3">信用证 90 天以内 90 天以上 承兑日期 / / 付汇日期 / / 期限   天</td></tr>
<tr><td colspan="3">托收 90 天以内 90 天以上 承兑日期 / / 付汇日期 / / 期限   天</td></tr>
<tr><td colspan="3">预付货款   货到付汇(凭报关单付汇)   付汇日期 / /
报关单号   报关日期 / / 报关单币种   金额
报关单号   报关日期 / / 报关单币种   金额
报关单号   报关日期 / / 报关单币种   金额
报关单号   报关日期 / / 报关单币种   金额
报关单号   报关日期 / / 报关单币种   金额</td></tr>
<tr><td colspan="3">(若报关单填写不完，可另附纸。)</td></tr>
<tr><td colspan="3">其他   付汇日期   / /</td></tr>
<tr><td colspan="3">以下由付汇银行填写
  申报号码：</td></tr>
<tr><td colspan="3">业务编号：   审核日期： / / (付汇银行签章)</td></tr>
<tr><td colspan="3">进口单位签章</td></tr>
</table>

➢　进口付汇到货的数据报审

1. 概念

进口付汇到货报审是进口单位根据《进口付汇核销监管暂行办法》的要求，按月将"贸易付汇到货核销表"及所附单证报送外汇局审查的业务过程和手续。

2. 业务审核单据

根据《进口付汇核销监管暂行办法》规定，进口单位"应当在有关货物进口报关后一个月内向外汇局办理核销报审手续"。进口单位在办理到货报审手续时，须对应提供下列单据：

(1) 进口付汇核销单(如核销单上的结算方式为"货到付款"，则报关单号栏不得为空)；

(2) 进口付汇备案表(如核销单付汇原因为"正常付汇"，企业可不提供该单据)；

(3) 进口货物报关单正本(如核销单上的结算方式为"货到付汇"，企业可不提供该单据)；

(4) 进口付汇到货核销表(一式两份，均为打印件并加盖公司章)；

(5) 结汇水单及收账通知单(如核销单付汇原因不为"境外工程使用物资"及"转口贸易"，企业可不提供该单据)；

(6)外汇局要求提供的其他凭证、文件。

上述单据的内容必须真实、完整、清晰、准确。

3. 办理进口付汇报审业务手续

(1) 进口单位须备齐上述单据，一并交外汇局进口核销业务人员初审；

(2) 初审人员对于未通过审核的单据，应在向企业报审人员明确不能报审的原因后退还进口单位；

(3) 初审结束后，经办人员签字并转交其他业务人员复核；

(4) 复核人员对于未通过审核的单据，应在向企业报审人员明确不能报审的原因后退还进口单位；

(5) 复核无误，则复核员签字并将企业报审的全部单据及 IC 卡留存并留下企业名称、联系电话、联系人；

(6) 外汇局将留存的报关单及企业 IC 卡通过报关单检查系统检验报关单的真伪，如无误，则将 IC 卡退进口单位，并在到货报审表和报关单上加盖"已报审"章，如报关单通不过检查，则将有关材料及情况转检查部门。

➢　进口付汇备案手续

进口付汇备案是外汇管理局依据有关法规要求企业在办理规定监督范围内付汇或开立信用证前向外汇局核销部门登记，外汇局凭以跟踪核销的事前备案业务。

1. 企业在办理下列付汇或开立信用证业务时，须办理备案手续：

(1) 开立 90 天以上(不含 90 天)的远期信用证；

(2) 信用证开立日期距最迟装运日期超过 90 天(不含 90 天)；

(3) 办理 90 天以上(不含 90 天)承兑交单的承兑业务；

(4) 提单签发日期距付汇日期超过 90 天(不含 90 天)的付汇交单业务；

(5) 付汇日期距预计到货日期超过 90 天的预付货款；

(6) 超过合同总额的 15%且超过等值 10 万美元的预付货款；

(7) 报关单签发日期距付汇日期超过 90 天(不含 90 天)的货到汇款业务；

(8) 境外工程使用物资采购的付款、开证业务；

(9) 转口贸易的付款、开证业务；

(10) 不在名录内企业付汇、开证业务；

(11) "受外汇局真实性审核进口单位名单"内企业的付汇、开证业务；

(12) 经外汇局了解认为确系特殊情况，有必要重点跟踪付汇业务。

　　企业在办理上述备案业务前，须对应报审已签发的预计到货日期在上月 1 日前的备案表的到货情况；否则，不予办理。

2. 进口单位在办理备案业务时，须对应提供下列单证：

(1) 进口付汇备案申请函(申请函内容应包含申请备案原因及备案内容)；

(2) 进口合同正本及主要条款复印件；

(3) 开证申请书(如备案原因为"远期信用证"，则该开证申请书上应有银行加盖的签章)；

(4) 进口付汇通知单及复印件(如结算方式不为"托收"，则企业可不提供该单据)；

(5) 电汇申请书(如结算方式不为"汇款"，则企业可不提供该单据)；

(6) 进口货物报关单正本、复印件及 IC 卡(如备案原因不为货到汇款、信用证展期，则企业可不提供该单据及 IC 卡)；

(7) 结汇水单/收账通知单或转口所得的信用证(如备案原因不为"境外工程使用物资"、"转口贸易"，则企业可不提供该单据)；

(8) 预付款保函(如备案原因不为"90 天以上到货"、超过 15%且超过等值 10 万美元的预付货款，则企业可不提供该单据)；

(9) 进口付汇备案表；

(10) 特殊备案情况下，外汇局要求提供的其他凭证、文件。

　　上述单据的内容必须真实、完整、清晰、准确。

3. 企业在办理进口付汇备案业务时应根据不同的备案情况对应提供上述单据，并按照下列要求完成备案手续：

(1) 企业应提前三个工作日将有关单据交外汇局核销业务人员初审；

(2) 初审无误，审核人员将单据报送主管领导审批；

(3) 业务人员应于企业备案当日(或次日，"受外汇局真实性审核进口单位名单"内企业除外)将通过初审的单据报送主管领导审批，主管领导在次日(或第三日，"受外汇局真实性审核进口单位名单"内企业除外)将审批结果退审核人员，对于审批未通过的备案，审核人员须及时向企业讲明原因。

(4) 审批通过后，由审核人员通知企业(或由企业主动查询)备案结果，并将加盖"进口付汇核销专用章"的备案表及所附单证退还企业，同时，将备案表第四联及有关单证复印件一并留存、输机。

Practice 操作练习

　　浙江立新贸易有限公司刚刚从法国进口了一批葡萄酒，付款方式为信用证，金额为USD98,500.00，现在打算去外管局核销，请问核销时应准备哪些单据？

图书在版编目（CIP）数据

国际贸易操作实训 / 董佩佩，王珍主编. —杭州：
浙江大学出版社，2009.4(2019.1重印)
（高职高专商务英语、应用英语专业规划教材）
ISBN 978-7-308-06697-6

Ⅰ.国… Ⅱ.①董…②王… Ⅲ.国际贸易—贸易实
务—英语—高等学校：技术学校—教材 Ⅳ.H31

中国版本图书馆 CIP 数据核字（2009）第 052401 号

（本教材配有练习答案，请需要的老师进入我社网站免费
下载。网址：http://www.zjupress.com）

高职高专商务英语、应用英语专业规划教材
国际贸易操作实训
董佩佩　王　珍　主编

策　　划	张　琛　张颖琪　樊晓燕
责任编辑	李　晨
封面设计	卢　涛
出版发行	浙江大学出版社
	（杭州市天目山路 148 号　邮政编码 310007）
	（网址：http://www.zjupress.com）
排　　版	杭州中大图文设计有限公司
印　　刷	浙江新华数码印务有限公司
开　　本	787mm×1092mm　1/16
印　　张	13.5
字　　数	405 千
版 印 次	2009 年 4 月第 1 版　2019 年 1 月第 5 次印刷
书　　号	ISBN 978-7-308-06697-6
定　　价	34.00 元